To Diane
Best Regards

A
BILLY YANK
GOVERNOR

Bernard A. Olsen

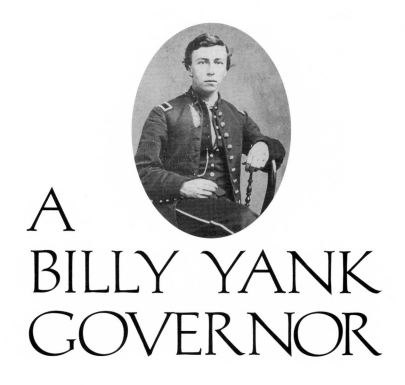

A BILLY YANK GOVERNOR

the life and times of New Jersey's Franklin Murphy

Bernard A. Olsen

with a foreword by

James M. McPherson

PHOENIX PUBLISHING

West Kennebunk, Maine

Library of Congress Cataloging-in-Publication Data

Olsen, Bernard A.
    A Billy Yank governor : the life and times of New
    Jersey's Franklin Murphy / Bernard A. Olsen.
        p. cm.
    Includes bibliographical references and index.
    ISBN 0-914659-90-1 (alk. paper)
    1. Murphy, Franklin, 1846-1920. 2. Governors—New
Jersey—Biography. 3. New Jersey—Politics and government
—1865-1950. 4. Soldiers—United States—Biography.
5. United States—History—Civil War, 1861-1865—Biography.
I. Title.

    F139.M87 O45 2000
    974.9'041'092—dc21
    [B]   00-058441

Printed in the United States of America

To
the Memory of My Parents
Bernhardt and Marion

Contents

Acknowledgments   x

Preface   xi

Foreword   xiii

Right for the Times   1

Gone for a Soldier   19

Marching with Sherman   47

Swords Into Plowshares   121

By Their Fruits   130

The Twilight Years   177

Appendices   201

Endnotes   203

Sources   212

Index   215

ACKNOWLEDGMENTS

I am indebted to many institutions and their staffs for assisting me with the research required for this volume. There are, of course, key individuals who helped guide this project through to fruition without whose dedication and generosity this book could not have been completed. Chief among these is Joan Ellis, descendant of Franklin Murphy, who opened her family archives and gave me access to the fabulous memorabilia and private papers that became the kernel of the project. I am most appreciative of the advice given me by Dr. James M. McPherson of Princeton University on the Civil War sections, as well as from my brother, Dr. John Olsen, Eastern New Mexico University for his many helpful suggestions.

Other individuals and/or institutions that provided invaluable assistance included: Timothy J. McMahon, New Jersey historian and life-long friend; Frederick (MD) Historical Society; Maureen Cattie, Free Public Library of Philadelphia; Freehold (NJ) Public Library; Rebecca A. Ebert, Archives Librarian, Handley Library; The Library of Congress; J. Michael Giebas, Marlboro High School; Maryland County Historical Society; Monmouth County (NJ) Historical Association; Guggenheim Library, Monmouth University; The National Archives; National Park Service; Dr. Greg Williams and Dr. Ken Meyers, Archivists, New Jersey Historical Society; Robert Mallalieu, Head Librarian, Newark Academy; Margaret M. Sherry, Reference Librarian/Archivist Rare Books and Special Collections, Princeton University Libraries; Red Bank (NJ) Public Library; Edward Skipworth, Archivist, Alexander Library—Special Collections, Rutgers University; Ellen Callahan, Greg Gill and Bette Epstein, New Jersey Department of State, Division of Archives and Records Management, New Jersey State Archives; Dr. Harry Wilson, Summit High School; Dr. Richard Sommers, Archivist—Historian, U.S. Military History Institute; Alan C. Aimone, Senior Special Collections Librarian, U.S. Military Academy Library; Alice S. Creighton and Gary A. LaValley, Archivists, Nimitz Library, U.S. Naval Academy.

I am also indebted to the following individuals for their generosity in ways too numerous to mention: Michael DuPont esq., Professor Michael Fowler, Dr. Gregory Halligan, John Kuhl, John Kuras, Barbara Loftus, Jane McCormick, Edward J. McKenna, Jr., esq., Donald Reinhart, Rose Tosca, and Allen Weldon. My wife and best friend Kathleen deserves special thanks for her infinite patience and encouragement when the research seemed overwhelming. I am especially grateful to our sons, B.J., Chris, Andy, and Ted, who, each in his own way, buoyed me up and kept me at my task.

B.A.O.

Preface

Many years ago during the early 1960s, I had the pleasure of meeting an elderly lady, Mrs. Helen Kinney, who lived in a beautiful home on the Navesink River near New Jersey's Atlantic Highlands. The house was appropriately called, "Distant Shore." Mrs. Kinney was the daughter of Franklin Murphy, a prominent New Jersey citizen who had distinguished himself in the Civil War and miraculously survived, then started the Murphy Varnish Company in Newark, New Jersey, during 1865, and ultimately became Governor of New Jersey at the turn of the century.

Through my mother, a registered nurse who cared for Mrs. Kinney, I had occasion to visit her home, a wonderful throwback to Victorian times. The house had been, for the most part, preserved by this matriarch of a prominent family that traced its lineage back to colonial times. I remember entering the front vestibule made of beautiful Italian marble and seeing the grand circular stairway that ascended to the heavens. Each landing was embellished with stuffed wild animals and intricate tapestries typical of wealthy homes of the period. The library was a literary treasure of priceless collections shelved in magnificent bookcases made of Indonesian teak. The dining room was equally palatial, its closets filled with china and crystal from the Hapsburgs and Hohenzollerns—all this the legacy of a most remarkable man.

The years passed and with them Helen Kinney and her beautiful Distant Shore. It was not until some forty years later and after the death of Helen's last surviving daughter, that destiny renewed my contact with the family. I had in the meantime pursued a career teaching history and my research was published as a book, *Upon the Tented Field*, a Civil War history of New Jersey soldiers who participated in that struggle.

In the subsequent settlement of the Kinney estate, the property went to a granddaughter who, familiar with my historical research, contacted me and asked me to examine an attic full of old family treasures which had never been shown to anyone.

As I started to examine this long-hidden collection, I immediately felt a definite spiritual connection to the past spread out before me, as well as to my own past, because of my long interest in researching the Civil War. Here was a literal treasure trove of nineteenth-century memorabilia centering, in large part, on the papers of Mrs. Kinney's father, Franklin Murphy. There were his diaries he had kept during the last months of the Civil War when he participated in Sherman's final campaigns; another journal written when he served as Governor of New Jersey; and two composed after he had retired from the state-house. The latter give a vivid picture of the values of an early progressive Republican whose views span the chasm from promoting workers' fringe benefits and controlling the growing pollution of the Passiac River, to pensions for the Grand Army of the Republic, tariff and money issues, and immigration problems.

There were photographs of him with Woodrow Wilson at Princeton University, Teddy Roosevelt at Sea Girt, and a group picture of a number of prominent public figures with William Howard Taft at Murphy's home. In addition there were copies of his speeches commemorating and analyzing the significance of special anniversary events with titles such as "The Battle of Monmouth," "Antietam," and "New Jersey Day at Saint Louis," to cite just a few. What I found particularly fascinating and indicative of his keen analytical skill was "An Assessment of the Costs of the Civil War."

All of the above and much more presented a wonderful opportunity to tell the story of a man who was "right for the times," a man who believed that his country was "the fairest land the sun ever shone upon," and its flag the "unsullied emblem of human freedom."

I hope I have done him justice.

Bernard A. Olsen

Little Silver, New Jersey
April 14, 2000

Foreword

Many of my students are astonished to learn that a century ago the Republican party was the more liberal of the two major parties. Born of the slavery controversy, Republicans elected Abraham Lincoln as their first president, prosecuted the Civil War to victory, abolished slavery, enacted equal civil and political rights for freed slaves, and used the strong arm of the national government to enforce these rights. In the 1870s, however, economic depression and Northern weariness with Reconstruction gave Democrats enough power in Congress to frustrate further efforts by the federal government to promote civil rights and social justice. In those days the Democrats were the party of limited government, state's rights, white supremacy, and the solid South. Republicans commanded the allegiance of African-Americans, the Northern middle class, many Northern farmers, skilled workers, and entrepreneurs whose economic energies and innovations were transforming the face of American society.

These economic and social transformations created new problems associated with urban overcrowding, agricultural distress, economic exploitation, industrial pollution, and extremes of wealth and poverty. Political factions in both major parties as well as third parties such as the Populists and Socialists proposed to address these urgent problems. But it was the liberal wing of the Republican party under President Theodore Roosevelt and such state governors as Franklin Murphy of New Jersey who led the way with reform legislation and executive actions that came to be known as the Progressive movement. In New Jersey, Murphy's administration (1902-1905) laid the groundwork for further reforms under the Progressive Democratic governor Woodrow Wilson (1911-1913), who became president in 1913 and began the transformation of the Democrats to the more liberal party during the course of the twentieth century.

Franklin Murphy exemplified the Republican party's great achievements during the first half-century of the party's history. At the age of sixteen he (like thousands of his contemporaries) lied about his age to enlist in the Union army in 1862. Fired by a patriotic devotion to national unity Murphy saw a great deal of action during his three years in the 13th New Jersey Volunteer Infantry. Rising from private to lieutenant, he fought at Antietam, Chancellorsville, Gettysburg, Chattanooga, in Sherman's Atlanta campaign, then marched with Sherman to the sea and through the Carolinas.

After the war, Murphy became one of the more responsible as well as successful entrepreneurs of the Gilded Age. He established a varnish manufacturing business in Newark which made a superior product sold all over the country and abroad. He pioneered in the creation of profit-sharing and a pension system for his employees. Entering local and then state politics, Murphy won election as governor in 1901, the same year Theodore Roosevelt became President. Murphy turned New Jersey into a smaller version of T.R.'s Square Deal. He cleaned up the polluted Passaic River, cracked down on violations of New Jersey's child labor laws, enforced progressive tenement house codes, instituted primary elections and ballot reforms that democratized state politics, supported public health measures to attack the scourge of tuberculosis, and launched a road-building and improvement program that made New Jersey's roads among the nation's best in the early twentieth century. In a sense, Murphy's tenure as governor brought him full circle from his youthful days as a soldier: as he had fought for a more progressive nation in the 1860s, he worked for a more progressive state forty years later.

Bernard Olsen has rescued Murphy's career from the undeserved obscurity in which it has languished. Using letters, diaries, speeches, photographs, and other sources to which Murphy's great-granddaughter gave him access, he has constructed a dramatic narrative of Murphy's three careers as soldier, businessman, and governor. This is a book that will interest students of the Civil War, of American economic history, of the Progressive era, and of New Jersey history. Lavishly illustrated with previously unpublished photographs, it is a book that its possessors will be proud to own.

James M. McPherson

Princeton, N.J.
August 4, 2000

A
BILLY YANK
GOVERNOR

"Let it be the mission of our society to kindle afresh from time to time the sparkling fires of patriotic love, so that our flag which represents that which our fathers fought to establish, and some of us here fought to maintain, remains forever the unsullied emblem of human freedom."

FRANKLIN MURPHY, JANUARY 3, 1900

1

Right for the Times

THE WORLD AT ANY AGE presents its people with particular circumstances which belie the oft uttered cliché that history repeats itself. These circumstances are never the same as those of bygone times nor will they ever be quite the same again although the hopes and aspirations and the strengths and weaknesses of human beings serve as a sort of common denominator that transcends the ages.

It is into these unique settings that people are born further defined by their adaptation and acceptance to their peculiar circumstances. They are destined to occupy some place for a flicker of time until they, too, mix their ashes in the dust of the millennia. The question of why some people leave their mark for posterity more conspicuously while others do not is a mystery as complex as human nature itself. Does the person create the times or do the times create the person is a question that is often posed to historians. Although frequently associated with Andrew Jackson, it applies to other eras as well. Historian David McCullough's response to this question in reflecting on the life of Theodore Roosevelt asserts that, "there is no answer to that

. . . he was exactly right for his times." He fitted in perfectly in ways he could not have, either before or since.

Similarly, if the times were right for Theodore Roosevelt, they were equally right for a lesser known yet immensely significant Roosevelt contemporary, a man who would leave a subtle yet indelible mark on his country, his state, and his community. His name was Franklin Murphy: Civil War Soldier, Captain of Industry, and New Jersey Governor. Here is his story which begins on a cold winter's day in mid-nineteenth-century America. McCullough continues, "We can never know enough about those in whose footsteps we follow. We can never tire of their stories. As much as has already been found in the records of the past there is still more to be found, much more."[1]

America Before The Civil War

Franklin Murphy was born on January 3, 1846, in Jersey City, New Jersey, at the beginning of the Victorian Era. The year 1846 dawned brightly on America with all the hopes of a young republic plunging headlong into what New York journalist

James K. Polk

John O'Sullivan labeled its Manifest Destiny. It was the year that would see the final settlement of the troublesome Oregon boundary issue. The forty-ninth parallel was continued to the Pacific Ocean despite the harangues of Senator Edward A. Hannegan of Indiana and other opponents who called for "fifty-four forty or fight."[2] Two thousand miles away at Harvard University, young Charles Sumner devoted a significant part of his Phi Beta Kappa speech to peace.[3] His future vituperations in the "Crime Against Kansas" diatribe would result in grave personal injury and contribute to sectional intolerance and civil war. It was also the year that saw President James K. Polk ask Congress to declare war on Mexico for "shedding American blood on American soil." A skeptical young congressman from Illinois, Abraham Lincoln in the "Spot Resolutions" demanded disclosure of the exact location, which foreshadowed domestic discord, dissidence, and civil disobedience. The results of the war as embodied in the Treaty of Guadalupe Hidalgo extended America's boundaries from sea to shining sea. Ominously, the glimmer of those rays would diminish as North and South maneuvered for influence and power in the newly acquired territories. While Dred Scott sued for his freedom, Northern interests attempted to exclude slavery from those territories acquired from Mexico in the so-called Wilmont Proviso of 1846 while many in the South coveted Cuba. The latter found expression eight years later in the Ostend Manifesto.

By 1846 Native-Americans continued their forlorn attempt at stemming the incessant incursions by whites onto their ancestral lands. Wagon trains poured endless streams of new settlers westward over arteries such as the Oregon and Santa Fe Trails. These pioneers were undaunted by ubiquitous perils which often led to disaster or death. Such was the fate of the 1846 Donner Party. The clash of cultures produced endless confrontations which cost the lives of innocent people, red and white alike. As Doctor William Morton made progress with anesthesia, the white man's diseases decimated the Native-Americans, drastically reducing their populations. The tribes retaliated and the resulting retribution created a vicious cycle as atrocity begot atrocity. Tragedy fell on the Whitmans when they were murdered by the Cayuses at their mission at Waiilatpu, Oregon.[4]

Meanwhile, the Northeast continued to experience the Industrial Revolution surreptitiously extracted from England by the legerdemain of Samuel Slater. Indeed, America had reached, what the economist W.W. Rostow called the "take-off"; "it was initiated by a more narrowly economic process . . . a sharp relative rise in export prices and/or large capital imports, as in the case of the United States from the late 1840s . . ."[5] It was sustained by what seemed to be endless natural resources and ample immigrant labor. Between 1840 and 1850, 1,797,317 souls would tramp down the gangplanks looking to share in the benefits of the New World.[6] Insatiable consumer demand created an endless spiral of spectacular inventions such as Elias Howe's sewing machine patented on September 10, 1846.[7] There were 143 other important inventions patented in the United States between 1790 and 1860.[8] "The greatest sight in Washington, to multitudes of visitors, was not the capitol but the patent office."[9] There were other marvels such as the venerable academic repositories that began to grace the nation's capitol. So it was that through the generosity of an Englishman, the Smithsonian Institution was chartered on August 10, 1846.[10]

While the activities of the Industrial Revolution confined themselves primarily to the North, a different kind of economic progress was taking place in the South. Agriculture had always been dominant and the South became increasingly dependent on imported manufactured goods. Therefore, it vehemently opposed tariff duties, although some less than others. The Walker Tariff of 1846 was President Polk's response to this controversial issue. It reduced the duty to 30 percent "ad valorem."[11] This stimulated the South's economy by solidifying plantation agriculture, and its system of bonded labor as the "Peculiar Institution" helped make cotton "King."

The great reforms of the Jacksonian Era reached a crescendo in the America of the 1840s. Great strides were made in a multitude of areas including advances in the penal codes, care for the mentally ill, and the quest to harness "demon rum." These reforms saw the abolishment of imprisonment for debt and the overall discontinuation of

Abraham Lincoln

public floggings and executions, although lingering excesses such as the brutal hanging of mutineers aboard the U.S.S. *Somers* suggest that reform was gradual and inconsistent. The horrid executions were justified by one contemporary when he wrote, "The annals of the world . . . do not afford a more impressive scene than that of the young commander of a small ship, away from his country, at sea, in the exercise of what he believes to be a solemn duty, ordering the execution at the yardarm of a brother officer, the son of a distinguished minister of state." Among the condemned was Philip Spencer, the son of the Secretary of War. Charles Sumner quoted Plato when reflecting on the man responsible for ordering the executions, "He who has slain a man, however justly, is not to be envied."[12] Envied he was not, and a pall descended upon Commander Alexander Slidell MacKenzie. He became tormented by personal attacks on his actions until death finally released him from his ordeal some six years later. As for the brig *Somers*, a gale sent her to the bottom in 1846 with severe loss of life, miraculously not including its new captain, Raphael Semmes. He was to go on to fame commanding the Confederate raider C.S.S. *Alabama*. Rear Admiral Livingston Hunt, U.S.N. retired, suggested that, "our judgement of the occurrence should include a knowledge of the times as well as of the individuals."

The quest to harness "demon rum" was spearheaded by Maine's first prohibition law in 1846.[13] The national mood was illustrated by a popular lithograph of a Newark, New Jersey, temperance group known as the "Washingtonians."[14] John B. Gough, a reformed drunkard, would chide imbibers, "Crawl from the slimy ooze, ye drowned drunkards . . . and with suffocation's blue lips speak out against the drink."[15] Perhaps most strikingly were those reforms that concerned the women of the Republic at mid-century. Long subjugated by conventional restraints, many woman gradually and persistently recoiled from their traditional roles of submission. No doubt,

this movement was the recipient of the egalitarianism of the Jacksonian Era. It found its most vocal expression not on the frontier, as one might expect, but rather in the more conservative enclaves of the Northeast, in places such as Seneca Falls, New York. It was led by strong-willed personalities, prominent among whom were Elizabeth Cady Stanton, Lucy Stone, Lucretia Mott, and Susan B. Anthony. They were influenced by domestic and foreign forces of which many of them were ignorant. These, in turn, created their own self-sustaining momentum which would leave a lasting imprint on the temper of the times. For example, there were the forces and ideas of the transcendentalists, many of whom supported the feminist movement. "They unconditionally accepted women as the intellectual equals of men and would later support the women's suffrage movement."[16] Margaret Fuller and Elizabeth Peabody exemplified this leadership. Sarah Ripley, with the support of her husband George, founded the social utopian experiment of Brook Farm, Massachusetts,[17] while in New Jersey, the Phalanx sought to achieve a symbiotic will-o-the-wisp where "women had equality in all things." When some of them went into town at nearby Red Bank wearing a kind of Turkish trouser called a "bloomer," many locals were scandalized.[18] In addition, there were pacifist forces who endorsed such lofty and idealistic crusades such as the one which would have outlawed war. They hoped to achieve this by guaranteeing collective security through an international organization of sovereign states. Little would its champion William Ladd have realized that his clarion call would blaze a trail followed by such august statesmen as Frank B. Kellogg, Aristide Briand, and the indomitable Thomas Woodrow Wilson.

The America of 1846 also struggled to shed its dubious reputation for being a cultural and literary wasteland. John Greenleaf Whittier wrote "Voices of Freedom" in 1846.[19] Henry Wadsworth Longfellow's work, *The Belfry of Bruges*, enlightened Americans on European geography and culture.[20] *Typee*, a "peep at Polynesian life"[21] was an early contribution of Herman Melville. Nathaniel Hawthorne, surveyor at the Boston Custom House, was about to gain fame with the *Scarlet Letter*[22] while young Walt Whitman was gaining recognition as the editor of the *Brooklyn Eagle*.[23] Henry

Phalanx, Lincroft, N.J.

David Thoreau meanwhile was sent to jail for refusing to pay taxes in support of the Mexican-American War.[24]

The beauty of America's Landscapes can be seen in the work of the Hudson River School. Artists such as Asher B. Durand, John Kensett, and Thomas Cole became highly popular in the 1840s. One collection of Cole canvases entitled "The Voyage of Life" attracted large crowds in New York City.[25] In music, perhaps none other succeeded in projecting what was typically American than Stephen Collins Foster. Unsuccessful in gaining admittance to the military academy at West Point in 1846, he turned instead to working for his brother in Cincinnati. It was there that he met W.C. Peters who published many of his early songs. The excitement of the times was seen in the exuberance of the "Forty-Niners" as they trekked to the California gold fields singing "Old Susanna."[26]

The Garden State

The little state of New Jersey, nestled snugly along the Atlantic seaboard, shared proudly in the nation's accomplishments. As expatriated African-Americans were settling Liberia in 1846, the "Garden State" abolished slavery when its legislature substituted the "Apprentice System."[27] It was not without its tragedies, however. A February nor'easter the same year doomed eight ill-fated vessels off the Jersey coast including the stout packet *John Minturn*. Horror-stricken bystanders watched helplessly while the ferocious Atlantic pummeled the stricken vessel. Finally, after eighteen grueling hours, the fractured hull slipped beneath the frothy waves

United States Life Saving Station, West End, Long Branch, N.J., circa 1850

Franklin Murphy circa 1860

casting thirty-nine passengers and crew into the frigid waters. Captain Stark, his wife, two children, and Thomas Freeborne, the New York pilot sent to help, were among those who perished.[28] The enormity of the disaster inspired the state of New Jersey to spearhead pioneering efforts that resulted in the establishment of the United States Lifesaving Service. As if to symbolically balance the melancholy trauma of the maritime disasters of that year, New Jersey hosted the debut of what would become the national pastime—baseball. On June 19, 1846, at Elysian Field in Hoboken, New Jersey, the New York Nine beat the New York Knickerbockers 23 to 1 to the cheers of enthusiastic fans.[29]

It was in the midst of these events and countless others that Abby Hager Murphy gave birth to her son, Franklin, on January 3, 1846. Scarcely two weeks after Franklin Murphy's birth, his distant relative, George Washington Doane, D.D., LL.D., Episcopal Bishop of New Jersey, delivered the first historical address to the New Jersey Historical Society at Trenton. Fittingly, it was entitled the "Goodly Heritage of Jerseymen."[30] It was to this heritage that the young boy would become devoted. He accom-

Jersey City circa 1844, after Barber & Howe

plished more in one lifetime than most might do in two or more. He would leave a lasting imprint and legacy on his times by volunteering in his country's service at the outbreak of the Civil War. He survived the internecine carnage of America's most deadly conflict where one in five did not. At war's end, he returned home and became an immensely successful "Captain of Industry" and finally, instilled with a sense of "noblesse oblige," dedicated the remainder of his life to public service. His dedication rewarded him with the pinnacle of success when the people of New Jersey elected him their thirty-first governor in 1901. Here is his story, epitomizing and projecting those natural rights—life, liberty and property ownership—into tangible success through hard work and patriotism in the "land of opportunity." Hopefully, these same opportunities will persist and become a beacon of inspiration to future generations so that they will not belie Franklin Murphy's assertion that "we have the fairest land the sun ever shone upon."

January 3, 1846, dawned cold and cloudy in Jersey City, New Jersey,[31] which lies on the west bank of the Hudson River opposite New York City.

The Native-Americans called it Arese-heck. "The patroonship of Pavonia, embracing the area from present Jersey City through Bayonne, was granted by the Dutch East India Company to Michael Pauw of Amsterdam in 1629."[32] This name underwent various changes during the colonial period from Areseck-Houck to Paulus Hoeck. Finally, on January 28, 1820, the state legislature incorporated the City of New Jersey.[33] It was a small city in those days, with a population of 4000 and was well laid out with wide streets and elegant dwellings, many dating back to when it was New Jersey's first nucleated settlement.[34] It was the seat of justice of Hudson County and a port of entry of New York City. Young Franklin Murphy spent the first years of his life in this thriving mid-nineteenth-century American city surrounded by great cultural and industrial activity. " There were five churches, a female academy (Misses Edwards, principals) and an excellent high school for males (W.L. Dickinson Esq. Principal).[35] Prominent among its enterprises were the American

View of Montgomery Street, Jersey City circa 1844, after Barber & Howe

Pottery Company and the Jersey City Company. There were newspaper offices, lumber yards, iron foundries, and many stores and mechanic shops."[36] Franklin Murphy was not a poor young immigrant like so many of his urban peers in those days but rather a descendant of a long line of distinguished ancestors. This lineage and his overall station in life spared him the disdain showered on many of his Irish brethren. The fact that he had been born in America and not on the "Emerald Isle" naturally distanced him from recent arrivals.

A Stain On Our Past

The ugly specter of nativism manifested itself in mid-nineteenth-century America as it has done before and since. This most often coincided with a large influx of immigrants which was the case then.

"The stream of immigrants reached a flood by the 1850s; the number of foreign born persons in the state doubled between 1850 and 1860 from 60,000 (12%) to 123,000 (18%)."[37] Clandestine organizations such as the Order of the Star Spangled Banner euphemistically dubbed the "Know-Nothings," heaped indignities on the newcomers. Storefronts of this period commonly sported in capital letters "NINA": No Irish Need Apply. "Meanwhile, antagonism occurred wherever natives and foreigners rubbed shoulders. New Jersey natives assaulted Irish Catholics and damaged or burned some of their churches. On September 5, 1854, nativist rowdies marched through the streets of Newark, spoiling for a fight."[38] The Irish were but one group of many that suffered from what some have called the "plight of the newcomers." Consider the remark of young James Horrocks, an English immigrant, who sailed for America in 1863 to escape the accusations of a pregnant sixteen-year-old girl who claimed that he was the father. "The English are very unpopular here and so are the Irish even more so . . . but the Scotch are a sort of go-between that the Yankees have no particular spite against, ergo, I became—Andrew Ross." He enlisted in the Fifth Light Artillery Battery, New Jersey Volunteers and survived the Civil War.[39]

There has been a cloudy page in the Republic's history that has seen abuse and discrimination meted out to the most recent arrivals until such time as they became assimilated into the mainstream and their cultural idiosyncrasies diminished with time. Paradoxically, these same immigrants often became intolerant of the next wave of immigrants, what modern psychologists might classify as the "abused becoming the abusers." Take for example, Irish-born Dennis Kearney and his gang of thugs who viciously abused the Chinese in California. There is no evidence that young Franklin Murphy endorsed any of these nativist views but he was certainly exposed to the media of the times. Thomas Nast, the most famous illustrator and cartoonist of this era, came to America in 1846, the very year that Franklin Murphy was born. One of his many popular drawings depicts the "Martyrdom of St. Crispin"[40] patron saint of all shoemakers who were threatened by Chinese immigrants. The message, of course, suggests that cheap immigrant labor threatened American industry. While caution should be taken not to read too much into the effects of such messages, it was no insignificant coincidence that Murphy's father derived his family's living from the shoe manufacturing industry. Murphy reflected a sense of nationalism in his judgment of immigrants, regardless of their nationality. He wrote, "We are even now in the brilliant morning of the world's great day, and before the sun shall have reached its meridian American influence will dominate the world. Let us welcome those who are in the condition to become useful and sympathetic citizens and let us exclude everyone else."[41]

The Murphy Family

The origin of the Murphy family has been definitely traced to the twelfth century as descendants of the Royal House of Leinster. MacMurrough "pronounced Murruff, hence Murphy" was lord of Hy-Kinsellagh County, Wexford, Ireland, until 1193 A.D. He was directly descended from Cathirus Magnus who was the king of Leinster in the beginning of the second century. His posterity founded the principal families of Leinster to include the McMurroughs (MacMurphy or Murphy).[42]

Among the many distinguished founders of the Murphy family was Art M'Murrough, a chieftain, knighted by Richard II in 1399 A.D. King Richard II ruled England during a stormy period of the Hundred Years War with France 1337-1453. He did this, in part, by marrying the daughter of the French King, Charles VI. Relations between the monarchy and Parliament continued to deteriorate. Events came to a climax when Richard went to Ireland to put down a revolt. It was at that time (1399 A.D.) that he knighted Art M'Murrough, Franklin Murphy's ancestor. Upon Richard's return to England, the Parliamentary opposition, led by his cousin Henry of Lancaster, forced Richard to abdicate. England thus achieved another milestone on her march toward constitutional monarchy.[43]

"The Martyrdom of St. Crispin" by famous political cartoonist Thomas Nast

Murphy

Murphy Coat of Arms – Arms: Quarterly, argent "slivery" and gules "red" four lions rampant countercharged: over all a fesse "broad horizontal band" three garbs "sheaf of grain" or Crest: a lion rampant gules holding a garb.

Murphy's family line also included Dermot, King of the Danes and Leinster, 1137-1169. The clan Murphy furnished the lords of Hy-Felimy County, Wexford and according to a petition still preserved among the state papers in the British museum, the clan held its lands by the English laws of primogeniture not by tanistry "popular vote" which was the Irish custom. The chiefs retained their armed soldiers through the sixteenth century and held their lands as allodial possessions, "ab initio," "no obligations from the beginning." The territory of the Murphys to this day is known as the "Morrows" and embraces the barony of Ballaghkeen in the county, Wexford.

Another distinguished ancestor of Franklin Murphy was Nicholas Knapp, who had sailed from England with John Winthrop in 1630. Stern Puritan values saw Winthrop choose as colonists for New England many who were "men of high endowments, of large fortunes; scholars, well-versed in the learning of the times; clergymen who ranked among the best educated and most pious of the ranks."[44] Murphy could look with pride to his Revolutionary War descent from Captain Josiah Crane of the "Eastern Battalion" - Morris-Continental Army.

Robert Murphy, the American progenitor of the family to which Murphy belonged, was born in Ireland and emigrated to America from England about 1756. He settled in Connecticut where he taught school for a number of years. Robert Murphy married Ann Knapp, a daughter of Joshua Knapp, of Greenwich, Connecticut. They had a son, Robert Jr. who was born in Connecticut in 1759, and at the outbreak of the American Revolution, he enlisted in the Bergen County, New Jersey troops and served under General Nathanael Greene at the Battle of Long Island and other engagements. Robert Jr. Married Hannah Doane and their son, William Murphy, was born on April 23, 1795. He married Sara Lyon, a daughter of Benjamin and Phebe "Crane" Lyon of Elizabethtown, and a descendant of Henry Lyon, a soldier under Oliver Cromwell and the first of the family to come to America. They had William Hayes Murphy who was born in Newark, New Jersey, April 15, 1821, the son of William and Sarah "Lyon" Murphy. William Hayes Murphy married Abigail Elizabeth Hager and their son Franklin Murphy, who was born in Jersey City, New Jersey,

Lower Green or Military Common, Newark, N.J. circa 1844, after Barber & Howe

on January 3, 1846, is the subject of this biography.[45]

Franklin Murphy's immediate family was as distinguished as his lineage. His father attended the Newark public schools, the preparatory school at Wilbraham, Massachusetts, and graduated from the Collegiate Preparatory School at Carlisle, Pennsylvania. He entered business in Jersey City, and remained there for seventeen years before returning to Newark. He served as Alderman from the 3rd Ward and was twice elected member of the Methodist Episcopal Church, the New Jersey Society, and the Sons of the American Revolution. Young Franklin was ten years old when his father moved the family to Newark to conduct a shoe manufacturing enterprise.[46] He had the good fortune to come from a family of substance and distinction.

Newark had been settled in May of 1666 by emigrants from Connecticut who prided themselves in having dealt fairly with the Native-Americans. They were quick to point out that all land acquisitions were fairly purchased, a claim few others could make. An early "committee of eleven" consisting of Captain Robert Treat, Lieutenant Samuel Swain, and others introduced self-government in the Mayflower Compact tradition. They resolved "to be ruled by such officers as the town should annually choose from among themselves, and to be governed by the same laws as they had, in the places from whence they came."[47] Franklin Murphy wrote of the early settlers of Newark, "they were adventurers from Connecticut . . . they were healthy of body and healthy of soul. They did not come here as gold seekers, but as home builders. They were not companions of lawless and freebooting men— they were groups of families, the women and children sharing in the heroic struggle."[48] Robert Murphy, an ancestor of Franklin, had been among these early settlers from Connecticut.

Newark Becomes An Economic Powerhouse

A mid-nineteenth-century description of Newark, New Jersey, portrays the city as an important port of entry and capital of Essex County.

It is on the west side of the Passaic River, 3 m. from its entrance into Newark Bay and is the most

View of Cross Street, Newark, N.J. circa 1844, after Barber & Howe

populous and flourishing place in the state. The river is navigable to this place for vessels of 100 tons burden, and the New Jersey railroad and Morris Canal pass through it. The Morris and Essex railroad commence here. The place is regularly laid out, the streets are several of them broad and straight, and many of the houses are neat and elegant. Two large public grounds in the heart of the city, bordered by lofty trees, add much to the beauty of the place. The city is abundantly supplied with pure water brought by a company from a fine spring 2 m. distant. Several of the churches are handsome buildings. The courthouse is built of brown freestone in a commanding situation in the west part of the city and is a large and elegant building of Egyptian architecture . . .

In 1843, there were 25 churches . . . There are three banks, an apprentices' library, a circulating library, a mechanics' association for scientific and literary improvement, and a young man's literary association. The commerce of Newark is considerable and increasing. The coasting trade employs 65

vessels of 100 tons each. A whaling and sealing company incorporated in 1833 is prosecuting that business. The tonnage of this port in 1840 was 6,687. In 1840, there were 2 foreign commercial, and 2 commission stores, cap. $15,000; 114 retail stores, cap. $321,250; 6 lumberyards, cap. $38,000; fisheries, cap. $60,000; precious metals, value produced, $154,312; 5 printing offices, 2 binderies, 1 daily and 3 weekly newspapers, and 3 periodicals, cap. $32,300. Total cap. In manufac. $1,511,339. 6 acad. 319 students; 30 schools, 1,955 scholars. Pop. In 1830, 10,950; in 1840, 17,290.[49]

The rapid growth of Newark and indeed most American cities during the second half of the nineteenth century and well into the next is captured by an observation made years later by Franklin Murphy, "One of my misfortunes in a busy life is that I am not able to see more and know better the many men who are now engaged in Newark's activities . . . there was a time when I knew nearly everyone in Newark . . . [this] rapid growth has come within the recollection of many . . . but it has always been a city of industry. The family life was simple and the community life was in accordance with the family life. There were no rich and few poor. It was a God-fearing and self-respecting community."[50] When young Franklin Murphy moved to Newark in 1856, "no less a political leader than William H. Seward referred to Newark in the Senate during the debates of 1856 as one of the largest manufacturing towns in the United States." Although adversely affected by the Panic of 1857, it quickly recovered when good times returned. The outbreak of the War Between The States found Newark the 6th largest manufacturing city of the United States, annually making more than "22.5 million dollars worth of goods—standing at the head of New Jersey's industrial column."[51] At about this same time, Joseph G. Martien was hard at work in Newark, attempting to meld cast iron by the use of a blast of cold air.[52] Martien's efforts were too late. By the summer of 1856, news of the Bessemer Process reached America. "The Athenaeum, which circulated widely in America, published Bessemer's paper on the manufacture of steel without fuel on August 23; while a brief account of the discovery appeared in the New York Tribune of September 16 and the National Intelligence of the 18th."[53] Newark was also involved in pioneering efforts in the field of surgical instrument manufacturing. There is an amusing episode surrounding one Jacob Wiss who was traveling through the city of Newark during the mid-1850s. It seems that at this time the city exacted a property tax on transients. The resulting $4.00 levy on two of Wiss's St. Bernard dogs proved a sufficient inducement to a change of plans. He settled in Newark and opened a successful surgical instrument enterprise.[54] New Jersey's participation in these vigorous economic activities serve to underscore Benjamin Franklin's witticism that "New Jersey was like a cider barrel, tapped at both ends."[55] The challenge then as today, was to reconcile this industrial activity and preserve the beauty of the state's towns and countryside. A contemporary of the times, Bishop George Washington Doane recalled a comment made by Henry Clay who spoke of New Jersey, as "the state of beautiful villages."[56]

The Murphy family's contribution to Newark's economy was in shoe manufacturing. Although very young and enrolled as a student at the Newark Academy, Franklin apparently had rather extensive

William H. Seward

experience in this field. Perhaps this experience instilled in him a natural proclivity toward free entrepreneurial capitalism that burgeoned in later years. A letter written years later supporting Franklin Murphy's candidacy for governor testifies to this experience and the spirit within the guild. (See illustration nearby.)

The economy of Newark and much of New Jersey became increasingly intertwined with that of the South and, indeed, the prosperity of many northern families depended on shoe manufacturing. "Early in the 19th century, Southern planters in their northern journeys were impressed by the fine shoes made in Newark. That was a beginning of a shoe trade which increasingly shod the feet of whites and blacks in the cotton belt until Newark became a household word in the South. Shoes were a simple item though an important one; great quantities of clothing, carriages, harnesses and saddlery were bought from Newark workshops which achieved reputations for excellence in strength, style, finish, and beauty."[57]

ORDERS BY MAIL RECEIVE PROMPT ATTENTION
ILLUSTRATED CATALOGUE PRICE LIST SENT FREE ON APPLICATION

Alfred J. Cammeyer,

DEALER IN ALL KINDS OF

Boots, Shoes, Slippers, & Rubbers.

CAMMEYER
STAMPED ON A SHOE
MEANS STANDARD OF MERIT

SIXTH AVENUE, COR. 20TH STREET,

New York Oct. 8th 1901.

Mr. Franklin Murphy,

Newark, N. J.

Dear Sir:-

When we were boys, (many years ago,) you and I were clerks together in a whole-sale Boot & Shoe Store, at 69 Murray St., N. Y., with French & Taylor.

I am now a resident of Long Hill, N. J. and on election day I will vote about a dozen of my people for you for Governor.

I will go to the polls with them in person, and they are all pleased to do me this favor.

My neighbor Mr. Sol Sayles a Democrat, has promised me to vote for you and to do everything in his power to get some other votes.

I am sure of his influence and his vote.   I knew your father very well, and he was a representative man in our business, and to exemplify the old saying, "there is nothing like Leather" One must stick to the fraternity, and use our best efforts for your election.

You have my kind wishes, and I will do every thing I can to further your election.

Very truly yours,

Alfred J. Cammeyer

Letter from Alfred J. Cammeyer to Franklin Murphy, Oct. 8, 1901

The Gathering Storm

The economic connection of Newark to the ante-bellum South coincided with a staunch rejection by many of the views held by the abolitionists. Whether by happenstance or things more tangible, it found its most vocal expression in the pulpits of the ministry. The message in the homilies of numerous denominations of this period rejected the notion of manumission.[58] As a devout communicant of the Methodist Episcopal congregation, young Franklin was exposed to the beliefs expressed by his ministers. It is interesting to note that his relative, the Right Reverend George W. Doane, Episcopal Bishop of New Jersey, shared many of these pro-Southern sentiments and had many Southern friends who became important figures in the Confederate States of America.

It is no wonder then that despite young Murphy's economic dependence on the political and economic status quo and his obvious exposure to doctrinaire conservatism that he would become so eager to abandon these values. A possible explanation rests with the wave of patriotism that spread throughout the North when General Pierre Beauregard's guns opened fire on Fort Sumter. There was a significant change among northern clergy as well, as they turned, in large part, to supporting enthusiastically the war effort. Patriotic zeal poured from the pulpits. As Murphy observed, "All over the land there are no men more patriotic, as a class, than the ministers of the gospel. Volumes could be written of the courage of those who could fight and preach."[59] Mercantile interests held similar views. In 1861, one Newarker responded as follows to the loss of the Southern trade and the economic depression that gripped much of the North and his city, "Such privation is a capital test of patriotism. Newark has towed the mark manfully, and proved to the world that she values this unequaled Union at a higher figure than ten times the money she ever made out of the South."[60]

Newark Academy

Franklin Murphy lived at 285 Mulbury [*sic*] Street in Newark, New Jersey, and attended the Newark Academy just prior to the outbreak of the Civil War. It was a short distance from his home to the school which was at the corner of High and William Streets.[61] It was a distinguished institution tracing its origin to a town meeting on March 8, 1774, ". . . it was voted, that a school house may be built on any of the Common Land in Newark-and the particular Place shall be where a major Part of the subscribers in value shall appoint."[62] There was a unique balance between the public and private orientations of the school. "It catered to the sons of the prosperous but also accepted young ladies."[63] It was opened to the public but required a tuition from the "subscribers." It was considered an "English school as opposed to a classical or Latin school and was designed for those who desired education beyond the common school level but were not necessarily headed for college. These were often boys preparing for a mercantile or business career."[64] This would have been appropriate preparation for young Franklin in anticipation of entering his father's shoe manufacturing business. In ensuing years, the Newark Academy varied its curriculum and many of its graduates did, in fact, go on to college. Franklin Murphy, however, did not; tragic national events would interrupt his formal education permanently, although not his ultimate success.

The nature of American education in the mid-nineteenth century often conjures up images of lengthy recitations painstakingly delivered by pupils before tyrannical schoolmasters who subscribed to the "3 R's" and a liberal "sprinkling of the rod." Upon close examination, however, these stereotypes were often exaggerated. This is not to suggest, that what was proper school decorum during the nineteenth century approximates what is often acceptable today. It is amusing, however, to notice

Newark Academy at High and William Streets circa 1850 as depicted on a Wedgewood plate commissioned in 1929 by the Newark Art Club

that the inclination of the "older generation" has been to consider their posterity decadent and depraved. For example, parents of the 1920s were aghast when they observed "lounge-lizards" whisking "flappers" away in "tin-lizzies." "British visitors in the century after the Jacksonian era, like their predecessors before them, continued to find American children detestably precocious, not truly childlike, spoiled by their parents . . . saucy, self-reliant, wild, spontaneous, immodest, independent, demanding, irreverent."[65] Although this appraisal by the British aristocracy may be jaded by anti-Yankee sentiment, it did not dissuade other giants of the age such as the quintessential American observer, Alexis de Tocqueville, to conclude, "that an egalitarian society narrowed the gulf between generations as it had between the social orders."[66]

It appears that the Newark Academy that young Franklin Murphy attended seemed to strike a balance. On the one hand, it would not tolerate the martinet excesses of overzealous pedagogues yet it expected the proper propriety of its young people. The former is exemplified by at least two examples: the first had to do with a Mr. Baird, a geography and mathematics teacher whose conduct towards his students resulted in the following entry in the Trustees' Minutes, "September 1, 1800. Resolved, that Mr. Baird be continued a teacher in the Academy another quarter, unless he shall misbehave, especially by abusing some pupil of the Academy . . . and the fact being proved by any two of the trustees . . . shall be dismissed from the Academy."[67] In a separate more serious case which took place on November 27, 1801, concerned a Mr. Delargny, a French teacher who had ". . . struck and kicked divers times, his pupil, Master Tavaraz. The facts being fully proved and Mr. Delargny, having been heard in his defense, the Board, on account of the ungovernable passion of Mr. Delargny, resolved that he be dismissed from his office in the Academy."[68] The latter, on the other hand, was made crystal clear in the Program of Course Instruction. "The discipline of the Academy will be mildly yet firmly administered, appealing to the conscience and self-respect of the pupil. Any boy continuing to refuse cheerful obedience will be quietly dismissed from the Institution."[69]

The merits of public versus private education is a subject much debated today, but it is also one that has been at the heart of many a spirited discussion of yesteryear. Consider the 1857 speech by George S. Boutwell to the American Institute of Instruction entitled, "The Relative Merits of Public High Schools and Endowed Academies."[70] In it he clearly suggests the superiority of public education while admitting that under certain circumstances private academies serve a function to society ". . . where there is not enough property sufficient to enable the people to establish a high school, then an endowed school may properly come in to make up the deficiency, to supply the means of education to which the public wealth, at the present moment, is unequal. Endowed institutions very properly, give a professional education to the people."[71]

This concept may still have relevance if one were to contemplate the impact on American education should all the private and parochial schools shut down. The Newark Academy provided the best of both worlds by combining those elements of public education that fostered independent thinking and self-reliance. Boutwell goes on ". . . I will not say a knowledge of the English language—but worth

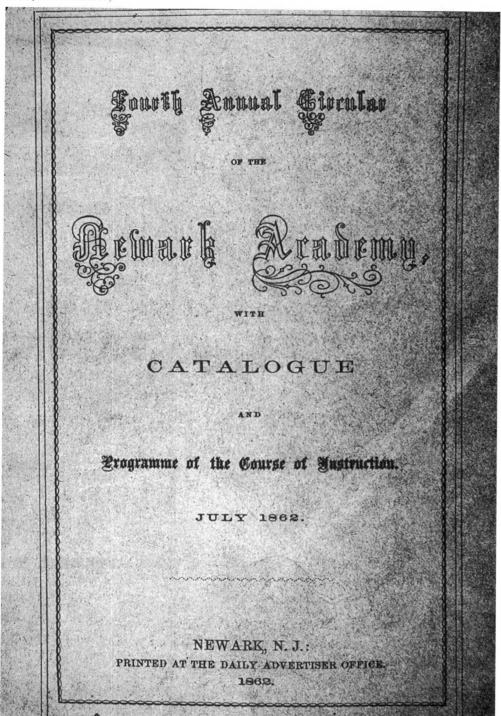

Fourth Annual Circular

OF THE

Newark Academy,

WITH

CATALOGUE

AND

Programme of the Course of Instruction.

JULY 1862.

NEWARK, N. J.:
PRINTED AT THE DAILY ADVERTISER OFFICE.
1862.

Cover of Newark Academy Catalogue of Instruction, 1862

more than the Latin or Greek . . . The Great Lesson of self-reliance is to be learned . . . the system of public instruction is equally beneficial to the rich."[72]

It is clear that Franklin Murphy combined the benefits of both systems and developed a strong sense of independence and self-reliance at a very young age. These were soon dramatically to manifest themselves as the nation was torn asunder by civil war. Washington Irving observed the spirit of this independence and self-reliance gleaned from Murphy's experience at the Newark Academy when he referred to the school as one "full of windows; sunshine excellent to make little boys grow."[73] And grow they did into strong young men willing to sacrifice all that they held dear to preserve the Union. At the root of this sacrifice was a sincere love of country which inspired Murphy to pen these lines, "patriotism is a virtue that is never absent from a properly constructed citizen of any country, but civil war more than any other war or more than any other cause, intensifies it."[74] For Murphy and many of his fellow countrymen, the benefits of education and material success held little value in the darkness of a divided land. To them, secession meant treason and the dissolution of the Republic. The Civil War historian James McPherson places the value of patriotism in a broader context: "The patriotism of Civil War soldiers existed in a specific historical context. Americans of the Civil War generation revered their Revolutionary forebears . . . The crisis of 1861 was the great test of their worthiness of that heritage. On their shoulders rode the fate of the great experiment of republican government launched in 1776."[75] Franklin Murphy was ready to bear this burden and show his worthiness to that heritage. His own words express it best, "The lesson of the hour, standing out clear and bright, is the lesson of patriotic sacrifice."[76] "The national fraternity is ours to cultivate . . . [we must] forget the East and the West and the North and the South . . . [and be] one people with one country—all of us proud to be Americans and devoted to our American Republic."[77]

Indeed, Franklin Murphy was a product of the times, left a legacy on the times, and was exactly right for the times!

2

Gone for a Soldier

HISTORY IS AN everlasting possession, not a prize composition that is heard and forgotten,"[1] wrote the historian Thucydides when he began the colossal task of chronicling the events of the Peloponnesian Wars. These ended in the destruction of the Golden Age of Greece. It was one of the most ruinous civil wars to that time and one that has striking similarities to the American Civil War some two millennia later. Take for example, the motivation of the people of Athens. Thucydides continues ". . . that Athens owed her strength to her democratic institutions and manners . . . Athens belonged to her citizens; her profits and glory were theirs, and it was for this reason that they were so restless and daring in her service, and so resolute in fighting on amid growing difficulties."[2] Americans displayed the same patriotic devotion. In reflecting on America's Civil War, Franklin Murphy, a young recruit in Company A, 13th New Jersey Volunteers maintained that ". . . the most conspicuous condition of that time may be said to have been the intensity of patriotic feeling which existed throughout the entire North . . . It [the war] was an experience so intense that nothing will ever equal it."[3] One of Murphy's comrades recalled a dream he had had in a letter home, "By the way, I dreamed I was home the other night. I was over to your house and was enjoying a cozy chat and laugh with the folks. When I woke up and found myself sleeping in a canvass house, heard the rushing of artillery and cavalry up the road and heard the orders given to our regiment to fall in, the feeling was indescribable. I felt rather sad, but then old patriotism stepped in and I was very soon satisfied with my condition—George." Yet the results were different. While the Peloponnesian War succeeded in fragmenting Greece and dividing the country, and postponing indefinitely national unification, the American Civil War shaped and defined the United States into a strong federated union capable of facing the challenges and responsibilities of a great world power in the twentieth century. It would take, however, a conflagration of enormous proportions, indeed a "storm of leaden hail" before this would come to pass. "The terrible war which

19

Abraham Lincoln

Lieutenant Franklin Murphy

ensued on disunion must be taken as the result of a profound and long-continued conflict between the political and social systems of North and South, with which slavery had a conspicuous connection."[4] Professor Woodrow Wilson asserted that America had evolved into two separate nations ". . . these two great forces, of the North and of the South, un-questionably existed, were unquestionably project-ed in their operation out upon the great plane of the continent, there to combine or repel, as circum-stances might determine."[5] Repel they did for four long years between 1861 and 1865 until the one side with all its power and might prevailed over the tenacity of the other and brought about that com-bination. As President Lincoln eloquently observed on March 4, 1865, "Both parties deprecated war, but one of them would make war rather than let the nation survive, and the other would accept war rather than let it perish, and the war came."[6] Histo-rian Hans J. Morganthau explains that "the existence and destiny of the Unites States were more deeply

Jefferson Davis

Alexander Stevens

affected by the domestic events of the Civil War than by the international policies leading up to it."

Some of the Causes

By 1860 the North had developed a dynamic way of life, possessing a diversified economy of manufacturing, banking, shipping, and agriculture. The population of about twenty-two million was growing and immigration added strength and cultural diversity.

The South, on the other hand, evolved quite differently. Twelve million people lived south of the Mason-Dixon Line by 1860, four million of whom were enslaved black Africans. Predominantly agricultural, the small yeoman farmers were dominated politically and socially by a planter aristocracy. Slavery, the South's "peculiar institution," had become ingrained in the social fabric of its society by the 1840s. Perhaps the industrial revolution and the invention of the cotton gin contributed most to the

South maintaining this institution. There were sound arguments, however, that called for its abolishment in favor of a more diversified economy. Nevertheless, on the eve of the Civil War, slavery came to be considered a positive good and was doggedly supported by most of white Southern society. Poor whites, whose economic circumstances precluded any chance of their owning slaves, supported the system which invariably placed them socially and politically above the bondsmen. Confederate Vice President Alexander H. Stevens, in a speech at Savannah, Georgia, on March 20, 1861, said that "the foundations (of the new government) are laid, its cornerstone rests upon the great truth that the negro is not equal to the white man, that slavery—subordination to the superior race—is his natural and normal condition."[7]

By mid-century, the South had clearly fallen behind the North in wealth and political power and became increasingly dependent on the North's banking and shipping facilities. The political center in Congress had also shifted from the old system whereby a tenuous equilibrium had more or less maintained itself in the Senate despite the North's numerical advantage in the House of Representatives.

With the election of Abraham Lincoln in 1860, the South seceded from the Union and formed the Confederate States of America. They perceived Lincoln as a wily abolitionist bent upon destroying their way of life. They justified secession by a "compact theory of states' rights" which held that the state entities were superior to the central authority. They believed they could righteously nullify Federal law and, indeed, abrogate the Constitution. This clash of federal and state authority had been seen earlier in the Republic's history. Jefferson's and Madison's Kentucky and Virginia Resolutions and John C. Calhoun's Nullification Proclamation were examples. Perhaps the difference in 1860 was that the spirit of compromise and thus the ability to do so seemed to have vanished. The answer may lie, in part, to the passing of those great statesmen who had seen the country through earlier crises.

The North had quite a different concept of what had been accomplished at Philadelphia in 1787. It believed that the Union as established by the Constitution was the solemn will of the people. The laws which were passed by the Federal government as established by the Constitution were the laws of the people, and the states had no right to disregard them.

It is clear that both the North and the South would have preferred a peaceful solution if it could have been arranged on their own terms. The South wanted independence; the North wanted preservation of the Union. It is also probably true that neither side would have opted for war had it realized the cost. The South would ultimately be vanquished and lose its entire way of life. The North would gain victory but at the cost of 360,000 of its young men. Both sides were confident of a quick victory. Senator

John J. Crittenden of Kentucky introduced an amendment which would have allowed slavery in the territories south of the old Missouri Compromise line and, in effect, guarantee its existence in the slave states. Lincoln, perhaps mistakenly, refused to consider it. Thus, the compromise failed, and the disparate political, social, and economic forces that had been at work for decades erupted in the early morning hours of April 12, 1861, when Confederate guns opened fire on Fort Sumter. This action abruptly ended more than seventy years of delicate compromises which had somehow held the Union together. The Civil War had begun.

New Jersey Unprepared

The state of New Jersey was totally unprepared for war. Many years of peace and the conspicuous lack of external or internal danger saw the state turn her energies toward the economy; agriculture flourished and the manufacturing of the industrial revolution was taking hold in the northern sections of the state. The 1861 report of Adjutant-General Stockton illustrates the inadequacy of the state's military condition.

The proclamation of the President of the United States, which appeared on the 15th day of April last (1861), calling out the militia of the several states to suppress rebellion already commenced in the portion of our country, found the state of New Jersey almost wholly unprepared for such a call . . . many years of profound peace, and the absence of any feeling of alarm, had left our reserve militia entirely unorganized, and to a great extent unenrolled throughout the state, while the active militia . . . amounted in the aggregate to about four thousand four hundred officers and men.[8]

New Jersey quickly responded to the crisis in a number of ways. Her population of about 676,000 people required a military quota of four regiments of 3123 men.[9] This was in response to President's Lincoln's initial call for seventy-five thousand volunteers. Men flocked to the colors. Among these were Judson Kilpatrick-Cadet Lieutenant at West Point, William S. Truex-Lieutenant Colonel of militia, and William B. Hatch who had recently served in the Czar's cavalry at St. Petersburg. Through the skillful administration of Governor Charles Olden state banks raised $451,000 in a short time.[10] The state's communication facilities were improved when the state took over a defunct company's telegraph facilities and continued the line to Cape May. In addition, Fort Delaware on Pea Patch Island was reinforced as a buffer against possible invasion across Delaware Bay. Governor Olden recognized the vulnerability of the state's long coastline and sought appropriate naval forces. He wrote from Trenton on May 15, 1861, "I have written to the Secretary of the Navy, recommending that a steamer carrying two or more guns . . . should cruise on the bays and inlets of this state . . . [to] prevent privateering."[11] These initial preparations soon proved inadequate as the war mushroomed which belied the optimistic comment of a contemporary politician that the conflict would spill no more blood than could be wiped up with a pocket handkerchief. As the conflict escalated, President Lincoln found it necessary to make a third and fourth call for thousands more volunteers. Franklin Murphy was proud of his state and her efforts to further the Union cause when he wrote,

> The support which the State of New Jersey gave to the general government was constant and loyal. Her War Governors, Charles S. Olden and Joel Parker, differing in their political affiliations, but united in their patriotic purpose, held up the hands of the President and sustained the army in the field by responding with promptness to every call made upon them. The State not only furnished all the troops required by the various calls of the President, but sent a surplus of over ten thousand, the number actually furnished being 88,305.[12]

Franklin Murphy Enlists

July 19, 1861, dawned clear with an easterly wind which brought unusually cool temperatures for mid-summer. The high of 71 degrees and a low of 58 degrees were not typical Jersey weather which was commonly hot and humid.[13] Young Franklin Murphy had made up his mind that morning to leave home and enlist in the newly formed 13th New

Joel Parker

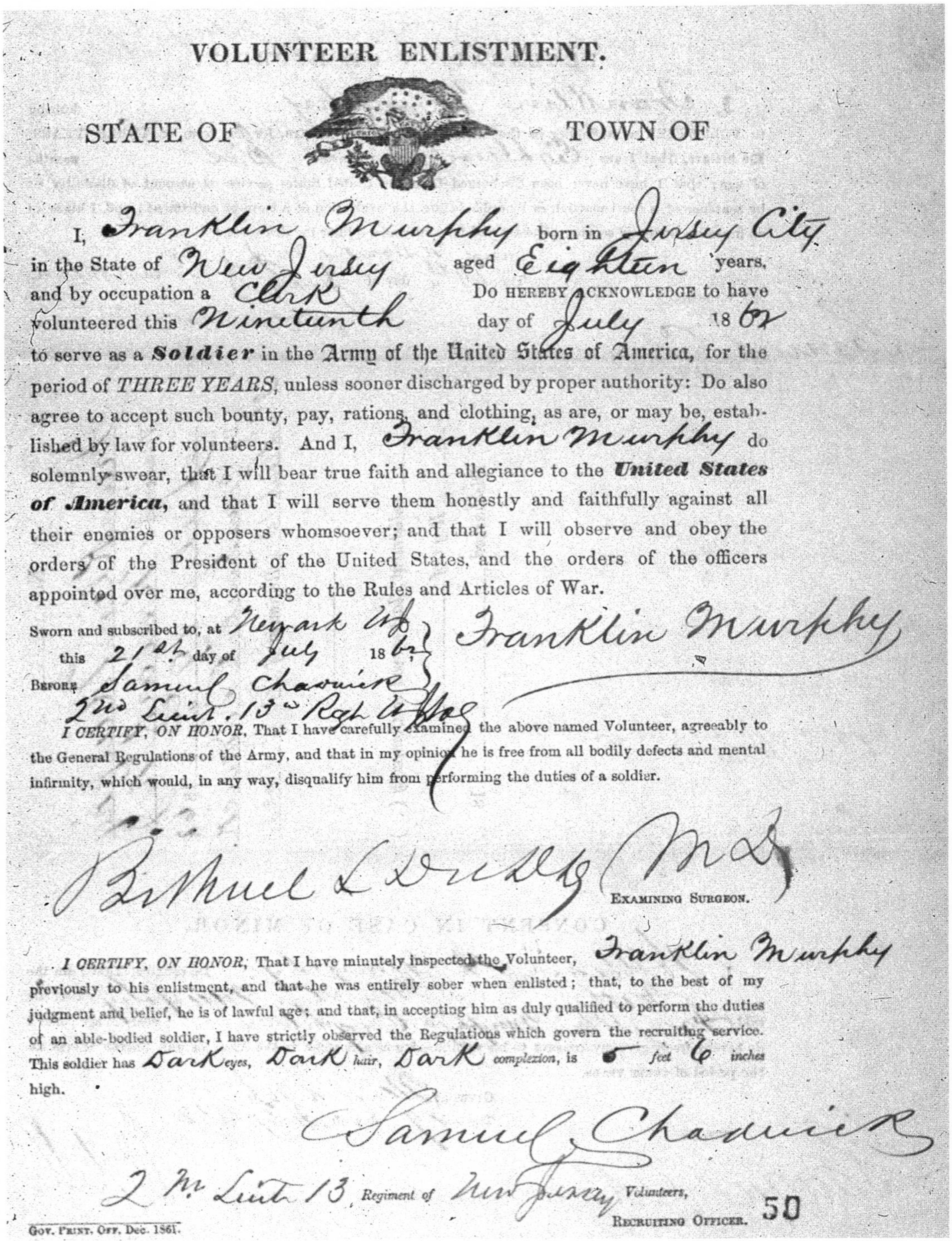

VOLUNTEER ENLISTMENT.

STATE OF   TOWN OF

I, *Franklin Murphy* born in *Jersey City* in the State of *New Jersey* aged *Eighteen* years, and by occupation a *Clerk* Do HEREBY ACKNOWLEDGE to have volunteered this *Nineteenth* day of *July* 18 *62* to serve as a **Soldier** in the Army of the United States of America, for the period of *THREE YEARS*, unless sooner discharged by proper authority: Do also agree to accept such bounty, pay, rations, and clothing, as are, or may be, established by law for volunteers. And I, *Franklin Murphy* do solemnly swear, that I will bear true faith and allegiance to the **United States of America**, and that I will serve them honestly and faithfully against all their enemies or opposers whomsoever; and that I will observe and obey the orders of the President of the United States, and the orders of the officers appointed over me, according to the Rules and Articles of War.

Sworn and subscribed to, at *Newark N.J.* this *21st* day of *July* 18 *62*   *Franklin Murphy,*

Before *Samuel Chadwick 2nd Lieut. 13 Regt N.J Vol*

I CERTIFY, ON HONOR, That I have carefully examined the above named Volunteer, agreeably to the General Regulations of the Army, and that in my opinion he is free from all bodily defects and mental infirmity, which would, in any way, disqualify him from performing the duties of a soldier.

Bethuel L Dudley (M.D)

EXAMINING SURGEON.

I CERTIFY, ON HONOR, That I have minutely inspected the Volunteer, *Franklin Murphy* previously to his enlistment, and that he was entirely sober when enlisted; that, to the best of my judgment and belief, he is of lawful age; and that, in accepting him as duly qualified to perform the duties of an able-bodied soldier, I have strictly observed the Regulations which govern the recruiting service. This soldier has *Dark* eyes, *Dark* hair, *Dark* complexion, is *5* feet *6* inches high.

Samuel Chadwick

2nd Lieut 13. Regiment of *New Jersey* Volunteers,

RECRUITING OFFICER.   50

Gov. Print. Off., Dec. 1861.

Franklin Murphy's enlistment document

Jersey Volunteers at Camp Frelinghuysen in Newark, New Jersey. He was just sixteen-years-old and knew he would have to lie about his age. He was confident however that maturity gained from experience in his father's shoe manufacturing business coupled with his exemplary education at the Newark Academy would serve to underscore his claim that he was eighteen. His confidence was affirmed with the signature of the enlisting officer, Samuel Chadwick, Second Lieutenant 13th New Jersey Volunteers, and was finalized when he took the oath that I, Franklin Murphy do "solemnly swear, that I will bear true faith and allegiance to the United States of America, and that I will serve them honestly and faithfully against all their enemies . . ."[14] It was a splendid regiment commanded by Ezra A. Carman, a veteran who had served as Lieutenant Colonel of the Seventh New Jersey Volunteers. These were three-year volunteers, proud and dedicated men who had not rushed off in the exuberance of the first days of the war but rather responded when the enormity of the conflict became evident. Echoing the thoughts of fellow historians John Kuhl wrote, ". . . that those regiments formed in mid-1862 contained a higher proportion of the best type of volunteer. These men had had time to see that the war was not going to be short, nor its human price cheap. They were serious and stable people who enlisted anyway, out of some true sense of obligation . . . New Jersey recruited five infantry regiments in this mid-1862 period, the 11th through the 15th. All five marked up exemplary records characterized by battlefield achievement, correspondingly high casualty rates, and a special sense of unit identity."[15]

A Soldier Trains

Camp Frelinghuysen was organized in July 1862 under the command of Colonel Cornelius Van Vorst and became the center of Essex County life.[16] It was a rendezvous located "on the east side of Roseville Avenue, north of Orange Street, where a large field, having a gentle slope to the Morris Canal, accommodated an encampment of several thousand men. The canal provided bathing facilities and was used in the morning, after reveille, by all the men not on the sick report."[17] All through the summer of 1862 Camp Frelinghuysen was the focal

Colonel Ezra A. Carman, commanding officer of the 13th N.J. Volunteers

point of life in Essex County. Throngs of well-wishers visited daily laden with assorted favors as if to lighten the load of their beloved who had, as many of the men would later write, "gone for a soldier." The dedication of the citizenry could be seen in their willingness to come long distances, from the Oranges for example, and other far away places. The men settled down to the routine of camp life. To most Civil War soldiers, this included some close-order drill, a rudimentary familiarization with their newly issued Springfield rifle-musket and perhaps a spattering of the "manual of arms" or the "French bayonet" drill. One New Jersey soldier, Sergeant Albert Harrison, described camp routine as follows, "We have breakfast at 7 o'clock, then get on our equipments at 9, drill until 11 o'clock, have dinner at 12 o'clock, equip ourselves again and drill from 2 until 4 o'clock, have a dress parade at 6 o'clock lasting half an hour."[18] Private Jacob Wolcott, Company B 14th New Jersey Volunteers, wrote his

Typical military encampment, 1860s

friend Powers on August 24, 1862, "I suppose you would like to know what I think of camp life-it is harder work than I had any idea of. We have to drill 6 hours every day and then have two dress parades every day. We are called in line at sunrise and answer to the roll then march down to the spring to wash for breakfast. We drill three hours then march back to our tent—black our shoes and put on our dress coat. Then we are marched on the parade ground and formed in line when we are inspected by the officer of the day . . ."[19]

There were lighter moments that punctuated the tedium of camp life which inspired historian David Lawrence Pierson to write, "the members of the 13th regiment managed to enjoy the weeks spent on the tented field in Newark. Starting in the morning with a splash in the canal, the balance of the day was spent in drilling, receiving friends and concocting schemes for initiating the newest recruit."[20] For example, the "blanket toss" was popular. An unsuspecting recruit would be tripped backwards onto a blanket while his chums would all grab a corner and fling the fellow upwards with as much force as they could muster. A more serious episode involved what came to be known as the "Great Skedaddle." Upon hearing that orders were received for a hasty departure for Washington D.C. and that there would be no farewell passes issued, one thousand men abruptly left camp. Pierson continues, "away they went, nearly one thousand men,

in the uniform of blue, out Roseville Avenue, to Orange Street, on a double time, with officers following and shouting at them to halt and return to camp. Within a few hours the men reported and one company engaged a band of music and came in with flying colors." The men were promptly forgiven as the time came for departure. An impressive ceremony was held at 6 P.M. on the evening of August 29, 1862. A group of ladies from Newark accompanied by the Reverend Mr. Levy presented Colonel Carman and the 13th Regiment with a beautiful bunting flag.

"Colonel Carman: In behalf of Miss Landell, it is my agreeable duty to present to your Regiment this flag." The message was candid in its expectations of the men as the flag was symbolic of the hardships that lay ahead. It was not an ensign for peaceful parades but intended instead for the "smoke of battle, the rallying object in the hour when you and the enemy shall meet face to face." The citizens offered prayers for the success of Murphy and all of the 13th Regiment yet braced themselves for the loss that would surely follow ". . . and while your regiment is far away from home and loved ones, tender hearts will be praying for your success, and gentle hands will be preparing to wreathe your brows with honor, or strew your graves with flowers."

Colonel Carman was obviously touched by this support and responded by assuring the citizens that he and his men would fight and if need be die beneath its folds.

"We go forth as Jerseymen, to sustain the honor of our State which is already noted for the bravery of its soldiers, the noble deeds of its citizens, and I may add, the beauty and patriotism of its women . . ."[21] This ceremony had the effect of boosting the morale of the men as they fell into formation on the parade ground that Sunday morning, August 31, 1862. The troops were solemn, however, as they marched toward the railroad depot. All that could be heard was the weeping of the women. Private Franklin Murphy vividly recalled these events, "My own time came in the summer of '62. I was a boy of sixteen, and judging from my own experience and what I know of boys of sixteen, I think they are as patriotic at that age as they are at any age. I was a man in size if a boy in years, and enlist I

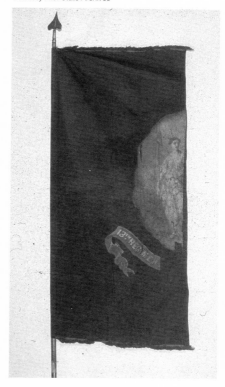

Flags of the 13ᵗʰ N.J. Volunteers

must. The Thirteenth Regiment under Colonel Car-men was being formed at Camp Frelinghuysen and I enlisted in Company A. The Regiment was quick-ly recruited and on the last day of August we start-ed for the seat of War. Never shall I forget nor will any who were there, the hot and weary march from Camp Frelinghuysen on that hot August Sunday. Down Orange Street to Broad, down Broad to Chestnut and then to the railroad where a special train was waiting for us. We were in heavy march-ing order. Knapsacks full, blankets and overcoats on our Knapsacks, Haversacks full, canteens full— but soon emptied—and with our muskets and ac-coutrements we were loaded down with such a load as none but a raw soldier ever dares to carry. Months afterward when we were hardened to our work and had learned how little is really necessary to a soldier's comfort, we had many a laugh over the heavy load we carried that day. But it was no laughing matter then. We thought we must take everything and we took it. The whole town turned

out to see us off, as a matter of course. Services in the churches were suspended or shortened, and the interest in the event was intense. Every departing soldier laddie met his sweetheart somewhere on the way, and many, sad to say, never saw them after . . . It was a long ride to Philadelphia which we en-tered at Kensington. Then a march to Broad Street Station of the Baltimore road with breakfast on the way, for it had taken us all night to reach Philadel-phia. Then the train for Baltimore, crossing the Sus-quehanna at Havre de Grace on the old ferry boat, the march through Baltimore and the final ride to Washington—all of these, and the day and a half they occupied are still well remembered as the first of my war experiences."[22]

The Thirteenth Regiment left Camp Freling-huysen and by September 2, 1862 had taken up position at Fort Richardson on Arlington Heights

Fort Richardson, Arlington Heights, Va.

outside of the capitol. It was deployed construct-ing earthworks and rifle pits to oppose the antici-pated Confederate movement toward Harpers Ferry and the upper Potomac. The unit was placed into Brigadier General Gordon's Third Brigade, Second Division, a part of Banks' old corps commanded by General Mansfield. On September 6, 1862, the reg-iment crossed the Potomac at Aqueduct Bridge and marched to the vicinity of Rockville and then on to Frederick, Maryland. It was so overloaded with equipment that much of it had to be discarded. Murphy and the men would later laugh in spite of themselves at the folly of their inexperience.

The Battle of Antietam

While the Battle of South Mountain raged, the 13th Regiment force-marched sixteen hours across fields, over the Catoctin Mountains west of Freder-ick and through the Middletown Valley. The Confederates in the meantime had moved toward the Sharpsburg Peninsula of the Potomac. Each army made preparations for the Battle of Antietam. It began at dawn. "Morning found both armies just as they had slept, almost close enough to look into each others eyes . . . on this open field, in the corn beyond, and in the woods which stretched forward into the broad fields like a promontory into the ocean, were the hardest and deadliest struggles of the day."[23] Sixteen-year-old Murphy was about to experience his first battle, what Civil War soldiers often referred to as "seeing the elephant."[24] At day-break on the 17th of September, 1862, these New

Burnside Bridge at Antietam

Jersey troops along with the Second Massachusetts Volunteers were ordered toward a wooded area near where Generals Hooker and Sumner had been driven. The blue line of battle passed through a cornfield reaching the Hagerstown Road north of the Dunker Church. Partially concealed by a slight ridge the Confederate troops opened a withering fire forcing the Union line to fall back several hundred yards. Murphy witnessed the horrors of war. As bullets tore through his keppie[25] (small military cap) he miraculously escaped injury as he watched his comrades fall wounded and dead, men such as Private Isaac Crawford severely wounded and Captain H.C. Irish killed instantly while attempting to cross a second fence west of the road.[26]

The 13th reformed under General Gordon's order and giving "three rousing cheers," charged in support of General Greene's position in the woods near the Dunker Church. While attempting to sup-

port Greene's right, these Federal troops were deceived by the Southerners into halting their fire. The Confederates made a gesture of surrender by grounding arms only to open a murderous fire into the blue flanks, forcing the Federal line to retreat. The men of the 13th New Jersey Volunteers lost seven killed and seventy wounded and twenty-five missing. These were their share of the total aggregate of twenty-three thousand that had fallen that day.[27] The total number of killed and mortally wounded was about six-thousand which was the highest single day total of the war. As Private Murphy wrote many years later,

Between daybreak and the setting sun of September 17th, 1862, over 93,000 men of kindred blood (56,300 Union and 37,000 Confederate) . . . engaged on this field in a desperate struggle and when the sun went down and mercifully put an end to the

Battle aftermath at Dunker Church

strife, 3,634 were dead and 17,222 wounded . . . It was the bloodiest day of American history . . . The most desperate fighting and the great part of the loss was in this vicinity. Here, within 1,200 yards of the Dunker Church, 55,728 infantry (Union and Confederate) were engaged. All this loss occurred before 1 P.M., more than three-fourths of it in the little over four hours from 6 o'clock to half-past ten, and on a field not over 1,500 yards from north to south, with an average width, east and west of nine hundred yards, an area of about 300 acres. No other equal area on the American Continent has been so drenched in human blood.[28]

The percentage of loss here for one day on the Union side, according to Franklin Murphy, was nearly 21 percent. The Confederate loss, killed and wounded was nearly 25 percent of those engaged. Lee was driven back, mediation and recognition of the South permanently deferred and Lincoln was in the position to issue the preliminary Emancipation Proclamation. Lincoln summed it up, "When Lee recrossed the Potomac I threw the Proclamation after him . . . on this field died human slavery."[29] Murphy reflected further on the battle as he analyzed it in context of previous events.

The issues of the battle were momentous and enduring. The three months preceding were the darkest in the history of the country. The Peninsula campaign had ended in failure. Buell's army in the west was on the retreat from Tennessee and Kentucky to the Ohio River. Pope's army was defeated in front of Washington, and nowhere was there a ray of hope. France and our English 'kin beyond the sea' had long desired a pretext for recognizing the southern confederacy, and intervening in its behalf, and has assured the southern leaders that recognition depended upon southern victories, and General Lee declared that one of the objects of his Maryland campaign was to gain recognition of the Confederacy, and achieve its independence, and when he crossed the Potomac he was playing for this great stake, and every man in his army, from general to drummer-boy knew it.[30]

General Gordon's official report to General A.S. Williams who took command at the death of General Mansfield gives insight into the role of the 13th New Jersey Volunteers at Antietam. "I received an urgent call from General Greene at this time holding a portion of the woods to the left, the right of which was occupied by the enemy in force. I directed the 13th New Jersey Volunteers, Colonel Carman, to support him. This regiment also for the first day under fire, moved coolly and in an orderly manner toward General Greene's position, and I am much gratified to report that the General has spoken to me of their conduct in terms of high commendation."[31] Colonel Carman's letter to Captain Smith A.A. General presents a concise view of the events of this momentous day.

Headquarters 13th Regiment New Jersey Volunteers

Camp on Maryland Heights
September 24, 1862

Captain:

I have the honor of reporting the part performed by my command in the action of Antietam Creek, near Sharpsburg on Wednesday September 17, 1862. At daybreak on the morning of that day, I was ordered to advance with the Brigade to the support of General Hooker's Corps then hotly pressed by the enemy. Advancing in Brigade line I formed to the right of the 107th New York when we were exposed for a few minutes to a very heavy artillery fire. I was then ordered by General Gorden to advance through the cornfield on our right, across the road and down into a thick wood to support General Sumner's Corps. Advancing through the cornfield up to the road I was fired into by the enemy who had driven General Sumner's Corps from the wood. I formed my line and prepared to dispute the advance of the foe. Their fire into my line was heavy and after a stand of a few minutes I was obliged to retire. I report with regret the loss of a gallant officer at this place, Capt. H. C. Irish, who fell at the head of his company, while directing their fire. After returning about 200 yards to the rear and reforming my command was ordered to support General Greene's Brigade then in possession of the wood near the schoolhouse but heavily pressed by a superior force of the enemy. I advanced to this position formed on the right of General Greene's Brigade and engaged the enemy for an hour. Being flanked on the right the whole Brigade was obliged to retire, which they did in good order followed by the enemy for a short distance. The farther pursuit of the enemy was checked by the rapid and effective fire of the battery attached to this Brigade under command of Capt. Cothran. I again formed my command into line waiting for an attack or an order to advance but was not again called on. I mention with pleasure the heroic conduct of Private James Kilroy of Co. G. of this Regiment who when the Color bearer was disabled volunteered to carry the honored emblem and did so, always pressing forward until severely wounded. I append a list of my killed, wounded, and missing.

I am Yours truly,
E.A. Carman
Col. 13th N.J.V.[32]

Many in the ranks resented the wanton slaughter of so many of these new recruits before they could be sufficiently trained. It has been tradition in the Republic's history since the days of the "minutemen" to muster citizen soldiers for the crisis at hand and then to quickly demobilize and send the boys home once it had passed. The scope and

Casualties at Antietam

depth of military training to meet these crises has been a debatable subject down to modern times. Take, for example, the "Ninety-Day Wonders." If a question can be raised about the competence of these hastily prepared officers of recent times, one can only wonder of the ability of many Civil War leaders who were in many cases given command of large numbers of troops with little or no real military preparation. This lack of training and the horrid carnage witnessed by those who survived prompted Murphy to write,

Seventeen days after leaving home we fought at the Battle of Antietam . . . In some respects the battle of Antietam was one of the greatest and most momentous of the Civil War. We had never had a battalion drill; some of us didn't even know what a line of battle was and they sent us into that fight against a lot of rebels who were protected by a natural breastwork formed by a ledge of rocks, to be butchered, a position untenable even to veterans. We stood up for a while and then we ran . . . They

Harper's Ferry

made us go in again, and we went—and then we ran again. That was our first experience. We left one hundred forty seven killed and wounded.[33]

Many senior officers were disillusioned or were under the false perception that the battle had little significance for all the carnage of that September day. Major General Jacob D. Cox lamented that "the result was that Lee retreated unmolested on the night of the 18th and that what might have been a real and decisive success was a drawn battle in which our chief claim to victory was the possession of the field."[34] What may rightly be considered a military standoff cannot dispute the wider results in terms of preventing European recognition of the Confederacy and altering the Northern objectives of the war to include ending slavery.

As darkness fell, Murphy and his comrades in the 13th New Jersey Volunteers remained in position on the battlefield, exhausted and waiting for the resumption of hostilities the next morning. But the day passed without further action and the regiment was ordered to Maryland Heights opposite Harper's Ferry.[35] A major of New Jersey Volunteers recorded the horrors in a letter home, "It is a terrible road from Frederick . . . the odor arising from the dead men and horses is sickening. Even the dead men are scarcely covered with dirt . . . The wounded Union men are still moaning at the railroad not one quarter of a mile off, and yet all this misery and suffering must be endured . . . It is the higher law that it shall be so."[36] The men mirrored President Lincoln's belief that the tumultuous struggle was Divine Providence when he wrote that "The Almighty has His own purpose." In the meantime, leaving this horror stricken field behind, the 13th

Regiment arrived at its new location on September 20, 1862. The men were engaged in cutting timber and erecting strong fortifications on the slopes and summit of the mountain. On the 27th of October they were visited by President Abraham Lincoln. This had a telling effect on morale as recorded by one of the men. "We had learned to love President Lincoln, and every man in the regiment was glad of the opportunity to look more closely into his kind face. The command was assembled on the parade ground, and as he passed along the line he was saluted and most heartily cheered."[37] Shortly thereafter, they received marching orders and moved up the Potomac River to Antietam Creek and encamped three miles west of Sharpsburg in the direction of Shepherdstown. The 13th New Jersey became part of the 12th Corps that relieved troops commanded by General Fitz John Porter. It performed picket duty on the northeast side of the river covering a portion of the Chesapeake & Ohio Canal and remained there until December 10, 1862, when it moved to Harper's Ferry by way of Hillsborough, Leesburg, and Fairfax Station to a point beyond Occoquan Creek. By the middle of the month, news of Burnside's disaster at Fredericksburg saw the unit countermarch to Fairfax Station and take up position on the north side of the Orange & Alexandria Railroad to Wolf Run Shoals back and forth through January and finally forward by way of Dumfries to Stafford Court House and winter quarters. At Wolfe Run Shoals Paymaster Stone distributed two months back pay and Marcus Ward, a distinguished Newark citizen who Franklin Murphy would call the "soldier's friend" for his many kind deeds arranged the means for the men to send their money home to their families. It was this same Marcus Ward who would be instrumental in establishing the army hospital at Newark, New Jersey, for wounded Union soldiers. One of these, Private Abram Medzgar, typified the support given New Jersey veterans by this man and his institution. Medzgar was severely wounded, had his arm amputated and survived, and was discharged at Ward U.S. Army General Hospital on December 30, 1864.[38]

Franklin Murphy and his comrades spent the winter of 1863 in relative comfort performing the routine duties of camp life. General Hooker replaced Burnside after the Battle of Fredericksburg.

Brigadier General Fitz John Porter, U.S.A.

Efforts were made to improve morale which had sunken to a low ebb among the Federal forces which had suffered so terribly before Marye's Heights. The components of the army were given a certain definition or identity by introducing unit insignias. He organized the cavalry into brigades and made this a very effective arm of the service eventually rival-

20th Army Corps insignia

Courtesy N.J. HIstorical Society

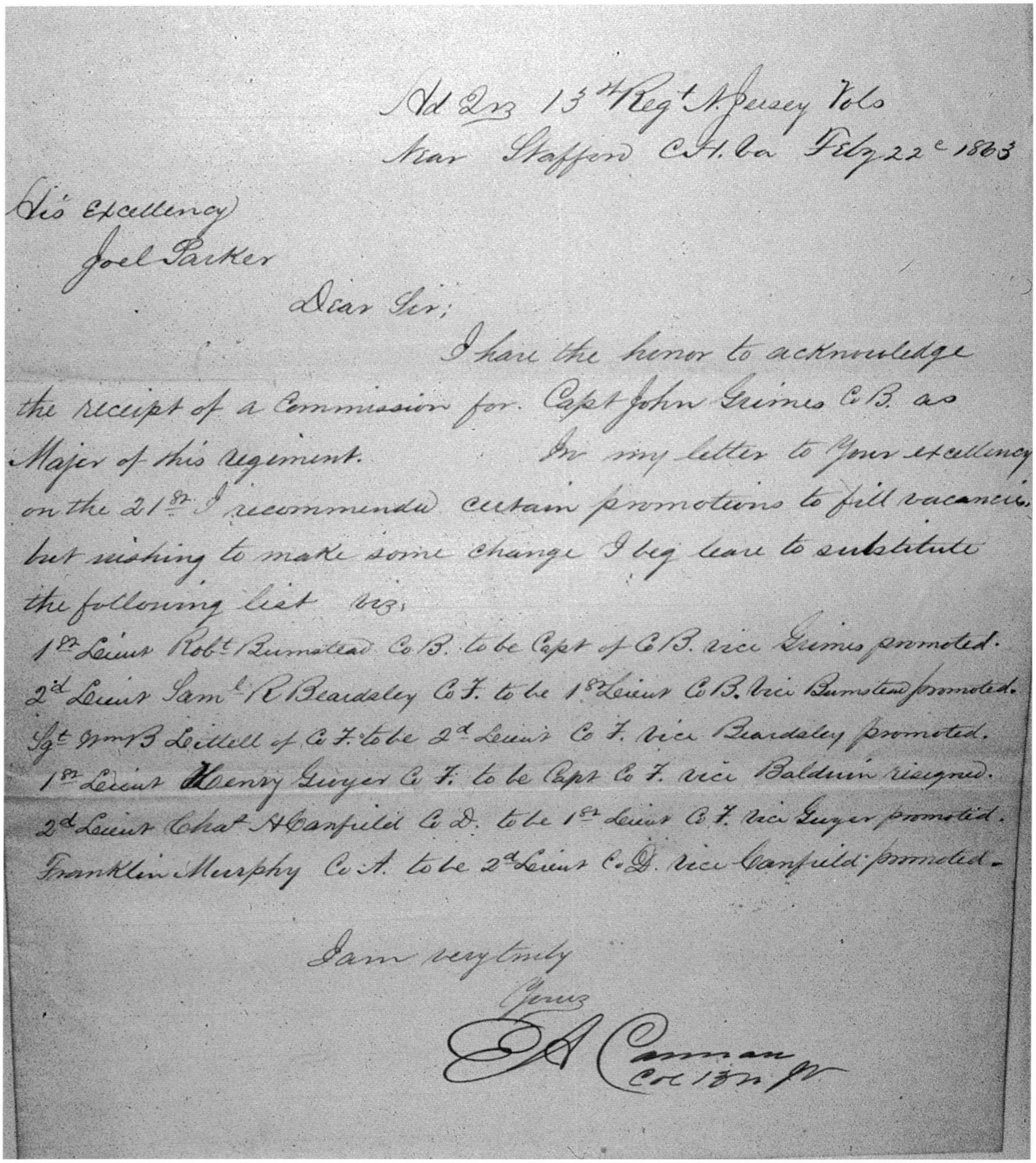

Hd Qrs 13th Regt N Jersey Vols
Near Stafford C.H. Va Feby 22d 1863

His Excellency
Joel Parker

Dear Sir;

I have the honor to acknowledge the receipt of a Commission for Capt John Grimes Co B. as Major of this regiment. In my letter to Your excellency on the 21st I recommended certain promotions to fill vacancies but wishing to make some change I beg leave to substitute the following list viz:

1st Lieut Robt Bumstead Co B. to be Capt of Co B. vice Grimes promoted.
2d Lieut Saml R Beardsley Co F. to be 1st Lieut Co B. vice Bumstead promoted.
Sgt Wm B Littell of Co F. to be 2d Lieut Co F. vice Beardsley promoted.
1st Lieut Henry Guyer Co F. to be Capt Co F. vice Baldwin resigned.
2d Lieut Chas H Canfield Co D. to be 1st Lieut Co F. vice Guyer promoted.
Franklin Murphy Co A. to be 2d Lieut Co D. vice Canfield promoted.

I am very truly
Yours
E A Carman
Col 13th NJ

Document recording Franklin Murphy's promotion to Second Lieutenant ing the prowess of the southern troopers under Jeb Stuart. General Kearny's idea of a corps badge was implemented by Hooker. "The First Corps was known by a Lozenge (full moon); the Second Corps by a Trefoil, the Third Corps by a Diamond, the Fifth Corps by a Maltese Cross, the Sixth Corps a Greek Cross, the Eleventh a Crescent, and the Twelfth Corps (Murphy's Corps) a Star. The First Divisions of all the corps were known by a red badge, the Second Divisions by a white, and the Third Divisions by a blue badge."[39] Commissioned officers during the Civil War had the prerogative of resigning from the service, enlisted men did not. Accordingly, on February 5, 1863, Lt. Colonel Swords resigned his commission which made Major Chadwick Lt. Colonel of the 13th New Jersey Volunteers and Captain Grimes major. Later that month four companies (E F G H) were detached from the regiment and sent to White House Landing on Aquia Creek on fatigue duty. They remained there through March 1863. The North generally relied on the lower ranks of enlisted personnel to perform the myriad of menial tasks associated with logistics while the South, wherever and whenever possible used slave labor. Historian John Hope Franklin writes, "Confederate and state governments relied on slave and free Negro labor to do much of the hard work involved in prosecuting the war."[40] Franklin Murphy was promoted to Second Lieutenant on February 22, 1863. He had been in service less than one year. The term "mustang" to denote rapid promotion would find its way into the slang of American soldiers a century later yet the process was nothing new to army life. Young Murphy had indeed, "mustanged" the ranks.

By the end of April 1863 General Hooker sent the Army of the Potomac toward Chancellorsville. The 13th Regiment, part of the 12th Corps broke camp early in the morning of April 27 and crossed the Rappahannock River at Kelly's Ford. They moved to the Rapidan River and crossed at Germania Ford capturing a recently constructed bridge built by the rebels.[41] By the 30th of April these New Jersey troops were in the vicinity of the Old Wilderness Tavern. They pushed on toward the Chancellor House and by May 1st marched to the United States Ford covering the crossing of the Third Corps. The 13th New Jersey Volunteers were or-

Major John Grimes, 13th N.J. Volunteers

dered to construct breastworks with abattis near the Plank Road. The Federal line ran some four miles east of the United States Ford on the left to the right of the Eleventh Corps. The right of the Eleventh Corps was exposed and vulnerable. Colonel Carman had been hurt earlier, although not seriously, during skirmishing with the Confederates. Private Samuel Toombs of Company F wrote that the Colonel was injured while crossing a fence which left Major Grimes in command. Grimes was an excellent drillmaster who prepared the men for the Battle of Chancellorsville. He did this in a number of ways including familiarizing them with the bayonet exercise.[42] Although the number of casualties sustained by the bayonet was relatively small during the Civil War there were few weapons which produced more fear among the soldiers. There is

Aftermath of the battle of Marye's Heights, Fredericksburg

little doubt that increased knowledge of its use added to this anxiety. Its intended purpose soon overshadowed its use as a candle holder, as General John Sedgwick was ordered to hit the Confederates at Marye's Heights. "On the third try, in one of the war's few genuine bayonet charges, the first wave of blue attackers carried the heights, captured a thousand prisoners, and sent the rebels flying."[43]

Battle of Chancellorsville

The 13th Regiment received orders to pursue the Confederates who were, it was believed, in full retreat. No sooner had they moved out of their defensive works than Stonewall Jackson's Corps mounted a furious attack on the right flank of the Union's 11th Corps down the Chancellorsville Road. This route was plugged by regiments of the 12th Corps, among others, including the 13th New Jersey and Best's Battery which "doubleshotted (the gun)

with canister."[44] The right flank was extended to the Rappahannock River so that each wing now rested on the river. Command of the Regiment passed to Captain Beardsley when Major Grimes was shot in the leg. He was assisted by Captains Ryerson and Harris. It was in this engagement at Chancellorsville that the South lost one of its most valuable commanders. As twilight descended on May 2, 1863, Confederate pickets under General A.P. Hill mistakenly shot and mortally wounded the indomitable Stonewall Jackson as he returned from reconnoitering the battlefield. It will prompt General Lee to remark that he had "lost his right arm." Lee continued, "I . . . desire to pay the tribute of my admiration to the matchless energy and skill that marked this last act of his (Jackson's) life, forming, as it did a worthy conclusion of that long series of splendid achievements which won for him the lasting love and gratitude of his country."[45] The next morning saw a resumption of furious fighting as the Confederates unleashed a savage attack on the Third and Twelfth Corps. One New Jersey soldier record-

A Billy Yank Governor / 36

Major George A. Beardsley, 13th N.J. Volunteers

ed, "The battle grew fiercer each moment. Above the unceasing rolls of musketry and the steady booming of cannon, the yells of the enemy and the cheering of our troops broke out at intervals."[46] The 13th New Jersey Volunteers first supported the Twenty-Seventh Indiana, were then sent to relieve the 2nd Massachusetts forming in line of battle and engaging the Confederates for two harrowing hours before it too, was relieved and sent to join its brigade in the rear. These Jerseymen sustained appalling casualties in these three days of fighting; one hundred and thirty killed, wounded, or missing including Major Grimes who was shot in the thigh; Adjutant T.B. Smith, shot in the arm; Second Lieutenant George G. Whitfield, killed in action and First Lieutenant James L. Layton also wounded to mention but a few. Overall casualties numbered some 13,000 Confederates and 17,000 Union.[47]

By May 5, 1863, the 13th New Jersey Volunteers were back at their old camp at Stafford Court House. It was re-clothed and supplied and fell into the "daily routine of brigade, battalion and skirmish

drills."[48] General Slocum reviewed the Corps on the 11th of May and a new stand of colors was formally presented by General A.S. Williams to Captain Beardsley as the Brigade band played some favorite "national airs." Franklin Murphy tells the story of an

incident which if not new, represents as well as any the sentimet that is always to be found in the soldier. In the early spring of '63 when the Federal and Rebel armies were confronting each other on the opposite hills of Stafford and Spottsylvania, two bands chanced one evening to discourse sweet music on either side of the river. A large crowd of the soldiers of both armies, gathered to listen to the music, the friendly pickets not interfering, and soon the bands began to answer each other. First the band on the Northern bank would play "Star Spangled Banner" "Hail Columbia" or some other national air, and at its conclusion the "boys in blue" would cheer most lustily. And then the band on the Southern bank would respond with "Dixie" or "Bonnie

General Thomas J. (Stonewall) Jackson, C.S.A.

"Tenting on The Old Camp Ground," one of the nostalgic melodies of the Civil War

Blue Flag" or some other Southern melody, and the "boys in gray" would attest their approbation with an old Confederate yell. But presently one of the bands struck up in sweet and plaintive notes which were wafted across the beautiful Rappahannock, were caught up at once by the other band and swelled into a grand anthem which touched every heart, "Home Sweet Home." At the conclusion of the piece there went up a simultaneous shout from both sides of the river; cheer followed cheer, and those hills which had so lately resounded with hostile guns echoed and re-echoed the glad acclaim. A chord had been struck responsive to which the hearts of enemies . . . could beat in unison, and on both sides of the river, something down the soldier's cheek washed off the stains of powder.[49]

Dealing with Desertion

There were some soldiers who could not endure the horrors of war. There was little understanding then of what psychologists in future generations would call "shellshock," "battle fatigue," or "combat stress disorder." Some men were simply homesick and longed to be back home; many of them had never been away from home. Others had less noble motivations. Desertions became common place. Regimental muster rolls include the records of numerous desertions including names, places, and dates. Some men simply vanished never to be heard from again while others slipped off making their way home or joining other units for the bounties offered. The technology of the nineteenth century made positive identification difficult. Men had gone into battle pinning scraps of paper to their uniforms containing scribbled names and addresses hoping to be identified should they become grotesquely disfigured in battle. After all, these were the days before "dog tags," dental records, fingerprints, and D.N.A. analysis. There was little distinction between what modern soldiers would call A.W.O.L. (absent without leave) and desertion. Punishments for desertion were inconsistent. In the beginning of the conflict they often consisted of reprimands, loss of pay and ostricism. As the war progressed creating manpower shortages, punishments became more severe. Court martial verdicts increasingly meted out death sentences to habitual

offenders, frequently by firing squads. "It became much harder for unhappy men to slip away and go home—a point of some importance, because desertions had been averaging two hundred a day; at the same time liberal grants of furloughs did something to ease the homesickness that caused the desertions."[50] A ghastly incident took place on June 19, 1863, at Leesburg which illustrates the horrors and finality of war. Private Samuel Toombs, 13th New Jersey Volunteers described the execution of two members of the 46th Pennsylvania Regiment and Christopher Krubart of the 13th New Jersey Volunteers all having been found guilty of desertion.

The wagons containing the coffins soon rumbled upon the scene, followed by an ambulance, closely guarded, containing the doomed men. Arriving at the spot where the three graves had been dug, a coffin was placed at the head of each, and the condemned seated upon them. Their eyes were blindfolded, their hands tied behind their backs and their feet fastened in front. The firing party comprised thirty-six men in all, eight being detailed to each of the condemned men, with twelve men in reserve . . . The death sentence was read, and Chaplain Beck, of the Thirteenth Regiment, offered a short prayer. The officer in command of the firing party gave the order, "Ready . . . Fire!" A sharp report followed, and three lifeless bodies fell backward upon their coffins. The troops were then marched past the graves and the men shudderingly looked upon the ghastly sight. Krubart's body was pierced by seven balls in the vicinity of the heart. No burial service was read. The bodies were placed in the coffins prepared for them, and at once consigned to mother earth.[51]

It was customary to leave one rifle unloaded so members of the firing squad would never know if they had fired the lethal shot. It was these horrid episodes that would stay with the soldiers like seventeen-year-old Franklin Murphy for the rest of their lives.

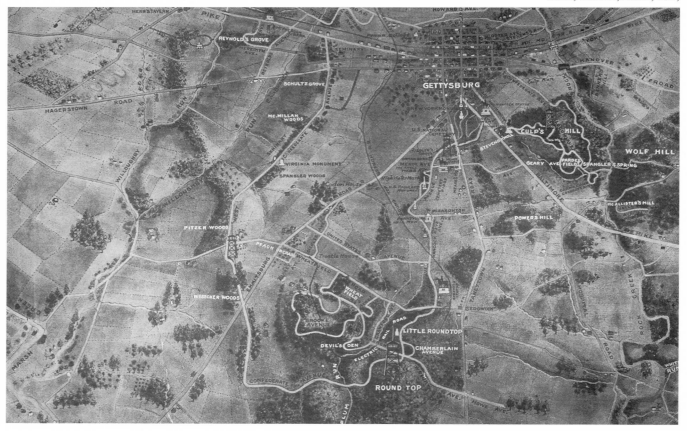

Map of Gettysburg

Battle of Gettysburg

In June of 1863 a dispute between Generals Hooker and Halleck over the use of troops located at Harpers Ferry resulted in Hooker's resignation and the appointment of George Meade as his replacement. As Confederate forces moved up the Potomac during this same month, the largest cavalry battle of the war took place at Brandy Station. The 13th New Jersey Volunteers marched at night through Dumfries to Drainsville. It paused briefly at Leesburg where it contributed to the construction of defensive works before crossing the Potomac at Edwards Ferry and moving on with the rest of the corps reaching the little Pennsylvania village of Gettysburg on July 1, 1863. The decisive conflagration had already began and Murphy and the men of the 12th Corps were quickly deployed to the extreme right opposing Confederate Johnson's Division of Ewell's Corps. The 13th New Jersey Volunteers dug in and prepared for its role in this momentous battle. In the meantime, Federal forces under General Sickles came under attack by General Longstreet's Corps in a desperate attempt to take the commanding position of Round Top. Murphy and his comrades were at first sent to support Sickles, leaving vulnerable part of their defensive line. The Confederates were quick to occupy these earthworks and rifle pits and put up stiff resistance before Union forces of the 12th Corps finally regained this position the following day. "Geary . . . charged boldly on the enemy, and as cheer after cheer resounded on the air it was known that the position had been regained . . . the slaughter on both sides was dreadful . . . The Confederate sharpshooters poured fire in the Federal line taking a terrible toll. When a stretcher bearer from the 27th Indiana was killed while aiding the wounded, the Federals retaliated by shelling the house from which the hostile fire originated. Only then did this activity subside."[52] The 13th New Jersey Volunteers formed in line of battle near Rock Creek. After a brief lull, there commenced the largest and most ferocious artillery duel that had ever been unleashed on the North American continent. "All along the Confederate line, out in the shallow open valley west of Cemetery Ridge, from the peach orchard to the rising ground directly west of Gettysburg, there were 140 Confederate cannon, and on the signal the gunners . . . ran to their posts. There was a long ripple of movement; then every gun in the Confederate line went off, in one long rolling crash—the loudest noise, probably, that had ever been heard on the North American continent up to that moment. The most stupendous bombardment of the Civil War had begun."[53] After some two hours of this exchange of "lead and hail" the Confederates launched their infantry assault on Cemetery Hill, their objective was a small grove of trees near the Union center. "Military men then had, and still have, a succinct expression: infantry is the Queen of Battles . . . when the final showdown came the foot soldier carrying a rifle was the important figure. The big guns had done what they could; now it was the infantry that would settle matters."[54]

This became one of the most famous charges in history as the precision marching Confederates moved out in splendid pageantry, battle flags unfurled. The charge was made by veteran Virginians of Pickett's Division and North Carolinians under General Pettigrew. A contemporary wrote, "then ensued a conflict which no pen can describe; a conflict so terrific, so grand in its display of heroism, so matchless in the stubborn tenacity with which loyal and rebel alike clung to the coveted position, that only those who saw it, or were participants in it, can ever appreciate its intensity or sublimity."[55] As Pickett's Confederates assaulted the Union center, the Jerseymen of the 13th Regiment led by Colonel Carman stood their ground nobly at Culp's Hill on the Union right flank sustaining twenty-one casualties among whom were Henry Downing of Company G killed, and Captains Ryerson, Arey, and Adjutant C.W. Johnson wounded. The enormous

Captain David A. Ryerson, 13th N.J. Volunteers

losses inflicted on the Confederate assaults proved a disaster. Lee broke off the offensive and retreated south. General James Longstreet who had opposed the charge reflected on the events of the Battle of Gettysburg . . . "Pickett's lines being nearer, the impact was heaviest upon them. Most of the field officers were killed or wounded."[56] Colonel Whittle, who had sustained casualties at Williamsburg and Malvern Hill, was hit several times and shot down. General Armistead's heroism is well-known as he impaled his hat on his sword and strutted out in a proud and defiant gate. The brave officer's finest hour ended as he died against the wheels of an

Captain John H. Arey, 13ᵗʰ N.J. Volunteers

enemy cannon. As for Pickett, he called off the charge when it became evident that the offensive failed and the northerners were reinforcing their lines. Thus ended the Battle of Gettysburg.

Murphy's comrade Samuel Toombs wrote of the carnage,

The scenes of the field of battle defied description. Beginning on the right of the Union line, the dead bodies of the enemy which lined Culp's Hill from its summit to the banks of Rock Creek presented a harrowing sight. They were so close together that it was impossible to walk over the ground . . . Behind the rocks and trees along the creek, and in the stone house from which the enemy sharpshooters did such effective work in the ranks of the 13ᵗʰ New Jersey and 27ᵗʰ Indiana Regiments, the dead bodies of several rebels were found, showing that the fire from these regiments had done severe execution.

America, North and South sustained some 50,000 casualties in what has become one of the most famous battles in history ". . . with the stalemate at Gettysburg having put an end to Lee's efforts to end the war by a quick strike into Northern territory, the Union command, now unified under General Ulysses S. Grant, resolved to wear down the South in a dogged march through Virginia."[57]

The battle is generally considered the "high water mark" of the Confederacy but there was a lot of war left to be fought. The survivors took heed in Lincoln's words, "It is for us the living, . . . be dedicated here to the unfinished work which they who fought here have thus far so nobly advanced. It is rather for us to be here dedicated to the great task remaining before us—that from these honored dead we take increased devotion to that cause for which they gave the last full measure of devotion."[58] Lieutenant Franklin Murphy survived and continued that dedication by serving as Lieutenant of Company D, 13tʰ New Jersey Volunteers. His daughter Helen Kinney recalled his role in the great battle and passed down the story to her descendants. Joan Ellis, Murphy's great-granddaughter recalls that during the skirmishing leading up to the major engagement three Confederate prisoners were brought into Union lines. Murphy was detailed to escort the Southerners to the provost marshal whose location was some distance from the position of the 13ᵗʰ New Jersey Volunteers. It took him seventy-two hours without sleep to successfully complete his mission. As the Confederate prisoners were turned over for interrogation the exhausted Murphy crawled under a thicket and went fast asleep. He returned to his regiment and took his position in line as the Battle of Gettysburg reached its climax.

Casualties at Gettysburg

The 13th New Jersey Volunteers maneuvered to support cavalry reconnaissance and returned and remained in its position on the line from July 4 through July 7, 1863. It was then ordered to join in the pursuit of General Lee and reached John's Cross Roads, near Hagerstown by July 11, Sandy Hook by the 19th and around the Blue Ridge encamping at Snickerville by the 23rd. It moved to Warrenton Junction and then to Kelly's Ford on the Rappahonnock River. On the 15th of August units of Murphy's brigade (2nd Massachusetts, 3rd Wisconsin, and 27th Indiana) under its commander, General Ruger were sent in support of the civil authorities who were continuing to suppress anti-draft sentiment in New York City. Although Murphy was obviously proud of his own regiment, he did not share in the provincial disdain of other units which was typical of the military during the Civil War. This disdain could and did result in the exchange of fire between Federal

soldiers. Sergeant Harrison in Company G of the 14th New Jersey Volunteers recalled an incident when he wrote, "Someone in the Fifth Corps fired shots at a crowd of our boys . . . who was sitting by the road side and throwing out insinuations at each other, about fighting etc. I tell you Clemmy there is a hard set of men in this army."[59] Murphy in contrast wrote of the 2nd Massachusetts Volunteers for instance, "it was my good fortune to serve in a brigade with the Second Massachusetts, and it is my pleasure to say . . . that there was no finer regiment in its personnel, in its discipline, in its courage, in its reliability, than the old Second Massachusetts of Boston."[60] Daniel Oakey, a captain in this regiment recalled meeting General Sherman who after acknowledging his salute continued in a friendly manner, "How do you do, Captain?" Scrutinizing the

The infamous Devils Den at Gettysburg

insignia on my cap, he continued, "Second Massachusetts? Ah, yes, I know your regiment; you have very fine parades over there in the park."[61]

The New York Draft Riots

Meanwhile the draft riots the previous month in New York had shaken the city and had caused great concern in the Lincoln government. There were many underlying forces that festered and caused resentment among the masses. A large number of these were recent impoverished Irish immigrants who were determined to make a living in the New World. Moreover, they resented both the propertied classes who employed them and the poor blacks that competed for their jobs. In addition, the spectre of religious bigotry reared its ugly head as the age-old Protestant/Catholic animosity contributed to these combustible forces. It was also clear that the poor lacked the wherewithal to avoid military duty by hiring substitutes or buying exemptions. This, no doubt, fueled resentment and gave some the perspective that the struggle was a "rich man's war but a poor man's fight." On July 12, 1863, the drawing took place and within twenty-four hours thousands of people took to the streets rioting, looting, and attacking innocent people. Noteworthy among the latter were many blacks, who for whatever reason were held responsible for the war and its resulting privations. Fires spread destruction and hundreds of people were injured and killed before order was restored by veterans of the Gettysburg campaign. With resumption of the draft on August 19th there was no guarantee that riots would not resume except of course for the deterrent of these battle hardened Federals.[62] The North could ill afford a repetition of the events witnessed by Anna Elizabeth Dickinson on Monday morning, July 13th,1863 in the upper part of Manhattan. Five or six hundred men stormed one of the draft enrolling offices destroying records, furniture and everything in their path while "the law officers, the newspaper reporters who are expected to be everywhere—and the few peaceable spectators, were compelled to make a hasty retreat through an opportune rear exit, accelerated by the curses and blows of the assailants."[63] By the end of the month tranquility returned to New York City and the draft

Private James Augustus Grimstead, 14th N.J. Volunteers

proceeded peaceably. A relative of James Augustus Grimstead, a soldier serving in the 14th New Jersey Volunteers wrote from Brooklyn on August 26, 1863,

August dear . . . other armies may have been more successful but none more brave or who have fought better. Why at the battle of Gettysburg I have seen it reported the men did not know who was leading them. Did you know part of your army had come north for their health? While they are here I suppose they will keep an eye on these Irish Copperheads just for pastime while the draft is in operation, it has been going on some days now very quietly. A rumor is going around that these troops are being collected here for some other purpose, that General Hooker is going to Texas with them. I am sure I don't know how true it is but its seems a little strange they should bring so many soldiers here just for the draft—though I heard "Uncle Abe" said he would send the whole Army of the Potomac here if it could not be done without . . . M.A. Day.[64]

The rumor turned out to be partially valid not to Texas but to Tennessee and beyond.

The glitter of martial pomp and circumstance was soon to wear off as the Civil War progressed. Gone was the precision marching of "spit and polish" militia units on parade. It was too uncomfortable and impractical to move large numbers of infantry long distances rigidly at "soldier arms" or "right shoulder shift." We have the following description of Federal soldiers on the march from a private in the 13th New Jersey Volunteers. "Marching orders were first announced by the Sergeant-Major to the Orderly-Sergeant and then to the troops. The camp is broken down. The sound of drums signal the men to "attention" as they are commanded to "take arms," "shoulder arms," "right face," "forward," column of fours." Each regiment was assigned a position on the road and after a short distance the soldiers discard the military formalities and proceed carrying their "equipments" in as comfortable a manner as they can find. Blanket rolls very often substituted for the bulky knapsacks. The regiments were assigned different positions in the line each day as are the brigades. This was done deliberately to give each unit an equal share in the honors associated with the [right of the line]."[65] A division column was led by the infantry followed by the artillery, ambulance corps, and finally, the wagon train.

3

Marching With Sherman

IN LATE SEPTEMBER 1863 orders came down detaching the Eleventh and Twelfth Corps, under General Hooker, from the Army of the Potomac for service in Tennessee. Murphy and his comrades in the 13th New Jersey were sent by railroad through West Virginia, Ohio, Kentucky, and Tennessee to Stevenson, Alabama. By October 4th they had traveled eleven-hundred miles and on reaching their destination were assigned the task of keeping open the lines of communication with the Federal army at Chattanooga. They did this by keeping a vigilant watch over the railroad to prevent the rebels from destroying the road. "The key was the railroad. Sherman worried that Confederate raiders and guerrillas might easily cut the road and shut off his supplies. He told a subordinate that the road had to be defended "if only fifty men have to fight a 1,000 . . . thirteen hundred tons of goods were required every day to feed and supply his huge force; this meant 130 railroad cars."[1] Murphy was stationed near Normandy never knowing when the 1000 rebels might attack. One of his comrades wrote, "we are frequently hearing of rebel depredations on the railroad, and are, therefore, constantly on the alert."[2] Partisan guerrilla bands behind the lines were always a source of fear and anxiety for Union soldiers operating as most did deep in enemy country. Although commanders like Sherman countered this threat as best they could by exacting large financial reparations from the local inhabitants for materials destroyed, the soldiers in the field were in constant fear of being captured and murdered by such notorious personalities as Nathan Bedford Forrest or John Singleton Mosby. These became the well known, but there were many others that have escaped the pen of the historian. James Bullman, a fellow New Jersey soldier in the 14th New Jersey Volunteers, wrote from Martinsburg, Virginia, on May 7th, 1863, "The notorious guerrilla chief Leopold, was captured and brought here two weeks ago today. I had a good look at the illustrious personage. He is a man about five feet eleven inches in height, of light, but compact build, light hair worn long, & gray eyes, 25 years of age. He has a commanding main, but bloodthirsty expression. He has been guilty of several murders in the western part

General Joseph Hooker, U.S.A.

of this state and in Maryland."[3] Andrew Leopold was from Shepherdstown, Virginia, and enlisted in Company F, First Virginia Cavalry. He was tried and convicted of murder by a Military Commission and executed on May 25, 1864.[4] He died a brave man convinced that his actions were in defense of his country. The scene was in many ways reminiscent of the death of Major John André, the gallant adjutant of Sir Henry Clinton, caught up in the Benedict Arnold conspiracy eighty-four years earlier. Thus have been the tragic fates for those who have chosen to conduct military operations outside the established codes of warfare.

In the meantime there had been a number of changes that took place in Franklin Murphy's 13th New Jersey Regiment. The Reverend Samuel C. Hay replaced Reverend Beck as Regimental Chaplain. Captain George A. Beardsley was appointed major and Lieutenant Pierson promoted to command Company D. Lieutenant Colonel Grimes returned to the Regiment from detached duty. The men settled into winter quarters and endured what turned out to be severely cold weather. On November 26, 1863, Thanksgiving Day, one of the men lamented that "there is no Thanksgiving dinner for us." Things began to look up by Christmas, however, "the men have been having a very pleasant time. The officers had contributed a sufficient amount to provide a fine dinner of turkeys, chickens, roast pigs, beef, etc. Tables were built on the parade-ground that accompanied the whole regiment at once. How

A Billy Yank Governor / 48

General Ulysses S. Grant, U.S.A.

they did enjoy it! Many citizens were present, and enjoyed the merry time. The boys had a concert in the evening with singing and dancing."[5]

Preparing for the Campaign Against Atlanta

By the spring of 1864 General Grant was appointed Lieutenant General and placed in command of the whole army while General Sherman commanded all Federal troops in the military division of the Mississippi. "Far more important than the title and authority . . . was the intimate understanding and sympathy between Grant, who was now personally to direct the armies in the East, and Sherman who—five hundred miles distant, and soon more—was to direct the armies of the West."[6] General A.S. Williams retained command of the First Division

General John Singleton Mosby, C.S.A.

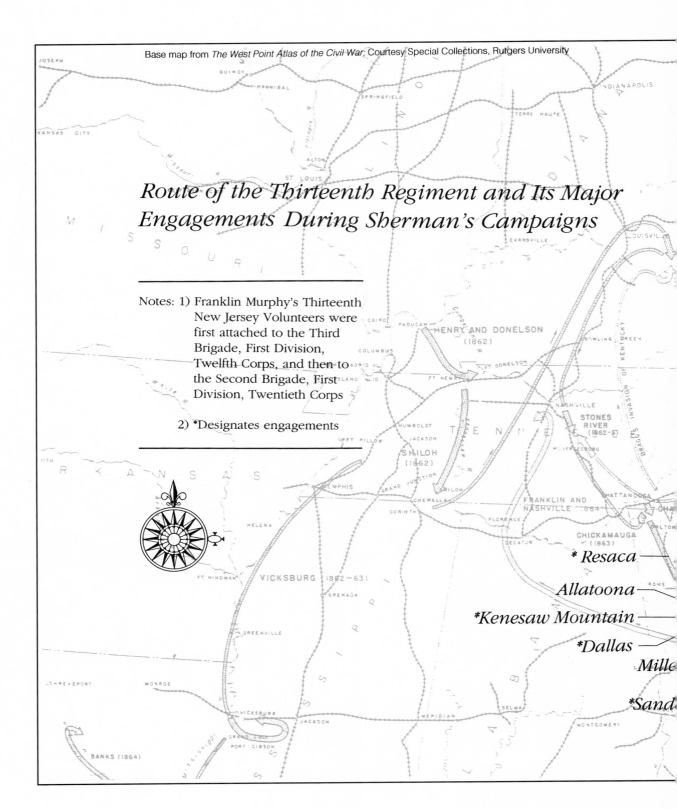

Route of the Thirteenth Regiment and Its Major Engagements During Sherman's Campaigns

Notes: 1) Franklin Murphy's Thirteenth
New Jersey Volunteers were
first attached to the Third
Brigade, First Division,
Twelfth Corps, and then to
the Second Brigade, First
Division, Twentieth Corps

2) *Designates engagements

*Resaca

Allatoona

*Kenesaw Mountain

*Dallas

Mille

*Sand

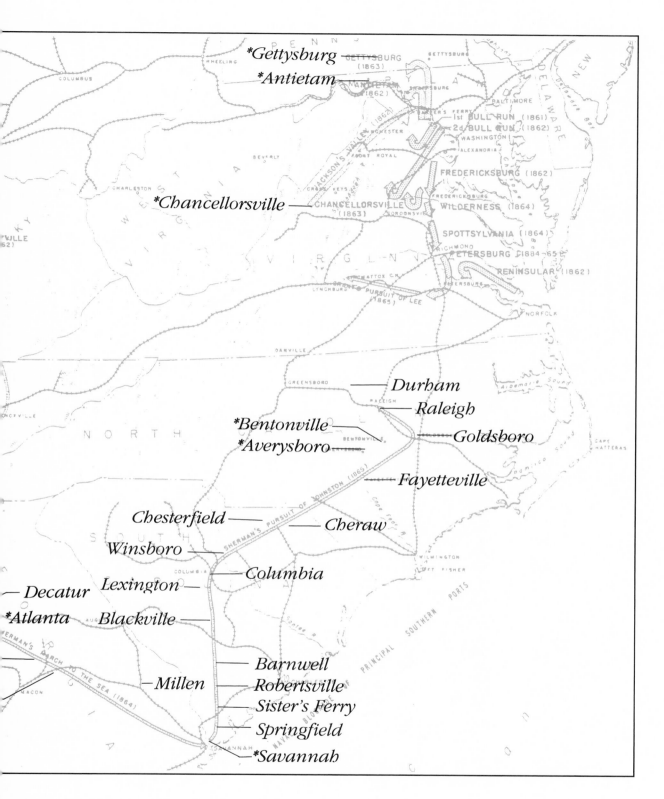

*Gettysburg GETTYSBURG (1863)

*Antietam

1st BULL RUN (1861)
2d BULL RUN (1862)

FREDERICKSBURG (1862)

*Chancellorsville CHANCELLORSVILLE (1863)
WILDERNESS (1864)

SPOTTSYLVANIA (1864)
PETERSBURG (1864-65)
PENINSULAR (1862)

PURSUIT OF LEE (1865)

Durham

Raleigh

*Bentonville
*Averysboro
Goldsboro

Fayetteville

Chesterfield
Cheraw

Winsboro

Columbia

Decatur
Lexington

*Atlanta
Blackville

Barnwell
Millen
Robertsville
Sister's Ferry
Springfield
*Savannah

The attack at Rocky Face Ridge

and General Ruger was in charge of the brigade to which the 13th New Jersey Volunteers belonged. Murphy captured the confidence that the soldiers had in Grant when he wrote, "Grant [is] that great silent soldier, whose praises will be told in all the future ages. How the hearts and the hopes of the nation turned to him and how superbly he responded. When he started on his campaign to final victory and his army had been lost in the Wilderness for three days and the anxiety of the nation

had reached its highest tension, how that first dispatch of his set all fears at rest and established a confidence in him that was never afterwards shaken."[7] But Murphy's fate was more immediately tied to Sherman and his grand army of 100,000 men divided into the departments of the Cumberland, Tennessee, and Ohio. The Confederate forces that opposed Sherman were under the overall command of General Joseph Johnston. These were divided into two corps which were led by Generals Hardee and Hood. They were supported by Wheeler's cavalry totaling about 44,000 men. The great campaign against Atlanta was about to begin. Murphy marched to Decatur, Alabama, on the crest of the Cumberland Mountains down into Battle Creek Valley and on to Bridgeport, Alabama. His unit continued through Lookout Valley via Rossville and Anderson, Georgia, and arrived at Ringgold by May 7. Confederate forces occupied Dalton and were shielded by the formidable mountain known as Rocky Face Ridge. "The country between Dalton and Resaca was a natural funnel, fifteen miles long, formed by the Connesauga River on the east and Rocky Face Ridge on the west. The railroad from Chattanooga came slantwise into the west side of this funnel by a slit near the top known as Mill Creek Gap. Snake Creek Gap was another slit near the bottom."[8] The Army of the Cumberland attacked Johnston's front while McPherson with the Army of Tennessee flanked his left near Resaca in the rear while Schofield pressed hard on the right. Sherman moved forward the Twentieth Corps to a point near Snake Creek Gap and by April 13, 1864, the 13th New Jersey Volunteers moved toward Resaca. The Confederates pushed hard on the left and charged an unsupported Union battery. Murphy and his comrades moved quickly to its support engaging the Confederates and preventing the capture of this ordnance. Private Toombs vividly recalled the rebel advance on this battery and how its Federal support broke and ran. General Hooker ordered the Red Star boys on the double-quick. "Captain, double-shot those pieces; they can't take your battery. My corps supports you . . ." As the troops reached the battery Hooker cried out, "I would rather be a private in that battery at this moment than a major general!" As the rebels were driven back, Captain Simonson, the battery commander, embarrassed that his

A Billy Yank Governor / 52

Commissary Department Rocky Face Ridge

own corps had not rescued him responded when he learned that the 13th New Jersey Volunteers were among those who came to his aid, "All right, I'm a Jersey man myself."[9]

The next morning the Second Division of the 20th Corps continued the advance and the 13th New Jersey Volunteers continued forward by the flank keeping to the left of the rebel battle line as it gave up ground. When the rebels offered stiff resistance these New Jersey troops formed in line of battle and advanced over a half-mile plain with the rest of William's Division, Knipe's brigade on the right, Ruger's in the center, and Robinson's on the left. On reaching high ground the Federals hastily threw up breastworks and prepared for a Confederate counter-attack. The rebels realized that their line had been flanked and became determined to drive the unionists back. In a letter to the *Newark Advertiser* it was stated, "Johnston . . . had sworn to break our lines at this point or perish in the attempt. He failed, though the loss was great on both sides."[10]

The battle raged for two hours as the southern troops tried in vain to break the Federal line. The shrill and piercing shouts of the "rebel yell" have become legendary. One New Jersey soldier described the rebels advancing, "yelling like demons." Finally the withering fire of the blue line of battle broke the Confederate advance. Murphy lost four comrades killed and twenty-three wounded including Robert C. Baldwin, Charles Remer, A.M. Mathews, R.G. Wilson, and John A. Spence. Their sacrifice along with the others resulted in forcing General Johnston to evacuate Resaca and retreat across the Oostanaula and fortify the hills south of Cassville. The Federal army pushed on forcing the enemy to retreat further and by May 20, 1864, crossed the Etowah River and advanced in the di-

Captain A.M. Mathews, 13ᵗʰ N.J. Volunteers

General John Sedgwick, U.S.A.

General Sherman's wagon train moving through Resaca, Ga. at night

rection of Dallas. Sherman sent a message to Washington, "I give two days' rest to replenish and fit up. On the 23rd I will cross the Etowah and move on Dallas. This will turn the Allatoona Pass. If Johnston remains at Allatoona I shall move on Marietta."[11] By the 25th the Confederates attacked General Geary's Second Division of Hooker's 20th Corps inflicting large numbers of casualties. The First Division was ordered to the left to reinforce Geary as the 13th New Jersey Volunteers were deployed as skirmishers to the right of the line along with the 82nd Ohio Volunteers. The Federals sustained serious losses in this encounter. Civil War medical treatment was primitive by today's standards and wounds that would not be considered life-threatening in modern times were often death sentences in the mid-nineteenth century. The accuracy of the standard issue Springfield rifled-musket with its lethal 58 caliber "minie ball" inflicted devastating wounds. Lieutenant Colonel Grimes and Lieutenant Baitzel were both wounded in action as was Jacob A. Freiday and John Booth; they survived while Moses Garra-

brant severely wounded in the leg did not. It was not just the enlisted men in the field who came under the deadly and often long range fire of improved technology. Sergeant-Major William Burroughs Ross wrote at 11 A.M. on May 9, 1864, "General Sedgwick commanding our Corps was killed about half an hour ago. He was standing right by our regiment and was shot directly under the left eye, the blood flying on some of our boys."[12] Ross met a similar fate five months later at Cedar Creek, Virginia. The impact of this carnage on the civilian population was understandably dramatic. M.A. Day, wrote to her nephew, Private James Augustus Grimstead 14th New Jersey Volunteers from Brooklyn, New York, on May 22, 1864:

Dear Augustus, How thankful I am to our Heavenly Father that He has still kept you safe & unharmed though shot & shell have fallen around you & death been very near you. Since these battles have been going on I have thought of you & wondered if

Do They Miss Me At Home.

Do, they miss me at home, do they miss me!
'Twould be an assurance most dear,
To know that this moment some loved one,
Were saying I wish he was here,
To feel that the group at the fireside
Were thinking of me as I roam,
Oh, yes, 'twould be joy beyond measure
To know that they missed me at home,
To know that they missed me at home.

When twilight approaches, the season
That ever is sacred to song,
Does some one repeat my name over,
And sigh that I tarry so long!
And is there a chord in the music
That's miss'd when my voice is away,
And a chord in each heart that awaketh
Regret at my wearisome stay,
Regret at my wearisome stay.

Do they set me a chair near the table,
When ev'ning's home pleasures are nigh,
When the candles are lit in the parlor,
And the stars in the calm azure sky?

Original script of James Bullman's poem

And when the "good nights" are repeated,
And all lay them down to their sleep,
Do they think of the absent, and waft me
A whispered "good night" while they —
A whispered "good night" while they —

Do they miss me at home— do they miss me
At morning, at noon, or at night?
And lingers one gloomy shade round them
That only my presence can light?
Are joys less invitingly welcome,
And pleasures less hale than before,
Because one is miss'd from the circle,
Because I am with them no more,
Because I am with them no more?

J. Bullman

your duties brought you in the midst of the strife or not. How my heart aches for the thousands of noble fellows who have gone to offer their lives for their country & more for those who have just escaped death & must go on through life maimed & crippled. God pity & comfort them. God comfort those who love them. How sad is the death of such men as Sedgwick, Wadsworth & Rice. The papers spoke of Sedgwick as Grant's right hand man. After all, what is life even in such a cause & what undying fame are you soldiers laying up for yourselves, the world will never forget it, nor will you ever forget the scenes you are witnessing every day. How terribly grand it must be to witness such battles as have been fought the last few days. I hope it will be decided soon, but whether soon or not the people have the utmost confidence in General Grant that he will win.[13]

There has been a great deal of analysis of Civil War letters and the impact these uncensored epistles have had on the modern understanding of this great conflict. Occasionally there surfaces other documents that capture the poignant inner feelings of the men who endured these times. A comrade of Franklin Murphy and fellow New Jersey volunteer wrote the following poem which vividly expresses the longing of the troops to be with their loved ones back home. It is entitled:

"Do They Miss Me At Home?"

Do they miss me at home, do they miss me?
T'would be an assurance most dear,
To know that this moment some loved one,
Were saying I wish he was here,
To feel that the group at the fireside,
Were thinking of me as I roam,
Oh, yes, t'would, be joy beyond measure
To know that they missed me at home,
To know that they missed me at home.

When twilight approaches, the season
That ever is sacred to song,
Does some one, repeat my name over,
And sigh that I tarry so long!
And is there a chord in the music,
That's miss'd when my voice is away,
And a chord in each heart that awaketh
Regret at my wearisome stay,
Regret at my wearisome stay.

Do they set me a chair near the table,
When ev'ning's, home pleasures, are, nigh,
When the candles are lit in the parlor,
And the stars in the calm asure sky?
And when the "good nights" are repeated,
And all lay them down to their sleep,
Do they think of the absent, and, waft me,
A whispered "good night" while they sleep,
A whispered "good night" while they sleep.

Do they miss me at home-do they miss me,
At morning, at noon, or at night?
And lingers, one gloomy shade round them,
That only my presence can light?
Are joys less invitingly welcome,
And pleasures less hales than before,
Because one is miss'd from the circle,
Because I am with them no more,
Because I am with them no more?

James Bullman 14th NJ Volunteers-killed in action Cold Harbor, VA, June 1, 1864[14]

Battle of Dallas

Meanwhile, Murphy and his comrades in Georgia confronted Confederate works which were impossible to carry by direct assault. The combat they experienced at this time became known as the Battle of Dallas which was actually fought near Pumpkin Vine Creek, a tributary of the Etowah River about thirty miles from Atlanta. Sherman became a master at flank movements which forced Johnston to abandon Allatoona, Georgia, in early June 1864 giving the Federals control of the railroad down to Kenesaw Mountain. Sherman had familiarized himself with this territory earlier in his career. He had a natural proclivity toward geography and committed the peculiarities of an area to memory. "While working with the inspector general in the 1840's, he [Sherman] had ridden around the Etowah River region, had climbed Kenesaw Mountain, and had passed through Allatoona Gap. He knew from that experience just how formidable Allatoona was, so he never considered a frontal

Typical chevaux-de-frise

attack on Johnston there."[15] The 13th New Jersey moved toward the railroad station at Ackworth not far from Kingston. The Federal battle-line faced south and ran in an east-west direction. The opposing Confederate lines extended from Kenesaw Mountain on their right west to Lost Mountain on the left including Pine Knob. Despite incessant rains which mired the roads and made movement difficult, Sherman ordered the shelling of Confederate positions. Simonson's Battery opened on the Confederates and a general engagement commenced on June 16th and 17th. Confederate General Leonidas Polk was killed in this artillery exchange which prompted Sherman to remark, "We killed Bishop Polk yesterday, and have made good progress today."[16] It was living in the midst of carnage which deadened the sensitivities of the combatants and made them almost take in stride the loss of life. In some cases the soldiers gently resigned themselves to their fate. Their writings express a sort of cavalier attitude exemplified in a letter signed only George which ended, "Now for a jolly good smoke, then a

few hours sleep and tomorrow—the Battlefield. Oh who would not be a soldier?"[17] The 13th New Jersey Volunteers suffered the loss of their brave young Lieutenant Peter M. Ryerson of Company C. His father, Major Ryerson had been killed at Williamsburg, yet another example of the multiple losses sustained by American families, both North and South.

Hard pressed, the Confederates yielded Pine and Lost Mountains and concentrated their defenses on Kenesaw Mountain, the right to cover Marietta and the left running across the Lost Mountain and Marietta Road covering the railroad track to the Chattahoochee. On the 22nd, the 13th New Jersey Volunteers were attacked as they built elaborate defenses between the woods and the open ground consisting of sharpened logs called chevaux-de-frise. The Confederates advanced in several lines of battle. These were seasoned veterans of Hindman's and Stevenson's Divisions of Hood's Corps. They moved forward in regal splendor displaying that superhuman courage which became the trademark of Civil War soldiers. They were undaunted by what they knew awaited them. "Some Civil War soldiers grasped intuitively, and more acquired by experience, the modern understanding that courage is not the absence of fear but the mastery of it."[18]

There can be little doubt of the soldiers' courage when considering what it must have taken to form in line of battle and advance across open fields into murderous fire. Franklin Murphy recalled, "As long as the nation endures the story of personal prowess and thrilling incident . . . will be told to interest the coming generations. No war engaged so many men, in none were the battles so numerous, in none were the issues more important . . . How all of us who are old enough to remember those days, remember incident after incident of individual bravery, not less than those examples of regimental courage whose record makes immortal the history of so many of our battlefields."[19]

The Battle of Kulp's Farm

The northerners opened fire at three-hundred yards inflicting devastating loses on the Confederates who fell back, regrouped and advanced a second time. Again the Federals poured a withering fire into the advancing foe who broke off the attack leaving many dead and wounded on the field. The battle was not over, however. The Confederates reformed in line of battle under cover of thick underbrush and opened a deadly and persistent fire which lasted nearly two hours. When the smoke finally cleared, ending this engagement that became know as the Battle of Kulp's farm, Murphy and his comrades in the 13th Regiment under the temporary command of Captain Harris sustained light casualties, none killed and six wounded.

On the 27th of June, 1864, Murphy with the Jerseymen moved in support of a field battery as part of a general assault against Confederate entrenchments. The assault failed and cost the Union army some 2500 casualties. This was unusual as General Sherman had characteristically avoided frontal assaults. He preferred to flank his enemy and force him to withdraw which minimized casualties on both sides. This had become so obvious a pattern, however, that he decided to do what the enemy least expected. Sherman reported, "I perceived that the enemy and our officers had settled down to the conviction that I would not assault fortified lines. All looked to me to outflank. An army to be efficient, must not settle down to a single mode of offence, but must be prepared to execute any plan which promises success. I wanted, therefore, for the moral effect, to make a successful assault against the enemy behind his breastworks . . ."[20] A contemporary general officer, Jacob Cox, lamented at the folly of these frontal movements. He wrote, "Our books of tactics, copying from the French, had taught that the regimental column of divisions of two companies, doubled on the centre was par excellence the column of attack. In spite of the fact that Wellington in the Peninsular War had shown again and again that such a column, even over open country, melted away before a 'thin red line' of British soldiers armed only with the old 'Brown Bess' with its buck-and-ball cartridge, the prestige of Napoleonic tradition kept the upper hand . . . So hard it is to free ourselves from the trammels of old customs and a mistaken practice!"[21]

The assault having failed, Sherman turned to doing what he did best, flank the Confederates and force Johnston to abandon Kenesaw Mountain. The 13th New Jersey Volunteers moved through Marietta

General William Tecumseh Sherman, U.S.A.

towards the Chattahoochee River and occupied a position in the right center of the army on July 7, 1864. It remained here until the 17th when it took part in the general advance crossing the Chattahoochee at Paice's Ferry bivouacking near Buckhead. It is a moving tribute to the human spirit that

Kenesaw Mountain from Allatoona Heights

Bridging the Chattahoochee River

A Billy Yank Governor / 60

a young soldier could set aside from all the death and destruction a perspective of the beauty of nature and its landscapes. Private Toombs recalled the majesty of the town of Marietta and the beauty of the surrounding countryside when he wrote, ". . . to our delight and surprise we found ourselves in Marietta. We halted at the Military Institute, a three story brick building, situated on an eminence on the outskirts of the town . . . From the lawn surrounding the Institute a beautiful view was spread before us in all directions." To the north of Marietta were the battle-scarred peaks of Kenesaw Mountain recently drenched in blood. Off to the left rose the majestic peak of Lost Mountain. Toombs continued, "Marietta lay nestled at the foot of Kenesaw, and stretching away eastward its beautiful broad avenues threaded their way through a forest of majestic shade trees which lined their sides. The place bore evidences of a wealthy, refined and cultured population."[22]

Battle of Peach Tree Creek

On the 18th Colonel Carmen led the 13th New Jersey Volunteers and the 82nd Ohio Volunteers in a reconnaissance to capture rebel cavalry positioned between the 4th and the 20th Corps. The skirmish at Nancy's Creek resulted in the deaths of two of Murphy's comrades, James Catford and Thomas Griffith. On the 19th the corps crossed Peach Tree Creek and was attacked by a strong force of rebels the next day. Command of Confederate forces changed hands when General Johnston was replaced by General Hood. Confederate authorities were displeased with Johnston's defensive inclinations and wanted bolder opposition to Sherman. General Lee would later lament this decision when he wrote, "The removal of Johnston at that critical juncture (and Hood's move into Tennessee)—at the very time when, as he (Johnston) affirms, he was about to attack the enemy—was a serious error . . . Sherman was now relieved from all organized opposition, and advanced leisurely to Savannah, and thence northward through South Carolina, leaving a broad track of desolation behind him."[23] The Battle of Peach Tree Creek is an example of the many misnomers in history. "There are no peach trees along Peachtree Creek. The name comes from the

General Joseph Johnston, C.S.A.

General John B. Hood, C.S.A.

Indians; it refers to a giant 'pitch tree' that had once stood on its bank. Two streams—called Peachtree Creek North and Peachtree Creek South—join northeast of Atlanta to form the creek, which flows in a generally westward direction until it empties into the Chattahoochee not far from the railroad bridge."[24] It was the last natural obstacle of any consequence between the Federals and Atlanta, five miles to the south. Hood massed his forces in the woods and launched one attack after another. There was "Stevens's Georgians charge once, then again, and each time withering fire repulsed them with heavy casualties . . . Brigadier General Thomas M. Scott's Alabamans and Louisianans, overran Geary's outpost hill, capturing many of the 33rd New Jersey and capturing its state flag . . . A fierce, 'almost hand-to-hand' struggle followed, during which Brigadier General Edward O'Neal's Alabama and Mississippi Brigade turned Williams's left . . . Union artillery cross fire raked their ranks, forcing them [the Confederates] back."[25] Franklin Murphy and his comrades in the 13th New Jersey Volunteers fought under Williams and distinguished themselves in this fierce fighting losing six of their number including William Backus of Company B who died on July 25th, 1864, of his wounds. "The 20th Corps had close to 1700 killed, wounded, and missing. Williams's division contributed the most to this total, 627 . . . Williams sadly wrote a friend, [his Division] was reduced in number to a brigade."[26] The Confederates abandoned the Peach Tree Creek defenses and fell back within the immediate defenses of Atlanta.

A Demonstration

Murphy and the 13th were ordered by Captain Guyer of Company F to position themselves on a hill about 500 yards from the Confederate works. This line remained the advanced Federal position for the remainder of the campaign and came under heavy rebel artillery fire. On July 27, 1864, the 13th New Jersey Volunteers were chosen as part of a planned offensive foray that was often referred to in Civil War verbiage as a "demonstration." Each division was to select a regiment that would decoy Union efforts to straighten their lines and pinpoint the positions of rebel forts. Several houses used by the rebels were torched by Murphy's comrades led

Brigadier General A.S. Williams, U.S.A.

Captain W.H. Miller, 13ᵗʰ N.J. Volunteers

by Captain Miller of Company A. It was necessary to eliminate these obstructions because they concealed the southern defenses. The Confederates lost heavily in killed and wounded and 33 rebels were taken prisoner. The Northerners did not escape unscathed; the 13ᵗʰ Regiment lost 2 killed and six wounded, including Orderly Sergeant Richard Brown who had his leg blown off and died quickly of shock and loss of blood. General Williams of the First Division had meanwhile replaced Hooker who had asked to be relieved from command. Murphy returned to Federal lines amidst the cheers of his peers and the message from his general that "you have done well."

"There were many instances of personal bravery displayed in front of Atlanta. The men were so frequently exposed to the fire of the enemy that the fear of danger was to a certain extent dispelled."[27] "The losses in Williams's division were heavier than Geary's in killed and wounded, and the reputation of that Division gives assurance that it gave quite as good an account of itself in the punishment of those who attacked it."[28] On the 28ᵗʰ of July General Hood attacked the Army of the Tennessee commanded by General Howard. It was during the fighting of the previous days that the Federal army suffered a terrible loss in the death of General James B. McPherson, one of Sherman's favorite officers. With the constantly shifting battle fronts

Engraving of the death of General McPherson

mistakes were made. McPherson rode directly into a Confederate line of battle, was confronted by the enemy who demanded his surrender. He reigned up his horse, tipped his hat in a salute-like gesture and galloped off. The Confederates opened fire and shot McPherson through the heart. The gallant officer was instantly killed by Corporal Robert Coleman of the 5th Tennessee Confederate.[29] When news of McPherson's death reached Sherman, he is said to have moaned with grief and sorrow. He quickly recovered and appointed John Logan temporarily to take his place. Logan, the volunteer, was in turn replaced by West Point's Oliver O. Howard which prompted Sherman to comment, "Logan will never forgive me for putting O.O. Howard in McPherson's place."[30] Presumably, he did not. Despite his deep feelings and tender sensibilities, time simply did not

allow Sherman to languish in this loss, after all he had Hood's determined offensives to repulse. And repulse them he did time after time until the Confederates had lost "so severely . . . that [Hood's] troops were losing their stomach for assaulting entrenchments."[31]

Concern in the North

In the meantime public opinion in the North was questioning Lincoln's conduct of the war and there were in fact many disgruntled groups who started to question the price of keeping the South in the Union. Grant's failure at the Crater and the successful Confederate raid at Chambersburg, Pennsylvania, put Lincoln into a melancholy mood. Several peace overtures were made to Confederate authorities. Historian Albert Castell writes, ". . . that thus twice within a matter of weeks Lincoln had approached the Confederate government in quest of

General James B. McPherson, U.S.A.

Horace Greeley

peace. This is not the conduct of a victor or of one who expects victory; it is how someone acts who is losing and knows it." It was a politically sensitive time as well because the Presidential elections were coming up in the fall. William Brown, a friend of President Lincoln's from Illinois captured a contemporary perspective when he answered a question about seeing the President.

"Ever see him again? He was asked, Yes, onct down in Washington, summer of 64. Things was lookin' purty blue that summer. Didn't seem to be anybody who thought he'd git reelected. Greely was abusin him in The Tribune for not makin' peace, and you know there was about half the North that always let Greeley do their thinkin' fer' em. The war wasn't comin on at all—seemed as if they never would do nuthin. Grant was hangin' on to Petersburg like a dog to a root, but it didn't seem to do no good. Same with Sherman, who was tryin' to take

Atlanta. The country was just petered out with the everlastin' taxes an' fightin' an' dyin. [32]

The inclination of many people in the North to "let the erring sisters go" became a source of anxiety and bewilderment to Federal soldiers who were fighting and dying to preserve the Union. It was best exemplified in The Chicago Platform of the Democratic Party of 1864 when it nominated former General George McClellan and called for an immediate cessation of hostilities. Sergeant Albert C. Harrison, a New Jersey volunteer who had responded to Lincoln's 1862 call, bitterly wrote on October 23, 1864, "I cannot chew that Chicago Platform fine enough to swallow it . . . No sooner will I die under the old Stars & Stripes. Don't talk about Mc. to the soldiers in the field. We have a better chance here of knowing the vast difference between the two men. Take the majority of the soldiers in the field, they would sooner vote for Jeff Davis himself . . . I tell you it don't go down with the 'blue bellies.' Uncle Abe the soldiers friend retains the chair for the next four years, if the Good Lord spares his life."[33]

Reflections about Lincoln

Tragically for the country his life was not spared and the tumultuous ramifications would resonate well into the next century. Lieutenant Murphy held similar feelings when he reflected on the President after the war.

How the great figures of the war time rise before us as our thoughts go back to those eventful days! Above them all is the sad and patient face of the immortal Lincoln. With a heart of love, a hand of steel, a brain that mastered every question and that kept the great question always in view; maligned at times, ridiculed at times, carrying almost alone in the dark days the burden of a nation's woe. How we came to love him and to trust him and to lean on him. Did the affection and confidence of a nation ever go out to any man as the affection and confidence of this nation went out to that giant of the prairies, raised up by an over-ruling Providence, to lead this great nation through fire and sword and slavery to peace and freedom and prosperity . . . Lincoln was a great President. I address some who perhaps knew him—as I did; I address many who remember those dreadful days of 61-65 when the country was almost torn asunder. How it seemed as if he was the only man in all this Nation whose gentleness and whose wisdom and whose unfailing courage was equal to the leadership of those trying days. We see him now, radiant with patriotic purpose and at times almost alone in his untiring faith and we know the result of all that he did in the civilization of this great country. Truly Lincoln was a great President.[34]

Lincoln, like Murphy, was thrust into a world not of his choosing, grappling as best he could with the forces thrust upon him. Theodore Roosevelt, a mere youngster at this time, would metaphorically liken these forces to cards dealt in the game of life. It would be forty years before his "Square Deal" would place the Federal Government in a position to referee that dealing. After all, this war, in large part, was a contest over what role that government should play vis-a-vis states' rights. Historian David Herbert Donald captures the feelings of Abraham Lincoln when the President wrote, "I claim not to have controlled events, but confess plainly that events have controlled me."[35]

Onward Toward Atlanta

There were many dreadful days ahead for Murphy and all the country as the summer of 1864 dragged on. The 13th New Jersey Volunteers were ordered to advance on enemy positions in early August. They engaged the rebels capturing some sixty prisoners and were ordered back to their old position where they remained until August 25th. Captain Harris was commissioned major and Lieutenant Johnson took command of Company E. A lot had happened in the Atlanta campaign in the meantime, most significantly General Sherman had succeeded in extending his entrenchments to East Point which gave him command of the railroads that supplied Atlanta. By early August Confederate General Hood sent Wheeler's cavalry in a dash to the rear hoping to disrupt the railroad and destroy the Federal lines of communication. Davis telegraphed Hood: "I concur in your plan, and hope your cavalry will be able to destroy the railroad bridges and depots of the enemy on the line to Bridgeport . . ."[36] Sherman responded in kind and sent Kilpatrick's cavalry on a raid on August 16th south and east of Atlanta. He succeeded in destroying the railroad at several key positions near Fairburn depriving the Confederates of much needed supplies. Then on the 18th, Kilpatrick aided by Garrand moved to Jonesboro, defeated Ross's Confederate cavalry and destroyed some of the railroad. He reported to Sherman that sufficient damage had been done to the railroad that it would take the Confederates a week or more to repair it. Although this turned out to be an exaggeration, he did well to inflict some damage and escape the combined cavalry and infantry of the Confederates.

Northern volunteer Frank Grimstead received a letter from his cousin Amanda asking,

> *What do you think of General Kilpatrick's raid? . . . I think that he is a very brave, bold & daring fellow to go so far into the very heart of the Rebel country . . . They had ought to have all the praise possible for such brave men ought to have their name exalted quite a high degree for undertaking such a perilous enterprise . . . and help demolish the Rebel railroads, pigs, poultry, and provisions at the expense of the Rebels (to their Bonnie Free Country.)[37]*

The perception of civilians at home often differed from those of soldiers in the field. James Grimstead wrote from Fairfax Station, Virginia, on October 18, 1863, "Kilpatrick I saw the other [night] as well as dense darkness, lighted up by a solitary lantern in his hand—would let me—it was a moment of great excitement—he had just threatened to shoot a quartermaster if he would not get his train out of the road and let his cavalry pass—he's an awful fellow. They say he likes to get surrounded and then cut his way out."[38]

Bombardment of Atlanta

Sherman in the meantime had ordered a bombardment of Atlanta by the awesome twenty and thirty pound parrot guns. He believed that the civilian population had evacuated the city. They had not. Many civilians became the innocent victims of war. ". . . on the night of August 3 a missile ripped through the house of J.F. Warner, superintendent of the gasworks, and exploded on the bed where he was lying with his six-year-old daughter Lizzie, 'mangling them horribly and producing instant death.' "[39] Those who survived did so by burrowing bomb-proof "gopher holes" into embankments or by taking advantage of natural caves to shield themselves from the deadly incoming missiles. This became reminiscent of what General Charles Cornwallis and his British regulars experienced at Yorktown eighty-three years earlier.

General Judson Kilpatrick, U.S.A.

A typical Atlanta cave

General Sherman and his staff at Atlanta

A Billy Yank Governor / 68

General Sherman and his staff before Atlanta

Brigadier General William J. Hardee, C.S. A.

The bombardment of Atlanta did not attain the desired results. With impending supply problems and expiring enlistments Sherman became impatient and decided to force the issue with a classic flanking movement, this time to the south by the right. Historian Ezra J. Warner in his book *Generals In Blue, Lives Of The Union Commanders* sums up Sherman's strategy when he writes, "Sherman assumed command of all troops in the western theater and entered upon a series of operations which would not only constitute the apogee of his career but would inaugurate the theory of modern war by which total destruction would be visited upon the civilian population in the path of the advancing columns. During the campaign which culminated in the capture of Atlanta, Sherman utilized his superior numbers to flank his opponent Joseph E. Johnston out of one defensive position after another." The siege was abandoned and the sick and wounded were ordered along with surplus supplies and equipment sent back to the Federal position on the Chattahoochee under cover of the 20th Corps. The rest of the Union army moved to the right southward and succeeded in getting behind Atlanta before the Confederates realized what was happening. General Hardee who commanded rebel forces at this point had fallen back to Lovejoy's Station. The 13th New Jersey Volunteers occupied abandoned rebel works in the rear by August 25th, 1864, expecting an assault by Hood's troops which never came. The next day most Federal forces were withdrawn from Atlanta leaving only General Schofield in front of the city. The Confederates rejoiced in what they thought was Hood's great victory over the Yankees. The reality was that he had simply been outmaneuvered. Murphy and his New Jersey comrades were ordered with two other Federal regiments to move out on reconnoissance and found a large force of two brigades of rebels and four pieces of ordnance opposing them. Again there was no engagement. Sherman had shifted his "whole army or the bulk of it, beyond the Confederate left, as he had done at Dalton, Allatoona, and Marietta, thereby leaving Hood, like Johnston before him, with a choice between attacking or retreating."[40] He chose to retreat ordering the stores burned and evacuated Atlanta.

Headquarters of General Sherman in Atlanta

Into Atlanta at Last!

The 13th New Jersey Volunteers marched into Atlanta with bands playing and colors flying just before dark on September 2, 1864, and encamped on the east side of the rebel breastworks near the Georgia Railroad. One soldier recalled that the "brigade band struck up a number of lively airs to the music of which we marched gaily into the city with flags flying."[41] Lieutenant Colonel Grimes resigned at this time and was replaced by Major Harris. The Atlanta campaign finally came to an end and the men rested for the first time in four months out of the range of hostile artillery. The Regiment lost about one hundred killed, wounded and missing. Franklin Murphy survived and reflected on these loses with

the terse statement that the "campaign which is apt to be and is usually in the popular mind overshadowed by the more brilliant campaign which followed, but the journey to Atlanta was a fight for every foot of the way."

Life was hard for the civilians in Atlanta in the fall of 1864. Mary Chesnut, wife of a Confederate official caught the melancholy mood when she confided to her diary on September 1, 1864, that "the battle is raging at Atlanta—our fate hanging in the balance . . . Atlanta gone. Well—that agony is over."[42] Inflation ran rampant as depreciated paper chased dwindling goods. One New Jersey soldier

General Slocum, U.S.A. and his staff

recalled that flour sold at $1.25 lb., salt $1.00, chickens at $7.00-9.00 each and coffee $19.00-20.00 lb.[43] Murphy and his chums enjoyed what soldiers in a later day would call "down time" during that September of 1864 visiting the ruins of the arsenal and railroad depot and meandering around once thriving hotels like the Trout House. General Slocum ordered a formal review of the Division at this time to keep military discipline and the troops focused on their task. One soldier recalled that it was a "fascinating sight." It was not all leisure, however, as the Federals were also busy building new lines of entrenchments. Murphy worked on these and performed routine picket duty. Meanwhile Confederate General Hood unsuccessfully engaged Federal units near Dallas, Georgia, before retreating into Tennessee.

Total War

On September 8, 1864, Sherman issued Special Field Orders No. 67 in what has become one of the most criticized decisions of the war; ordering some 1500 civilians evacuated from Atlanta. In a statement to the mayor of Atlanta Sherman exclaimed, "We don't want your negroes, or your horses, or your houses, or your land, or anything you have; but we do want, and will have, a just obedience to the laws of the United States."[44] This became part of Sherman's concept of total war—the destruction of the enemy's morale, civilian as well as military. Confederate General Hood responded that this order "transcends, in studious and ingenious cruelty, all acts ever before brought to my attention in the dark history of war" a response to Sherman's policy that "war is cruelty and you cannot refine it."[45] General Sherman's deliberate

Federal troops tearing down buildings in Atlanta

"scorched earth policy" was designed to end the war and end it as soon as humanly possible.

The apparent contradiction of unleashing total war upon civilians as well as enemy combatants was Sherman's concept of achieving that end. In his mind, it was absolutely essential to destroy the will of the South's population to make war on the legitimate government of the United States. He was not the vandal that his enemies depicted him as being. In fact, he was fond of the people of the South and had spent much time in their midst prior to the war. Wherever and whenever possible he avoided pitched battles when the objectives he sought could be accomplished without undue loss of life. His decision to cut lose from his supply lines, to "dive under," and drive his army through the rich heartland of the South has become one of the most daring and unorthodox military moves in history; one that would go down in the annals along with Hanni-

bal's crossing the Alps and Cortez burning his ships before moving on the Aztec capitol of Technochti-lan. The circumstances of war have often brought misery to innocent victims by their own government. Not all civilians in Atlanta, for example, were required to leave. Sherman's army allowed some civilians to remain behind to administer the mundane duties associated with providing services to an army of occupation. No doubt, some engaged in wartime profiteering while others simply sought employment. These people were generally considered disloyal by fellow southerners and in some cases were tried for treason. A letter written to Secretary of War James A. Seddon by Confederate General Howell Cobb dated December 22, 1864, illustrates this policy. In it he writes, "Since the reoccupation of the place [Atlanta] by our own people

The citizens of Atlanta leaving the city in compliance with Sherman's order

there were found soldiers and citizens who had remained there with the Yankees and had been employed by them in various occupations. When women and children were driven out by the heartless brute Sherman, and were forced to make their way to some place of refuge, those who remained subjected themselves, in my opinion, to the suspicion of treason. Acting upon this opinion I ordered Colonel Glenn, commandant of the post, to arrest all such and send them here . . . [for trial]" Seddon replied, "Adjutant-General-Inform General Cobb that his course of proceedings is deemed judicious."[46] In the meantime General Sherman finalized his strategy for the next "dive under." "The general [Sherman] commanding deems it proper at this time to inform the officers and men of the Fourteenth, Fifteenth, Seventeenth, and Twentieth Corps, that he has organized them into an army for the special purpose, well known to the War Department and to General Grant . . . and in Field Orders #120 . . . for the purpose of military operations, this army is divided into the wings viz: the right wing, Major-General O.O. Howard commanding, composed of the 15th & 17th Corps; the left wing, Major-General H.W. Slocum commanding, composed of the 14th & 20th Corps." [47] Sherman wanted to keep his options opened and the Confederates guessing just where he was going and why. On October 20th, General Sherman wrote to General Thomas, that he "proposed to organize an army of 60,000 or 65,000 . . . to destroy Macon, Augusta, and it may be Savannah and Charleston . . . see what we can haul and send back all else . . . one gun per thousand men will be plenty to take along."[48]

A Billy Yank Governor / 74

The Campaign for Savannah

The month of October saw Federal supplies dwindle to the point that foraging parties were once again ordered out into the countryside. By the 12th of the month, Murphy and the men of the 13th New Jersey Volunteers fanned out some twenty miles crossing the South River at Clark's Mills where they succeeded in commandeering large quantities of corn, wheat, and cotton and smaller amounts of bacon, sweet-potatoes, and chickens. By November the Campaign of Savannah had begun in earnest for Murphy and his New Jersey comrades. They marched some nineteen miles along the Atlanta and Augusta railroad in a southeasterly direction before encamping at the foot of Stone Mountain, in DeKalb County. The army was divided into two parts, or wings, the left corps (14th & 20th) under General Slocum, moving along the most northerly route, and the right (15th & 17th) corps, under General Howard. General Judson Kilpatrick and the northern cavalry moved with Howard. By November 22, 1864, the northern forces had crossed the Little River and marched into the Georgia capital of Milledgeville right down Jackson Street to Green Street with regimental bands striking up spirited "national airs." General Sherman occupied the residence of Georgia's Governor Brown while the Confederate legislature fled before the approaching bluecoats. A provisional legislature of sorts was organized which promptly repudiated the state's Ordinance of Secession. By November 26th the Federals made contact with the enemy and a spirited skirmish took place at Buffalo Creek near Sandersville. Three of Murphy's comrades were wounded in this action as the rebel cavalry under General Wheeler doggedly fought the invaders both on horseback and dismounted and deployed as infantry behind breastworks. The results once again saw the southerners yield to the superior Federal forces which forced the rebels out of Sandersville. Colonel Carman's report of the action of the brigade in this affair says:

November 26, 1864. The brigade had the advance, moved out of camp at half-past six o'clock, a.m. and after marching two miles, the Ninth Illinois Cavalry in our front encountered the enemy,

Lieutenant General Joseph Wheeler, C.S.A.

The rear guard, Sherman's march through Georgia

who posted on a small creek, the road through which had been obstructed by falled trees; the enemy were soon dislodged and pursued to Sandersville, at which place they made a stand, driving back our cavalry. I then deployed six companies of the Thirteenth New Jersey as skirmishers, with four companies in reserve, and advanced on them, the Ninth Illinois being disposed on the flanks. The enemy gave way before my skirmishers, and I entered the town at the same time as did the Fourteenth Corps, who came in on another road to the left. Moving to the right, I followed the enemy through the town and one mile beyond, skirmishing a little. My loss was two men wounded, belonging to the Thirteenth New Jersey.[49]

After driving the rebels through the town the Regiment moved south to Tennille Station #13 of the Georgia Railroad. The next day it moved to Davisborough and on to Spier's Station #11 as far as the Ogeechee River and burned a huge lumber yard filled with bridge timbers. Murphy and the other sixty-odd-thousand men of Sherman's army continued on crossing the Ogeechee on the 30th of November reaching the vicinity of Millen by December 3, 1864. It was here that another stark reminder of the horrors of war greeted these men— the Confederate prison stockade of Camp Lawton. The horrors of Civil War prison camps are a gruesome example that combine the ingredients of total war and the resulting incarceration of large numbers of men with conflicting ideologies. Confederate authorities would not consider Blacks combatants.

First Lieutenant James L. Carmen, 13th N.J. Volunteers

First Lieutenant William Bucklish, 13th N.J. Volunteers

They would not grant them the status of prisoners of war. This broke down the parole system that would have spared thousands the sufferings of malnutrition, disease, and exposure that ultimately cost many their lives and many more their health. An officer of the 13th Regiment New Jersey Volunteers described Camp Lawton:

> *At Millen, about nine thousand of our men had been kept as prisoners, and seven hundred and fifty had died. The prison-pen (Camp Lawton) is a stockade of logs about twenty feet high, and enclosing some twenty-five acres, with sentry-boxes around the whole about fifty yards apart. A small stream through the center of the enclosure, and a fort was built near commanding the ground. Here our men were turned loose without shelter (except the holes they were able to dig) from the scorching sun by day and the heavy dews at night, or the storms and cold of winter, and with only scanty provisions.*
>
> *The prisoners had all been removed a few days before our arrival.*[50]

Prison pen at Camp Lawton, Millen, Ga.

Another union volunteer Frank Grimstead received a letter from his cousin Amanda that summarized the perception of the folks back home. "If you come across any Rebels I hope you will use your new sabers & revolvers with a hearty good will and not let them take you prisoner when there is the least chance to escape for you know as well as I do how our prisoners fair down in Seceshiondom but take as many prisoners as you can the more the better for our cause . . ."[51]

Sherman's army trudged on moving forward day by day until by December 6, 1864, it had reached a point fourteen miles from Savannah. The Confederates had posted a small force of about three hundred infantry and a battery of artillery in a fort protected on both sides by swamps. These were called sand forts by the bluecoats and were not nearly as formidable as the rebels believed them to be. It was near a place called the Montieth Swamp that the Federals deployed their forces with Colonel Selfridge of the 46th Pennsylvania commanding the First Brigade on the left, Colonel Carman of the 13th New Jersey commanding the Second Brigade on the right. Murphy and Company D formed in line of battle and the Confederates gave way, abandoning their works. The dikes of several large rice fields had been flooded which slowed progress, but by the 10th of December the Regiment moved along the Montieth Turnpike and struck and destroyed some of the Charleston and Savannah Railroad. Within a few more days, it moved in line of battle between the Monteith Turnpike and the Savannah River near Pipemaker's Creek constructing elaborate breastworks along the entire regimental front. On December 16, 1864, the Regiment, with its Brigade crossed the Savannah River to Argyle Island where it fortified the northeast side of the island. The objective was a reconnoissance of the South Carolina shore and if possible to cut off the rebel retreat by taking the Savannah and Charleston Pike.

The war had many coincidences as the land occupied by Murphy and his comrades on Argyle

"Destruction of the Railroad" during Sherman's march to the sea

Island was owned by the Gibbons family of Morristown, New Jersey. That mattered little as the hungry men set to work putting the rice mill into operation. They met with little success and were forced to buy rice from local runaway slaves with whom they could barely communicate. The price for a portion of rice was as Private Toombs recalled, "One Dollah." The war was punctuated occasionally with episodes of humor. As the Confederates posted cannon along the Savannah River and had several gunboats shell Federal positions including the rice plantations, one member of the 13th New Jersey Volunteers recalled that incoming rounds exploded into buildings sending the soldiers and residents running for their lives. When a frightened slave was stopped and asked why he was in such a hurry he responded, "We guess 'tis' bout dinnah time." [52] James Augustus Grimstead, another New Jersey vol-

unteer, recalled an incident earlier in the war when Federal soldiers tried to have some fun out of the deadly game of war. He received a letter written from a friend and comrade from Camp Seminary, Virginia, on August 28, 1861. Signed only George, it read in part,

Our regiment is stationed about ¾ of a mile from the rebel batteries and this afternoon about a dozen of our boys went out towards them to reconnoiter. They approached within ¼ of a mile, where they had a full view. The rebels sent out two companies to act against them. To have some sport our fellows got a stove pipe and part of the running gear

Captain Raphael Semmes, C.S.A.

of an old wagon and mounted it upon it. They then got hold and pulled the old thing up and pretended to load it. Then they sighted it. At this the two companies turned back into the fort, and presently down came a large cannon ball, then another & another. The boys began to think it was rather warm for their health and made backward tracks quite fast. However they had their fun out and that was all they wanted.[53]

Savannah Falls

The retreat routes of the Confederate armies were increasingly cut off and the position of General Hardee was becoming desperate. By December 19, 1864, the only avenue of escape left to the Confederates was across the Savannah River. On the morning of the 20th, twelve companies from the Brigade and three from the 13th New Jersey Volunteers were sent out on a reconnoissance of Clysedale Creek in an effort to hit the Savannah and Hardeesville Road. Events were quickly reaching a climax.

Confederate Chief Engineer John G. Clarke achieved what some considered a miracle in finishing the pontoon bridge from Hutchinson's to Pennyworth Island and on across the river to the South Carolina shore. Historian Burke Davis believes the miracle was a result of the furious wrath of General Beauregard which hastened the completion of the bridge.[54] In any event, when Fort McAllister fell to General William Hazen's Federals the last major obstacle to Sherman's army had been overcome. It was yet another desperate advance into withering fire that came to typify Civil War combat. Across some two hundred yards of open fields the unwavering blue line of battle advanced undaunted by explosions of land mines that tore bodies apart. On they went crossing a deep ravine and up and onto the ramparts of the fort in desperate hand to hand fighting overcoming Confederate opposition and silencing the guns that threatened Ossabaw Sound. Sherman shouted his excitement to General Howard, "They're on the parapet . . . they took it, Howard. I've got Savannah!"[55] Indeed, Sherman had made Georgia howl destroying millions of dollars worth of property and disrupting civilian lives to the extent that it was no longer possible for southerners to support the war effort with the same level of enthusiasm. America had been ravaged by Americans and Georgia and her people would be a long time recovering from this carnage. Raphael Semmes, the intrepid captain of the notorious Confederate raider C.S.S. *Alabama* miraculously escaped the guns of the U.S.S. *Kearsarge* and made his way home from England. On a trip with his young son to the Confederate capitol of Richmond late in the war he observed, "I was two weeks making my way to the capital of the Confederacy, owing to the many breaks which had been made in the roads by raiding parties of the enemy, and by Sherman's march through Georgia! Poor Georgia! She has suffered terribly during this Vandal march of conflagration and pillage, and I found her people terribly demoralized."[56] Despite his many victories, Semmes too, was held accountable by his own people for the misery they endured. Mary Chestnut confided to her diary on July 25, 1864, that "Semmes, of whom we have been so proud—he is a fool after all—risked the *Alabama* in a sort of duel of ships! He has lowered the flag of the famous *Alabama* to the

Sherman's "bummers" foraging in South Carolina

Kearsarge. Forgive who may! I cannot."[57] This was yet another indication, albeit a small one, that morale was breaking down in the South. It was not just the blatant rifts such as the one between Jefferson Davis and Joseph Johnston that undermined southern resolve, it was the subtle attitudes of civilians that were apparently accomplishing that destruction to which Sherman was so intent on achieving. A Federal volunteer stationed before Petersburg observed, "The rebels do not fight with the courage and determination they once did. They seem to be utterly beaten. They know their cause to be hopeless and they don't care."[58] It was soon to get even worse as the northern columns turned their wrath on South Carolina, the mother state of secession.

A wave of euphoria, by contrast, spread across the North with the news of the fall of Savannah. This was expressed by all levels of society from prominent general officers to the rank and file enlisted men. General Sherman's famous message to President Lincoln read, "I beg to present you, as a

Christmas gift, the city of Savannah, with one hundred and fifty heavy guns and plenty of ammunition, and also about twenty-five thousand bales of cotton." to which he replied,

My Dear General Sherman:

Many, many thanks for your Christmas gift, the capture of Savannah . . . Please make my grateful acknowledgements to your whole army, officers and men.

Yours Very Truly,
Lincoln[59]

While Sergeant Albert Harrison wrote, "General Sherman still gladdens our hearts by his successful movements," fellow New Jersey volunteer Lieutenant Franklin Murphy described his march to Savannah with the 13th New Jersey Volunteers, "For grandeur and courage of conception that campaign [March to the Sea] will remain unique, but for the boys who felt none of the responsibility, it was a picnic. Sherman's March to the Sea will go down in history as one of the masterful military moves of modern times, but to those who didn't have to think it out, it didn't seem to be much of an undertaking. We had a right and left wing called respectively the Army of the Tennessee and the Army of Georgia. Two army corps were in each and we marched substantially five miles apart, and we lived on the country-and as we went along there was a strip twenty miles wide that didn't have a cow or a pig or a chicken left. We took everything in sight and some things not in sight. We destroyed the enemy's resources, we cut the Confederacy in two and we captured Savannah."[60] One of Murphy's peers, an Illinois Lieutenant ". . . described the march to Savannah as a 'pleasure trip' in comparison with the grueling Carolinas campaign . . ."[61]

Northern wrath became especially virulent as Sherman's troops began their march north through South Carolina. After all, it was South Carolina that had led her sister states out of the Union four years earlier and very well might have three decades earlier over the tariff controversy had it had sufficient support then. In addition, it was South Carolina that had committed the inexcusable crime of firing on the flag at Fort Sumter. If Georgia was made to suffer, South Carolina would surely be next, so thought the battle hardened veterans of Uncle Billy's legions. General Henry Slocum ". . . who had opposed the army's excesses in Georgia, now had to admit that at the very least . . . 'it would have been a sin to have the war brought to a close without bringing upon the original aggressors some of the pains.' . . . Unified as never before in a destructive policy, Sherman's army kept its word about ravaging South Carolina. Only the rare houses now escaped the torches of Sherman's men, who also continued to strip the land and then burn it . . . One chaplain gave his blessing to this focus of anger among the men; The wealthy people of the South were the very ones to plunge the country into secession, now let them suffer."[62] Dr. William Gilmore

Simms, a prominent South Carolinian sensed his peoples' anxiety and fear when he wrote, " 'Voe victis!'—woe to the conquered!—in the case of the people who had first raised the banner of Secession. The 'howl of delight,' sent up by Sherman's legions, when they looked across the Savannah to the shores of Carolina, was the sure fore-runner of the terrible fate which threatened our people should the soldiers be once let loose upon our lands. Our people felt all the danger. They felt that it required the abilities, the most strenuous exertions, the most prompt and efficient reinforcements, to prevent the threatening catastrophe."[63]

Franklin Murphy and his comrades in the 13th New Jersey Volunteers moved within the limits of Savannah on December 23, 1864, pitching camp on Warren Square on Habersham Street.[64] The men had marched over three hundred miles in one of the most remarkable campaigns and sustaining only six casualties, three wounded, and three captured. On January 14, 1865, they were ordered into the city to guard the supplies of the Quartermasters Department but within four days returned to the Brigade to guard the rolling stock [trains] until January 27th when it moved out on the Augusta Pike pushing forward, day by day until February 10th when it rejoined its proper command.

The Carolina Campaign

Franklin Murphy's diary survived the war and it is this pristine document that captures the Carolina campaign in many of its dimensions. The drudgery and monotony of the march, the incessant rain which mired the roads and slowed the progress, and the finality and death throes of the Confederacy, demoralized and exhausted and desperately grasping to the forlorn hope of a lost cause. The following are extracts from Lieutenant Murphy's diary.

January 17th (1865)

Started on campaign from Savannah. Crossed the river to S.C. and camped. In afternoon were ordered to build corduroy on the road.

January 19th

Laid quiet on the Savannah R. waiting for Hd. Qr.

Train to come up. Roads very muddy in consequence of rain & the wagons all stuck in the mud.

Details for the O.D. (Officer of the Day)
Jany 23d Capt. Guyer
   24th Capt. Johnson
   25th Capt. Pierson

January 27th 1865

Started from Savannah on campaign. Our Regt. Was ordered to guard the Corps supply train. We moved out in rear of Geary's Division on the Augusta road. The roads were badly cut up & in some places the going was bad. Went into Camp at 3:30 P.M. having made eleven miles. I was detailed for picket at night & went on duty with a detail of 21-4.

January 28th 1865

The experience of today fully convinced me that the fears I had entertained of having a hard time with the train were well founded. Drudged on all the afternoon & until 9 o'clk P.M. when the head of the Regt. Went into camp. The left did not get in until 11 P.M. camped near Springfield.

January 29th

About 7 o'clock the Regt. Again took the road. Our train this morning was near the right and as the road was good we travelled right along. About ten o'clock we reached Springfield where the train parked for about an hour. In the only yellow painted house in town was stuck up the sign of J.R. Haltiwanger M.D. The town consists of some eight houses & the ruins of about eight more. After leaving Springfield we marched some two miles further & halted for dinner. In the afternoon we pulled on & went into camp about five miles from Sisters Ferry.

The Federal army kept their promise to pillage and plunder South Carolina. "Yet the countryside by no means endured all the destructiveness. Towns and cities also suffered atrociously at the hands of Federal firebugs. Within the first three weeks of the invasion of South Carolina, portions or most of the following towns received the torch: Gillisonville, Grahamville, Hardeeville, McPhersonville, Springfield, Robertsville, Lawtonville, Barnwell, Blackville, Midway, Orangeburg, and Lexington.[65]

January 30th

Laid quiet all day. Heard no news & saw no strange event. Everything quiet along the lines except a Division of the Fifteenth Corps which passed us in the P.M. moving toward the river.

February 1st

Still no appearances of a move. To pass time away Capts. Matthews & Guyer & I concluded to go to the Brigade distant some ten miles to get our Blankets. Started about 9 o'clock. On reaching the river we found the bridge up & had to wait for a boat to take us to the upper landing—some two miles up stream. Gen. Slocum went up on the boat with us. Genl. Kilpatrick & Davis were also at the bridge. Found 1st Brig. encamped at the upper landing. Struck out for our Brigade which we found at Robertsville some four miles from the river. Got our Blankets & dinner & said bygones & started back for the river. Arrived there at dark and after procuring rations for the men we had with us we went on board the "Mary Benton" lying at the wharf & got supper—a very good one—slept in the cabin using my own blankets. Matthews remained with me & Guyer went to First Brigade Hdqrs.

February 2d

Woke at daylight. Saw the Steward of the Boat-paid him for supper last night & obtained a lunch of apple pie & coffee from him for Matthews & I. We then got on the "Jeff Davis"-a sort of a wheelbarrow concern & started down the river to the lower landing. On arriving at the pontoon bridge however we found it down & could not get through. Went on board the "Sylph" where we had breakfast after which we borrowed a small boat of the captain & rowed ashore. Pushed on for camp where we arrived at 9:30. In the P.M. had my pantaloons washed wearing my drawers in the meantime. Had dress parade in the P.M. but did not go out-had no breeches. Also received a mail bringing me several papers from home but no letters. Also recd. several "O.B.'s." Heard from my Ordinance returns for 3d Qr. Of 64 O.K. Went to bed just after dark.

Companies	Trousers	Blouse	Caps	Boots	Bootees	Stockings	Great Coats	Rubber Blankets	Woolen Do	Shirts	Drawers	Greatcoat tents	Shelter tents	Knapsacks	Haversacks	Canteens	Greatcoat Straps	Helmets
A	11	7	2		1	48	1	1		4	2							
B	11	3	1	1	1	74		3		7	7		3½	1	5	1		1
C	14	4	2	13	2	85			2	2	7	3	3	1	4	9		
D	4	1			5	2	78	2	7	1		45	2	4½	5	10	2	10
E	6	1			4	4	31		2			5		1	1			
H	12	4	3	1	5	59				3	4		3	3	3	1		
I	10	7	1	1	4	40	oo					7		1	8			12
K	10	3	1		1	42	2				7		2½	1	1			
	5	1	1		3	45			1	2	4							
						2												
Total	83	31	11	25	28	531	3	17	4	23	77	2	17½	13	38	18	22	6

Special requisition, 13ᵗʰ N.J. Volunteers, from Franklin Murphy's diary

Feb. 3

When I got up this morning I found it raining & found myself with no pants to wear. Got Henry to drying my wet ones. A hard job in rain but by holding them by the fire for some two hours he had them nearly dry & I put them on.

February 4th

Henry called me just before daylight to Breakfast, & soon after I was up. I had just time to eat Breakfast wash myself & pack up as the cry to fall in with the 2d Brig. 2d Div. To which we are temporarily attached. Col. Mindell of the 33d NJ is our new Brig. Commander. We marched to the river and crossed on pontoons to S.C. & marched to the upper landing where we halted for dinner & drew rations for the men. Capt. Matthews & I took dinner with Lt. Crawford & I played a game of chess with him. Had a good dinner. In the afternoon we started out again in the mud and after some seven hours plodding in the muddiest kind of road we encamped within a mile of Robertsville-having made three miles and a half since dinner.

February 5th

Laid quiet in the morning. Captain Matthews was sent out with fatigue detail at daylight to work on the road. At noon we marched. Passed through what

Sherman's march by torchlight through the swamps of South Carolina

was left of Robertsville. All the houses were burned down & nothing left but the church. The road was pretty good & by night we had made eight miles. Had a good camping ground.

February 6th

Started at 9 AM our Brigade was in rear guarding train. The day was very rainy and the roads were very muddy. We started out on the Lawtonville road. At noon the train packed & we had dinner-hard tack & muddy coffee. We trudged along until dark when we went into camp having made thirteen miles. Had a wet place to lay down in. It was some time before we could get a fire started. We finally succeeded & got dry & warm. Had some fresh pork for supper-the first of the campaign. My previous impressions of South Carolina were confirmed-that it is a very poor country to travel in-particularly on foot in rainy weather. Wouldn't give 285 Mulbury St. for the whole state. Every house & almost every Negro shanty was burned to the ground.

"The march northward from Savannah was aimed at Goldsboro, North Carolina, 425 miles away, where Sherman expected to be supplied by Union forces moving inland from Wilmington. Sherman's soldiers would have to cross nine substantial rivers and scores of their tributaries during what turned out to be the wettest winter in twenty years."[66] This goal, of course, was kept a careful secret and even within the Federal councils of war there were questions as to what exactly was Sherman's destination. One comrade of Franklin Murphy recalled the answer given to a general officer by Sherman when he was asked where he was going next? He replied, "If my shirt on my back knew where I was going I would take it off and burn it!" And this is the secret of his success. Sherman wrote to his wife Ellen of his intentions to "dive again beneath the surface, ". . . He warned her not to reveal his plan . . . "Don't breathe this, for the walls have ears, and foreknowledge published by some mischevious fool might cost many lives. We have lived long enough for men to thank me for keeping my own counsels, and keeping away from armies those pests of newspaper men . . ."[67]

Feb. 7th

Started out at 6:30 AM Brigade third in line. Had a little more rain & considerable more mud-for a change. The marching was very hard. The mud being very slippery. Halted for dinner at twelve o'-clock & laid quiet until half past four. Rec'd a small mail from Col. Mindell's Hd.Qrs. while halting. Also found where some sweet potatoes could be had & sent for some. Matthews went out with a foraging party of sixty-four men. He was only gone some two hours & came back with all the pork he could carry—every man had a pig. We crossed the Coo-sawatchie River & with a big swamp just at dark & camped on the opposite bank.

February 8th

Started this morning at daylight. During the night a hard wind had sprung up which blew away what remained of yesterday's storm. The day was very windy & rainy & cold. Nothing but very hard march-ing could keep one anyways comfortable. Halted for dinner at noon but as Shipman was behind with the mules we got no dinner but some crackers which Miller had in his haversack & some pork I begged off the men. The roads were very tolerable today-a great improvement in those of yesterday. We marched to Beaufort Bridge in the afternoon which we reached at half past four & camped. The three right companies of the Regt. Were on picket. The Rebels had very extensive works here & had a force of 400 Infantry & some artillery which com-manded the road, but they had to leave them. The approach to the place is through a very large swamp the road through which was commanded by artillery.

Sherman had divided his army to confuse the Confederates and to keep them guessing where he was going to strike next. They didn't know if he was going to strike Augusta to the south or Charles-ton to the north. His real objective was Columbia to

the northwest. "The General's basic strategy re-mained unchanged. He would avoid battle wher-ever possible, and would reveal the actual objective of his march only at the last practicable moment."[68]

February 9th

Started out this morning at daylight. Our Brigade on the advance. The weather had got cold during the night & the roads today were very good. We marched straight along without any delay until noon when we had 45 minutes for dinner. Marched on in the afternoon until 4 o'clock when we camped within a mile of Blackburn. Saw Gen. Slocum on the road. Also found plenty of forage of all kinds—Boys had all they could carry. We marched eighteen miles.

Note: Blackburn was actually Blackville, a station on the Augusta & Carolina Railroad.

February 10th

Marched to Blackville or Blacktown & halted some three hours. We then received orders to move to our Brigade. While waiting Kip & I spent the time rousting gubers—marched on the railroad & reached the Brigade at 5 P.M. Rec'd a mail and I got my dress coat & some papers. Was glad to get back to our division away from Geary.

By mid-February, Murphy and his comrades had marched from Savannah to Blackville. Their mission was to assist the Second Division protecting the wagon trains. On February 10, 1865, they re-ceived orders from the Corps Commander, General Williams, to rejoin their own "military home" in the Second Brigade of the First Division commanded by Colonel Hawley. While General Killpatrick's cav-alry moved to the left threatening Augusta, Georgia, the wings of the army moved on both sides of the Savannah River to Sister's Ferry. From there they shifted to the north side of the river threatening Au-gusta on the left and Charleston on the right while destroying the transportation and communication facilities. An officer of the 13th New Jersey Volun-teers explained how they attempted to confuse the Confederates when he wrote, "We leave the enemy concentrated in each place, and now turn to the north, moving in the direction of Columbia, South

Sherman's troops crossing the South Edisto River

Carolina-having moved the trains in safety to this point."[69]

February 11th

Started at 8 AM for Duncan's Bridge. Marched along without halt until 12 o'clock when we halted half an hour for dinner. Pushed on in the afternoon & reached the Banks of the Edisto-South Fork-at 3 o'-clock & were from that time until 8 crossing-all owing to somebody's mismanagement & a mud puddle-It should not have taken the whole division a half hour to cross the Bridge. As it was we did not camp until late. The Rebels had destroyed the Bridges which however were reconstructed in four hours by the 1st Mich Eng. Marched 14 miles.

The rapid progress of Murphy and his comrades in this seemingly invincible juggernaut astonished friend and foe alike. Sherman remarked, "It is impossible to conceive of a march involving more labor or exposure . . ." In a letter to Secretary of War J.C. Breckenridge on February 19, 1865, Lee wrote "I do not see how Sherman can make the march anticipated by General Beauregard, but he seems to have everything his own way."[70] Confederate General William Hardee was hard put to admit that " . . . I wouldn't have believed it if I hadn't seen it happen." General Joseph E. Johnston lamented that there had been few armies in history that compared with Sherman's when he commented, "I made up my mind that there had been no such army since the days of Julius Caesar."[71]

By February 12th the 13th Regiment was out in advance of their division guarding the train. Although off to an eleven o'clock start, they made rapid progress. The roads were good for a change and there were no delays. Murphy wrote, "I never saw better roads in the South than those of today. There were no bad places & the train neither stopped or jammed up-as they usually do. The men

Captain D. Van Resselear, 13ᵗʰ N.J. Volunteers

however, were pretty tired-marching so long without a rest. We camped between 3 & 4 o'clock having made 12 miles on the road towards Columbia. Heard some reports of cannon ahead which was said to be the Rebels over the river. Geary was afterwards reported to have lost 20 killed & wounded including one colonel."

February 13ᵗʰ

Broke camp about 8:30 AM & marched half a mile down the road & then stacked arms & halted until 12 o'clock. We then pushed on following the Third Division train. We marched along on the road to Columbia-crossing the north fork of the Edisto-until about 3 o'clock when we went into camp. The road was very good. We passed Hdqrs. Of General Slocum & Williams on the road. Had a good supper, a good tent pitched & a good bed. Made seven miles.

The quantity and quality of food was always an issue. It varied, of course, from too much to too little depending on the contingencies of the campaign. American army officers then, as today, are often responsible for providing for their own sustenance while enlisted personal were generally provided rations. This explains why the officers often "begged" food off the rank and file. A "mess" was kept small as it was every man for himself in a catch-as-catch-can campaign. Murphy wrote on February 14ᵗʰ, "Tonight our mess disbanded. Matthews & Kip messing themselves & Miller & I each going it alone. I got Coconag as cook. Our object in disbanding was to make the mess smaller, as ours was too large & inconvenient for a campaign."

To move 60,000 men over muddy unpaved roads often in the pitch darkness was a logistical nightmare. How it was efficiently accomplished is a tribute to the leadership of the officer corps and the dedication and tenacity of the enlisted men. Impassable roads or bridges washed out by freshets caused countless delays but they were always overcome. Murphy's diary entry of February 15, 1865, discusses these hardships.

February 15ᵗʰ

Had orders to move at 9 A.M. but it was about twelve before we started. Had lunch before starting. At half past one we halted in order to have a bridge built ahead. Started again at 5 P.M. & marched along at a very slow rate & the roads were bad and it soon became dark, and as the weather was stormy-the night was dark as pitch. The marching was very hard but we kept going until half past twelve when we camped.

February 16ᵗʰ

Today our Division was on the advance & we were not troubled with teams in the road. We marched forward on the road to Columbia, leaving Lexington C.H. (which we heard was occupied & destroyed last night by the 14ᵗʰ Corps) to our left. We crossed an unfinished railroad-the Columbia & Augusta in the morning. The road was graded but no rails laid. It has evidently been worked upon quite recently. We halted at noon where the men had dinner. I was detailed with my company to forage. Was gone all the afternoon but was only partly successful. Troops

Federal troops foraging

camped near where they had dinner. I run into the 14th Corps while foraging. Heard that Howard was bridging the Sauter River.

The foragers of General Sherman's army were called bummers. This Union army had cut itself off from its base of supplies and its survival depended on what it could scrounge from the countryside. The extremes of behavior of some sixty thousand or more soldiers enduring the hardships of a forced march under intolerable conditions can readily be imagined. They not only extracted from the local populace the sustenance to sustain themselves but served the important military function of protecting the flanks of the advancing columns. At times this

was inadvertent. There were also atrocities committed on both sides but the number and severity of these were relatively minor when compared to other armies of conquest. These bummers "were automatically formed and intelligently acted as a wide screen of scouts covering the front and flanks of the marching column. Thereby they not only protected it from surprise, but saved it time-wasting deployments. If enemy cavalry appeared on the scene, the laden foragers would pour out of barns and kitchen gardens like a swarm of angry bees, each party rallying to form a well concealed and

The "bummer"

extended firing line, while some of their number drove the laden mules to the rear."[72] As Franklin Murphy was only partly successful at Lexington Court House in procuring "eatables" or "victuals" as Civil War soldiers often called their food supplies, a fellow member of the 13th New Jersey Volunteers had better luck. Private Toombs wrote, "We accompanied the detail for about five miles and then taking a by-path through the woods struck off on "our own Hook" and soon reached a large plantation where we obtained an abundant supply of corn meal, flour, bacon, sorgham, beans, and two dozen eggs. We had heavy loads and after an hour's walk reached the Lexington Court House road about an hour before the Regiment came along. We made a fair division with the men who messed with us and had some to spare for others."[73]

By February 17, 1865, the 13th Regiment had reached the Saluda River. From a promontory on one side the men could see fires all the way to the horizon. Murphy described it this way. "Right on the bank of the River—the Saluda is a high hill where our Brigade lay for a short time, from which you can see for many miles, and as far as the eye could reach from left—south to north—the horizon was lit up with the reflection of fires, probably burning buildings. The camp fires of the whole army were also plainly visible. After waiting until half past nine we crossed the river & reached camp about ten o'clock."

February 18th

Laid quiet until about half past three in the afternoon waiting for the second and third divisions to pass. Started at that time and guarded the trains. Marched until half past nine when we halted for the night.

Columbia Falls to Sherman

The army continued northward. The Jerseymen of the 13th Regiment took their positions on the right of the brigade and marched four miles north in the direction of Zion's Church about six miles northwest of Columbia, South Carolina, where their wing crossed the Saluda River, a branch of the Congaree River. As they waited for the Fourteenth Corps to cross the river, elements of the Fifteenth Corps crossed about two miles below and by midmorning entered the city of Columbia hoisting the stars and stripes over the old court house "amid the cheers of soldiers and the playing of national airs by our bands." Late in the evening Murphy crossed the river and camped for the night on the peninsula formed by the Saluda and Broad Rivers. The Federal soldiers who entered the city continued their destructive reign of terror. The city of Columbia was nearly burned to the ground. To what extent it was the deliberate acts of Sherman's army or the result of accidental fires fanned by high winds is still debated among historians. Many contemporary accounts attribute the wanton destruction and in some cases the loss of life to the drunken state of the soldiers which inspired South Carolinian William Gilmore Simms to write, "Liquors were drank with such avidity as to astonish the veteran Bacchanals of Columbia; nor did the parties thus distinguishing themselves hesitate about the vintage. There was no idle discrimination in the matter of taste, from the vulgar liquor, . . . to the choicest redwines of the ancient cellars."[74] What is certain is the scene was one of indescribable horror as dwelling after dwelling, city block after city block succumbed to the flames. Simms continued, "No language can describe nor can any catalogue furnish an adequate detail of the wide-spread destruction of homes and property. Granaries were emptied, where the grain was not carried off, it was strewn to waste under the feet of the cavalry, or consigned to the fire which consumed the dwelling . . . But the reign of terror did not fairly begin till night. In some instances, where parties complained of the misrule and robbery, their guards said to them, with a chuckle: 'This is nothing. Wait till tonight, and you'll see hell'"[75] This seemed to answer the question of an old proverb, "Quis Custodiet Ipsas Custodes?"

Who shall guard the guards? So on marched the relentless columns, day after day, mile after mile. "Habitation after habitation, village after village—one sending up its signal flames to the other, presaging for it the same fate—lighted the winter and midnight sky with crimson horrors."[76]

February 19th

Moved out this morning at about 7:30. Passed the Second Division and marched along side of the Third Division. Halted at 12 o'clock when I had dinner. In the afternoon we pushed on and guarded the Third Division train. Halted at 3:30 and went into camp about one mile from Broad River.

February 20, 1865, dawned foggy as Murphy crossed the Broad River on pontoons barely able to "distinguish anything a rod ahead of me." He was able to march seven miles down the main road towards Winnsborough before pitching camp for the night.

The next day, February 21st, Murphy reached Winnsborough about 3:00 P.M. It was a beautiful village in northwestern South Carolina with well constructed homes and elegant gardens. The prosperity of the area centered on the Danville Railroad. In addition to the beautiful homes, there was a court house, several churches and a literary society. Murphy couldn't help a provincial comment when he wrote, " The gardens and grounds, however, were not well laid out and it wants northern energy and taste to make the place really beautiful" yet as it compared to other areas of South Carolina "the place services more civilization than it is usual to find in South Carolina." As these Federals marched through the town the hostility of the inhabitants was apparent. Murphy commented, "I noticed quite a number of men and more women, some of whom looked very down in the mouth while others were very defiant belonging I presume to the last ditch fraternity." They continued on and camped in the hills several miles outside the town. It was a welcome change of scenery for the bluecoats from the flat and swampy country that they had traveled in for so long.

Confederate authorities were determined to make a stand at Winnsborough and instructed General Beauregard to take measures that would delay Sherman's columns. He ordered Wheeler's cavalry to try to hold the Federals in check until he could come to their assistance. It was an unrealistic expectation given the troop strength and resources the South could bring to bear at this time and place. One of Franklin Murphy's comrades in the 13th Regiment wrote, "A rebel courier was captured at this place with dispatches to Wheeler from Beauregard. The courier stated that Beauregard desired Wheeler to keep the enemy in check at Winnsboro and he would send him reinforcements. Wheeler sent word back that it was impossible to hold Sherman's foragers in check let alone the main army."[77] As Murphy and the 13th pushed ahead with the 20th Corps, the 14th Corps moved by a different road on a parallel. Unfortunately the foragers beat the advancing columns and burned a substantial part of the town including the Episcopal Church. Sherman disapproved of the destruction but refused to castigate them for doing what he, at least indirectly, ordered them to do, i.e. destroy the morale of the people of the South to continue the war. He wrote, "Fighting is the least and easiest part of war, but no General ever was or will be successful who quarrels with his men, who takes the part of citizens against the petty irregularities or who punishes them unduly for gathering fire-wood, using wells and springs of water and even taking sheep, chickens and food when their regular supplies are insufficient."[78] He did try to exercise restraint by ordering the trains searched for plunder which resulted in uncovering huge piles of valuables which were systematically fired. One of the fortunate houses to escape the incendiary's torch was the Obear home. A young man named Leighton had fallen ill to fever which frightened the Federal soldiers away. The ladies of the house were caught up in the spirit of "sesesh" defiance as they sang "Oh, yes I am a Southern girl—I glory in the name."[79] Indeed from Franklin's Murphy's perspective they belonged to the "last ditch fraternity." And the blue columns pushed onward driving relentlessly forward anyone or anything in their path. Civilians melted away like snow before a warm spring sun. Diarist Mary Chesnut experienced these events when she wrote, ". . . we took up our line of march. And straight before Sherman's men, five weeks we fled together. By incessant hurrying, scurrying from pillar to post, succeeded in being a sort of avant-courier of the Yankee army. [Their] sleep was rudely broken into at Alston. 'Move on, the Yanks are on us.' So they hurried on, half-awake, to Winnsboro."[80]

On February 22, 1865, orders came down to move on earlier than the men expected. The diet of Civil War soldiers on the march consisted frequently of salt pork, bacon, and hardtack, washed down with coffee, sweetened if they were lucky. It was difficult to digest which made many sick when they were not allowed to rest. Murphy wrote, "moved out half an hour sooner than was expected and many men lost their breakfast in consequence." They set a record this day of eighteen miles which was the longest and hardest march of the campaign up and down the mountainous countryside. It was hard on the horses and mules as well. They passed Rocky Mount by the afternoon and reached the banks of the Catawba River as darkness fell. As the Second Division was left behind to destroy the railroad at Winnsborough, Murphy and his comrades were led forward by General Sherman. Murphy wrote, "General Sherman rode with our column today." The next morning [February 23rd] the 13th New Jersey Volunteers crossed the Catawba on pontoons. Progress was slow over the steep roads and the column halted about four miles out to wait for the trains to catch up. Foragers succeeded in commandeering supplies from the local area. As Murphy observed, "the foragers today were very successful. Mathews and Luger each getting a wagon load of meat, potatoes, flour, and meal. I was supplied from what they brought in."

It was on February 23rd that General Joseph Johnston was assigned command of all Confederate forces in North Carolina. "The Confederate Congress had . . . made Lee General-in-Chief of all their armies, and he had called Johnston from the retirement in which he had lived since the preceding July to assume the direction of the forces which were trying to prevent Sherman from closing in upon the rear of Richmond. Mr. Davis, the President of the Confederacy, had openly declared that he would never give Johnston a military command again, but the responsibility was now with Lee, and Mr. Davis could only acquiesce."[81] The rift between these two men gives insight into the dissention within the Confederate high command which eroded those forces of cooperation necessary to successfully conduct the war.

February 24th

The first thing that disturbed me this morning was the voice of the Corporal of the Guard at my tent, bringing me the Adjutant's compliments and a detail for picket with orders to report at Brigade Headquarters at 6:30 A.M. I had just time for breakfast when the detail was formed and I started. Capt. Bliven was F.O.D. The picket was all got together and we pushed on to follow the 3d Brigade. By the time we reached the 3d Brig. We found them halted & learned that the 17th Corps were marching on the road we were to take and in about an hour the division was placed in position & the pickets posted. I had my mule brought out to the picket line & my tent pitched as it was raining quite hard. The rain continued all day and night. Lt. Underwood & Lt. Thompson were on duty with me & I shared my tent with them. I had rather a pleasant time notwithstanding the rain & my wet clothes. We passed the day in "spinning yarns" and talking of the state of things generally.

February 25th

The rain of yesterday continued all night & this morning did not show much signs of any abatement. During the night one side of me got wet through the effects of laying in a puddle of water. It was with great difficulty I got my fire started but finally succeeded after sending a long distance for rails. I had a good breakfast & dinner. Underwood & Thompson both eating with me. While at dinner the relief came out & we soon went into camp. Take it all through I think I have had many harder tours of picket than this one. Arrived at the Regt., which by the way did not move today. I had my tent pitched & a fire started and at dark went to bed expecting to be drowned out before morning.

Captain C.H. Bliven, 13th N.J. Volunteers

February 26

I was not exactly drowned out last night but it rained hard and I did not sleep very sound. We recd. orders to move at 9:30 and we lay from that time until nearly dark before we started. At 5:30 we pulled out and in half an hour after that were fairly started. We found it a very muddy road to travel. The rains had made it so muddy that a great part of it had to be corduroyed. Our Brigade was the tail end of everything, bringing up the rear. We trudged along in the mud until about ten o'clock when we halted for the night. We made about five miles.

February 27th

This morning we pushed on at Daylight and worked along some four miles in the mud when we halted for the other two divisions to come up. Recd. orders here to have muster rolls made out for the muster tomorrow. I was busy all the afternoon on my rolls & then did not get them completed. They were near enough finished to muster on however.

"Corduroying" the road

By February 28th the men were mustered for pay by Major Harris and did not continue their march until about noon. They made steady progress despite the muddy conditions covering about eight miles crossing Little Lynch's Creek. As Murphy noted they had "to stop several times to fix the road." They did this by cutting logs and laying them down one against the other in a process called "corduroying." One can imagine the jolting that would take place driving wagons and teams across such a surface let alone the effects on the ankles of the marching men.

The men were up and out by daylight of March 1st and made eleven miles progress over the sandy roads in this vicinity before stopping for dinner near Big Lynch Creek. They continued another three miles before camping for the night in a light drizzle. The next morning the rain continued which began to grate on the men's nerves as Murphy noted in his diary. "Another day of rain and mud. Not hard rain but confounded drizzle that would go right through a fellow and make him feel put out with himself and everybody else." On they marched in three inches of mud almost on a "double-quick." About half past one in the afternoon they ran into rebel skirmishers and drove them back "on a run" to the bridges over Thompson's Creek near the town of Chesterfield. Flanking maneuvers finally dislodged the Confederates. Murphy's diary entry for March 2nd relates these events. "We had to run around some to clear them out which we finally did and went into position about dark near the town [Chesterfield]. The 5th Georgia I believe held the place before we came."

March 3rd

This morning I was detailed on fatigue duty to assist in repairing the bridge over Thompsons Creek which the Rebels had partially destroyed. I worked until 11 o'clock & then went to camp. After dinner

Federal troops entering Cheraw, S.C.

Kip & I went to the C.H. & after inspecting it we visited the jail. The Court House is a very peculiarly constructed one & has a fine Law Library in it. I also found some military works-some of which I brought away with me. The jail, like all other jails was a horrid looking place & I did not stay long in it. About 4 P.M. we moved through the Burg from Thompsons Creek & took up position some 3 miles from town & went into camp. Chesterfield is not much of a place and derives its importance from its being the county seat. It was rumored tonight that the 17th Corps was in Cheraw, a place of importance on the Great Pedee River which the rebels had fortified at which Joe Johnston was reported to be with twenty thousand Grey Backs.

The men received a well-deserved rest on the morning of March 4th, waiting for the advance divisions to pass. Murphy read a criticism in a southern review of Sue's "Wandering Jews." This was a story of a man who showed disrespect to Jesus on his way to crucifixion. He was condemned to wander

the earth until Judgment Day. It was written in 1844 by the French novelist, Marie Joseph Sue, and was strongly vulgar and anti-clerical.[82] This gives insight into his strong sense of morality, no doubt based on his religious convictions which were so much a part of his time. After all, Murphy was born and reared in the revival times of America's Second Great Awakening. He wrote, "At about 4:00 P.M. the 13th New Jersey broke camp and moved out on the left of the Brigade leading the Division. By 8:00 P.M. they had to stop to corduroy part of the road which took several hours and it was after 11:00 P.M. before they camped for the night about two miles from the Pee Dee River. There were rumors that the 14th Corps was at the river laying pontoons but, of course, they were not confirmed. The following day was spent quietly in camp and it was not until about

Destroying the railroad at Catletts Station

9 o'clock on March 6th that the campaign resumed as the 13th New Jersey Volunteers marched out leading its brigade and the division. By mid-afternoon they entered the town of Cheraw where they remained until 10:00 P.M. Murphy wrote,

About three o'clock P.M. we entered Cheraw— Band playing, Colors flying & Regt. marching in column by Company. In my opinion all a humbug. I don't believe in making such a squall before every Secesh place we come to. We stacked arms in the main street and lay quiet until 10 o'clock P.M. In the meantime many looked about town but I did not think it would pay & remained where I was. From what I could see of the place I should judge it to be a town of considerable size & has been quite a pretty place. Many of the fences were torn down & many of the houses burned or destroyed. A powder explosion which occurred here destroyed some buildings & killed half a dozen soldiers & citizens. I understand that Sherman captured some guns & Locomotives here but did not leave very many. Just at twilight I went to visit the spot called Marion's Grave and a sad looking place I found it. There was no monument & nothing to designate even the grave except a pile of bricks. The grave yard was a very old one and quite a pretty church stands in the center of it. Many of the graves are very old & some quite new with all kinds of grave stones around them & many with no designation whatever. A little after ten o'clock we started again-crossed the Great Pee Dee River and pushed on some five miles further on the other side. We halted at half past twelve A.M. tired & sleepy having made about fifteen miles."

March 7th

Started this morning about 8 o'clock. Our Brigade had gone on and the first two hours were spent in catching it. Our Brigade led the Div. & our Div. second in line. The roads were very good today as the rain had not had much effect on the sandy soil. Today was the first real pleasant day we have had in a long time. We passed several places where immense quantities of resin & pitch had been set on fire. We went into camp about 3 P.M. having made fifteen miles. We encamped at Mason & Dixon's Cut on the Lamb Hill R.R. The country passed through today was a great pitch country. Nearly all the large pine trees were topped, and the pitch was on some two inches thick.

The 13th New Jersey Volunteers succeeded in destroying much of the Wilmington, Lamb Hill and Charlotte Railroad and large quantities of cotton. "No command on either side, North or South, had the knack for destroying railroads like Sherman's army. An entire regiment or more lined up along one side of a railroad track and picked up the wooden ties at one end. Troops then broke off the ties and gathered them and telegraph poles and started fires, upon which they laid the rails. When the middle of the rails became red hot, the men destroyed them by picking up both ends and twisting them around trees . . ."[83]

The rain returned with a vengeance on March 8th and continued unabated all day long as the Jerseymen trudged along mile after mile. It was very poor country according to Lieutenant Murphy with few signs of civilization. " I only saw one house & that was on fire-a very pretty sight it was too. At 8 o'clk we camped. I was wet through from head to foot inside & out, and the prospect was very poor for my ever getting dry again for the rain kept on coming. At last I got a good fire started & finally got tolerable dry & went to bed with dryer clothes & a much better supper than I expected. In spite of the rain I read the first Vol. of 'The Lofty & the Lowly' by Miss McIntosh which I found very interesting."

Murphy Reaches North Carolina

There was a major change among Sherman's troops as they moved into North Carolina. Orders went out to avoid the wanton destruction of civilian property. North Carolina was not the cradle of secession but rather had been the last of the southern states to secede. Furthermore, significant numbers of her citizens had remained loyal to the Union. "As if the army had undergone a massive transformation overnight, North Carolinians received treatment similar to that of Georgians. Senior commanders issued orders to remind the soldiers that they were in North Carolina . . . a marked difference should be made in the manner in which we treat the people and the manner in which those of South Carolina were treated."[84] Sherman had an ulterior motive as well. There had always been a degree of hostility between the peoples of North and South Carolina dating back to early colonial times. Sherman thought he could exploit these ancient anomosities in his quest to divide and conquer. He wanted his men to "deal as moderately and fairly by the North Carolinians as possible, and fan the flame of discord already subsisting between them and their proud cousins of South Carolina. There was never much love between them. Touch upon the [South Carolina] chivalry running away, always leaving their families for us to feed and protect, and then on purpose accusing us of all sorts of rudeness."[85]

It had stopped raining by sun-up on March 9th as the men awoke in hopes that the weather would "clear off." They were on the road by 8 o'clock and by 9 o'clock it started raining again. They continued on stopping and starting for another twelve hours encamping about 10:00 P.M. for the night. The rain finally tapered off and Murphy found the time to jot down a few lines in his diary. "Just after I had my tent pitched the rain ceased. Matthews, Peirson & Bohwell took supper with me as their mule was not up. Mat & B slept with me." March 10th and 11th saw the blue columns push onward wading across huge swamps and down roads knee deep in mud over the Lumber River on pine tree bridges near what is probably known as Blue Bridge. By late in the day of the 11th Murphy and his comrades were moving out almost on a "double-quick." He noted, "We struck the plank road before dark and marched to within a mile & a half of Fayetteville where we camped having made 21 miles-the last 11 of which were made without halt or rest. We camped at 10 P.M.

Confederate General Robert Barnwell Rhett whose son Alfred was captured during the fighting around Fayetteville

The Confederates had about twenty-five thousand soldiers in Fayetteville and although they had made statements of their intentions to defend the city, they evacuated it as the northern troops approached. Some of the rebels were sent to Jonesborough while the rest were sent to reinforce Raleigh. The military significance of Fayetteville was the city's arsenal. It was one of the largest built by the United States Government spanning some twenty acres. One of Murphy's comrades wrote.

There are about twenty brick shops of various sizes for the manufacture of ordnance, where we found some of the original machinery of the arsenal, besides some that had been brought from Harper's Ferry by the rebels. These buildings and the dwellings, together with the machinery, ordnance

manufactured, and materials for the manufacture, in all stages of completion, were all destroyed, most of them by the Michigan Engineers, with an ancient weapon-a battering-ram. We came so suddenly upon the enemy that they did not have time to remove any of it. The city had an old and dilapidated appearance; formerly contained about five thousand inhabitants. The rebels had destroyed six steamboats it being the head of navigation on the Cape Fear River.[86]

March 12th

Laid quiet, In P.M. wrote a short letter home.

By March 13th the Federals had marched through Fayetteville and crossed the Cape Fear River on pontoons. Murphy was detailed to guard the flank of the brigade with the aid of a unit from the 107th New York Regiment. He found time to jot down in his diary his observations of Fayetteville. "Fayetteville is quite a large sized town of five or six thousand inhabitants I should think. There is an old government arsenal-a very large & fine one which however Sherman is destroying. A very heavy line of works guarded the town from the South but it seems the enemy did not use them. We marched through town in column by company & were reviewed by Genl Sherman & Slocum."

General Sherman did in fact destroy the arsenal at Fayetteville but he issued strict orders that the town was to be undisturbed otherwise. This policy of conciliation toward the people of North Carolina was in sharp contrast to the punishment meted out to their South Carolina countrymen.

March 14th

I passed the day on pickett. The Regt. & 2d Mass. Went on a recconnoissance some 9 miles up the road & returned about 10 P.M. I was relieved at dark & marched my detail to where the Regt. had camped & remained there for the night. Drew some cornmeal & Bacon for them. Took supper with Clark.

There is an expression in contemporary military slang, "hurry up and wait" as orders are often countermanded or canceled entirely. This was certainly a feature of army life during the Civil War as well. It is difficult from the modern perspective to grasp the reality of what Murphy and his comrades

General Judson Kilpatrick, U.S.A. and staff

endured in this relentless drive northward over un-paved roads and open terrain saturated by incessant rainfall. By March 15th another ten miles had been covered and the men took up position on the Cape Fear River near Bluff Church. The rain continued and the next five miles proved to be the most difficult of the entire campaign. Murphy wrote,

It rained in torrents from 1 o'clock till dark, but I got my tent up—had supper, & plenty of wood for a fire and was just making myself comfortable for the night when orders came to move immediately & I had to leave everything. In ten minutes we were off trudging through the mud on a five mile tramp to support Kilpatrick. The mud varied in depth from one foot to four feet & it was very sticky. Some shoes were lost in consequence. We had several streams to ford besides & with the intense darkness

& the rain it was decidedly the most disagreeable night march the Regt. has ever had. We finally reached the Cavalry—took up position & made ourselves as comfortable as the mud would permit & waited for morning.

Lieutenant Franklin Murphy moved out with his command from Fayetteville, North Carolina, on towards Averasboro in support of Federal cavalry under General Kilpatrick who was opposed by Confederate infantry. There were vast differences between the role of cavalry and infantry during the Civil War. Cavalry were generally considered the "eyes" of the army. It was their job to probe enemy positions, to wreak havoc on unprepared and un-

The Battle of Goldsboro

suspecting foes and then report back vital information to army headquarters. It was their ability to cover vast distances relatively quickly that enabled them to function much like later day commandoes. The infantry, on the other hand, was the pivotal mainstay of the army; it was on their shoulders that battles were won or lost. Whether it was Johnny Reb and Billy Yank during the Civil War, or the doughboy, GI, or Grunt of later conflicts, it was they who bore the brunt of the fighting. It was the infantry "line of battle" during the Civil War that constituted the strength of both armies. There were few instances where cavalry could stand up against infantry. General John Buford's troopers were an exception at Gettysburg as were Nathan Bedford Forrest's men at Brice's Crossroads. These forces were dismounted and deployed as infantry much like the dragoons of earlier conflicts.

Battle of Averasboro

On March 16, 1865, the Second Brigade was moved up in line of battle on the right and left of the Raleigh Road—cavalry protecting the flanks. Skirmishers were sent out who quickly engaged the Confederates in what developed into the Battle of Averasboro. Captain Pierson detailed alternating units from each company of the 13th New Jersey Volunteers. They were followed by the Third Brigade which flanked the Confederate lines as the Second Brigade advanced to the front. By about 2:00 P.M. the whole line advanced. The 13th New Jersey Volunteers passing through a deep swamp and coming within two hundred yards of the Rebel works engaged the enemy in desperate combat which lasted upwards of two hours. The Confederates abandoned their works and retreated in the direction of Goldsboro. The engagement cost Franklin Murphy's regiment two men killed and twenty-two wounded. Among those who gave their last full measure of devotion were Wickliffe Hardman, and Orem Warren while Arthur Donnelly, James H. Parliament, and Cornelius Westervelt sustained lesser injuries.[87]

March 16th

Soon after daylight the order was given to advance. We moved straight ahead our skirmishers driving the Rebels nearly or quite half a mile. Here they had a line of battle. We remained in this position some two hours during which the skirmishing was very heavy. Our line got out of ammunition & a new detail was sent out with Capt. Pierson. The rebels fired shells at us as well as bullets. Several of the men were wounded here. We were relieved here by the 3d Brig. Of the 3d Div. & fell back & moved to the right where we engaged the enemy. After this we occasionally changed position forward or to the right but we were fighting all day—sometimes with only a skirmish line & sometimes with our whole line of battle, when the work was very warm. We drove the Rebels I should think a mile & a half during the day & captured from them 2 pieces of artillery. As we advanced we passed by a number of dead Rebs & several of their officers. It rained more or less all day. Just before dark we were relieved by a Brigade of the 14th Corps and we fell back and took up position in reserve. Camped in column by division. The loss in the Regt. was two killed-21 wounded & 6 missing. Six of the wounded were from my company.

Sherman reflected on these events in a letter on March 17, 1865.

Hdqrs. Military Division of the Mississippi

In the Field,
Camp between North River and Mingo Creek
March 17, 1865

The enemy yesterday had a strong intrenched line in front of the crossroads, and had posted the Charleston Brigade about one third mile in front, also intrenched. The Twentieth Corps struck the first line, turned it handsomely and used the Charleston Brigade up completely, killing about 40 and gathering about 35 wounded and 100 well prisoners, capturing 3 guns, but on advancing further encountered the larger line, which they did not carry, but was abandoned at night. This morning a division of Williams' followed as far as Averasbor-

ough whilst the rest turned to the right, as I have heretofore stated. Slocum lost in killed and wounded about 300. He is somewhat heavily burdened by his wounded, which must be hauled. We left the Confederate wounded in a house by the roadside. The route of retreat of the enemy showed signs of considerable panic, and I have no doubt he got decidedly the worst of it.

Yours truly,
W.T. Sherman
Major General[88]

Equipment accountability has been a feature of the United States Army in times of war and peace. It would seem that under the immediacy of combat conditions that this accountability would be relaxed. This however, has rarely been the case. For example, on at least two occasions Franklin Murphy in his capacity as Company Commander 13th New Jersey Volunteers documented material loss. The details are indeed remarkable if one contrasts the cumbersome methods of recording all arms and equipment during the Civil War with the efficiency of modern armories manned by highly trained M.O.S. [military occupational specialty] supply sergeants who collect special weapon cards before arms are issued. Murphy wrote the following report on equipment lost during the Battle of Averasboro:

"I certify upon honor, that on the 16th day of March 1865 near Averasboro N.C. the stores enumerated below were lost under the following circumstances.

The Regiment to which my company belongs was directed to advance under fire of the enemy to take a certain position: in doing so, one private was killed and six wounded.

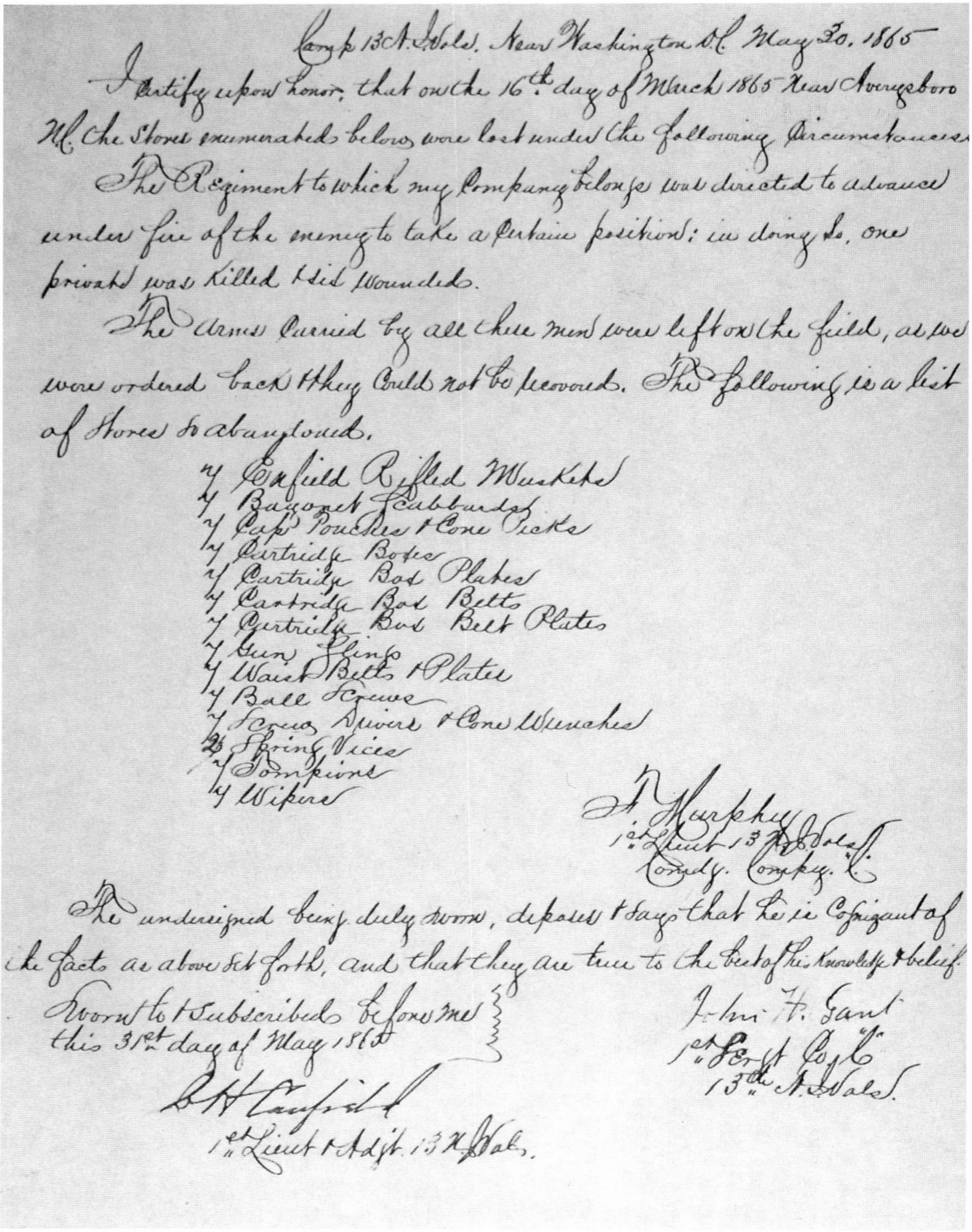

Camp 13th A.Vols. Near Washington D.C. May 30. 1865

I certify upon honor, that on the 16th day of March 1865 Near Averysboro N.C. the Stores enumerated below were lost under the following circumstances.

The Regiment to which my Company belongs was directed to advance under fire of the enemy to take a certain position: in doing So, one private was killed & six Wounded.

The arms carried by all these men were left on the field, as we were ordered back & they could not be recovered. The following is a list of Stores So abandoned.

7 Enfield Rifled Muskets
7 Bayonet Scabbards
7 Cap Pouches & Cone Picks
7 Cartridge Boxes
7 Cartridge Box Plates
7 Cartridge Box Belts
7 Cartridge Box Belt Plates
7 Gun Slings
7 Waist Belts & Plates
7 Ball Screws
7 Screw Drivers & Cone Wrenches
3 Spring Vices
7 Tompions
7 Wipers

F. Murphy
1st Lieut 13 N.J. Vols.
Comdg. Compy. C.

The undersigned being duly sworn, deposes & Says that he is Cognizant of the facts as above Set forth, and that they are true to the best of his knowledge & belief.

Sworn to & Subscribed before me }
this 31st day of May 1865

R H Canfield
1st Lieut & Adjt. 13 N.J. Vols.

John H. Gant
1st Sergt. Co. C.
13th N.J. Vols.

Lieutenant Murphy's report of equipment lost during the Battle of Averasboro.

The Battle of Bentonville

The arms carried by all these men were left on the field, as we were ordered back & they could not be recovered. The following is a list of stores so abandoned.

7 Enfield Rifled Muskets
7 Bayonet Scabbards
7 Cap Pouches & Cone Picks
7 Cartridge Boxes
7 Cartridge Box Plates
7 Cartridge Box Belt Plates
7 Gun Slings
7 Waist Belts & Plates
7 Ball Screws
7 Screw Drivers & Cone Wrenches
2 Spring Vices
7 Tompions
7 Wipers

F. Murphy
1st Lieut. 13 N.J. Vols.
Comdy. Compy. C." [89]

The march continued as the blue columns made their way northward crossing the Black River on March 18th and through a hundred yards of chest-deep swamp. They stopped for about an hour. Murphy wrote, "on the other side and dried ourselves by the fire . . . we were working hard all day building corduroy roads. At dark we went to camp having made about 8 miles."

Battle of Bentonville

Sherman's army moved relentlessly onward despite Confederate attempts to impede its progress. Murphy and his comrades in the 13th Regiment New Jersey Volunteers were among the troops that were ordered to move on the 19th of March on the "double-quick" in support of General Slocum opposing General Johnston near Bentonville. Major Harris was ordered to deploy the 13th New Jersey Volunteers on the right side of a ravine and to construct "such defenses as could be quickly made" to cover the rear of the 14th Corps. Heavy firing and retreating Federal soldiers indicated that the 14th Corps was in trouble and that a collapse was imminent. This, in turn, could become a rout which threatened to roll up the entire Federal line. As hasty defenses were shifted to protect the right flank of the Regiment, the rebels emerged in three lines of battle from the woods into a cleared field a short distance to the left on the opposite side of the ravine. Lieutenant Murphy steadied his men to hold their fire until the rebels were within two hundred yards. Then came the order to fire unleashing a torrent of leaden hail, the fury of which was seldom seen during the whole campaign. It was in some respects reminiscent of that decisive volley fired by Wolfe's Scottish Highlanders on the Plains of Abraham bringing to a close the Seven Years' War some 104 years earlier. On came the gray line of battle plunging themselves headlong into the volleys of shot and shell. This was a true testimonial to the courage and dedication of these Confederate soldiers that underscores the assertion that these men, on both sides, possessed a unique quality of bravery and heroism that would not be seen today. General John A. Wickham, commander of the 101st Airborne Division and Army Chief of Staff during the 1970s, while observing a Civil War battlefield that exacted similar feats of courage remarked, "You couldn't get American soldiers today to make an attack like that."[90] The southerners regrouped and advanced a second time again into the devastating fire of Murphy's 13th New Jersey Volunteers. This proved too much even for these dauntless veterans as their morale collapsed and they retreated leaving their dead and dying on the field. Thus ended the Battle of Bentonville, yet another union victory as the Federal pincers moved progressively northward. There were no further attempts by the Confederates to stem the advance of Sherman's army. The Brigade commander, Colonel Hawley commended the 13th New Jersey Volunteers. "You are entitled to the thanks of this whole army, for you have saved it."[91]

The Thirteenth Regiment played a key role in this, the last battle of the war in the Carolinas. They foiled General Joseph Johnston's attempt to overwhelm General Slocum before he could receive reinforcements. Had they not been able to stem the collapsing line, the battle most surely would have been lost. This, in turn, would have delayed for weeks the final victory over General Johnston's Confederates and cost the lives of untold numbers of brave men, including perhaps Lieutenant Franklin Murphy. The 13th New Jersey Volunteers helped to bring the long war to a close yet their days of soldiering were not yet over.

Murphy recalled the Battle of Bentonville in his March 19th diary entry.

March 19

We were off at the usual time this morning and, as usual, at work on the road which by the way was unusually bad as the 14th Corps passed over the same road ahead of us. About noon we heard artillery fire ahead of us some six mile which turned out to be the 14th Corps engaged with the enemy. We were soon after ordered forward as support and on coming up to the Battleground we took up position on the left of the 14th Corps our left retired in order to secure the flank. We had scarcely got in position before we heard the left of the 14th Corps was turned and the Johnnies were coming down upon us. We hastily threw up a few rails in front of us & had hardly done before the Rebs made their appearance in an open field on our left and front. They were in strong force (I should think a Brigade) & were coming to turn the flank of our 3d Brig. We gave them a very severe flank fire however & it was not long before they were running in the greatest confusion. We kept up the fire on them for some fifteen or twenty minutes & by the time we had driven them all back. The artillery—of which we had eight pieces in position on our right blazed away at them with grape & canister spherical case in front & we poured the bullets in their flank. After this the Rebs did not approach our works near enough for our fire to do much execution & we did not waste powder on them. They made an even distinct charge however just on our right & for three hours there was the loudest & most continuous musketry I ever heard. The slaughter on the part of the Rebs

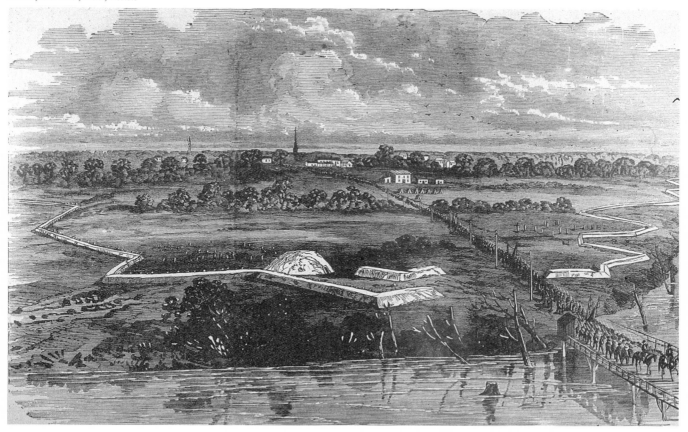

General Schofield's army marching toward Goldsboro, N.C.

must have been tremendous for they charged against our works—which however slight afforded considerable protection to our men. The lines of the Rebels were in plain sight of our artillery and Batteries I & M 1st NY did their prettiest, I tell you. At dark the battle ended for by this time I judged the Rebs had enough of charging our lines. Col. Hawley, our Brigade commander gave the Regt. great credit for its action saying we saved the day for the troops on our right. After dark the men were at work strengthening the works, and by 10 o'clk we had a line that was consequently strong & the men lay down with their equipments on. I was very tired for I had worked hard during the day. There was but one man wounded in the Regt. He was Corporal Stark of my company.

Fall of Goldsboro

The men rested for the next two days occupying themselves with strengthening their defenses and cutting down timber. They removed as many trees in front of them as they could in an effort to deprive the advancing foe of cover. There was intermittent skirmishing on the picket lines, what the Federals referred to as a "brush with the Johnnies" but it did not amount to anything. By March 22 they were off marching about nine miles down the road towards Goldsboro and pushing on towards the Neuse River. Murphy's friends Matthews and Kip "took supper and slept with me." They reached the river about noon on the 23rd and passed General Terry's command which consisted "of a division of the 24th, one of the 25th Corps," about a mile from the river. "Saw Terry himself," wrote Murphy.

March 24th

Pushed on at Daylight & reached Goldsboro about 9 A.M. While passing through the town we were reviewed by Gen. Sherman, Genl. Slocum, Schofield, Davis, Williams & several others were also present. We also passed Gen. Ruger & staff nearby. We pushed on through town & encamped about 3 miles outside. I was detailed for picket & went on duty about dark. I was senior officer and as the O.D. went away, I had to establish the whole line. It was a hard job and I did not get through till after nine o'clock.

On March 24, 1865, the 13th New Jersey Volunteers marched into Goldsboro with colors flying and drums beating passing in review of Generals Sherman and Slocum. Thus ended the campaign of the Carolinas. In seventy days the Union army had captured and destroyed millions of dollars worth of property, disrupted communications lines, and "made the mother-state of secession and rebellion feel in every nerve and fiber the war which she had causelessly provoked."

Lieutenant Franklin Murphy's last diary entry was on March 25th.

March 25th

Upon arriving in camp today, I found the Regt. had orders to build quarters where we were & thus ended our long campaign.

Captain Daniel Oakey, 2nd Massachusetts Volunteers, a member of the unit that Murphy respected, wrote of the Battle of Bentonville,

As we trudged on toward Bentonville, distant sounds told plainly that the head of the column was engaged. We hurried to the front and went into action, connecting with Davis's corps. Little opposition having been expected, the distance between our wing and the right wing had been allowed to increase beyond supporting distance in the endeavor to find easier roads for marching as well as for transporting the wounded . . . the Battle of Bentonville, which was a combination of mistakes, miscarriages, and hard fighting on both sides. It ended in Johnston's retreat, leaving open the road to Goldsboro', where we arrived ragged and almost barefoot. While we were receiving letters from home . . . Lee and Johnston surrendered, and the great conflict came to an end.[92]

Kilpatrick reported on the Battle of Bentonville to Sherman the following:

Headquarters Cavalry Command

In the Field, March 19, 1865

General W.T. Sherman,
Commanding Military Division of the Mississippi:

General:

The enemy in heavy force, and commanded by General Johnston in person, attacked the Fourteenth Corps today, captured three guns, and gained a temporary success; but our lines were finally re-established. The Twentieth Corps [Murphy's] and my cavalry came upon the field, and took up strong positions from 2 o'clock until dark the enemy made every effort to break our center, but he has failed in each attempt and certainly with great loss . . .

Kilpatrick
Brevet Major-General,
Commanding Cavalry[93]

Death of Lincoln

Murphy and his comrades remained at Goldsboro and on April 10, while waiting for a resumption of campaigning received news of the fall of Richmond. Sherman implemented his plans by ordering his columns to move against the Confederates concentrated at Smithfield. General Johnston withdrew his scant southern forces across the Neuse River hotly pursued by Sherman through Raleigh in a torrential downpour on April 13th. The chase continued onward to Martha's Vineyard near the Cape

Fear River, down the roads from Hillsborough to Greensborough when finally on April 14th Sherman received communication from Johnston, by a flag of truce, requesting an armistice. It was tragically the same day that John Wilkes Booth made good his fiendish plot to murder President Lincoln. The army was stunned at first but shock soon turned to rage. Everywhere there were calls for vengeance. "A mob of some 2,000 soldiers marched on Raleigh that night with the intention of destroying the city, and only the timely intervention of the Fifteenth Corps commander, Maj. Gen. John Logan, supported by field artillery, averted a second disaster. Fortunately for the people of North Carolina, Sherman and Johnston reached terms of surrender before the army began another march."[94]

The assassination of President Lincoln was a national disaster every bit as tragic for the South as it was for the North. Much has been written of its impact on Reconstruction and historians have speculated about what might have been had it not happened. All seem to agree that the years following the war would have been less turbulent had Lincoln guided the ship of state. "Feelings of good will, difficult enough to foster after four years of hatred and strife, were further endangered by the removal of Lincoln's influence and by gross injustice to Confederate leaders who were falsely accused of complicity in the assassination."[95]

Lincoln's last message to Sherman published years later by A.H. Markland in the *New York Daily Tribune* contained the following message. "Say to General Sherman for me, whenever and wherever you meet him, God bless him, and God bless his army. This is as much as I can say, and more than I can write."[96] A fellow New Jersey soldier, 2nd Sergeant A.C. Harrison wrote on April 17, 1865, from Burkes Station, Virginia, a letter home to his parents in Red Bank, New Jersey. In it he captures the emotions of the Union soldiers in the field.

But the worst news which was ever received in any army came to us night before last. A dispatch came to us stating that our President, Secretary & Son had been murdered. It is horrible. Today the news came official stating that the Pres was dead and the Secretary's Son could not survive but that the Father there were very faint hope entertained for

Major General John A. Logan, U.S.A.

his recovery. God grant he may yet live to see the end of this Wicked Rebellion. The best friend we Soldiers had on earth was Uncle Abe. He done all the good that lay in the power of man to do. And offered the Enemy every enducement to come back to the old Union. But they would not and now may the sword never be sheathed until the blood of every Traitor North and South is spilled to atone for the great crime. No quarters should ever more be shown to them. If they still persist they should wear the halter.[97]

General Sherman wanted to bring hostilities to an end as quickly as possible by offering General Johnston the same terms as Grant had offered Lee. He did not want petty political details to delay the capitulation and inadvertently offered political concessions that were unacceptable to Federal authorities. Ambiguities over the status of slaves and Confederate war debt exacerbated the situation. He feared that southern forces would dissolve into roving bands of guerrillas, take to the mountains to continue hostilities indefinitely. He wanted to avoid the predicament that General Charles Cornwallis had faced eighty years earlier during his Carolina campaign. American forces led by Nathanael Greene and Frances Marion had successfully eluded superior British forces while conducting guerrilla warfare exhausting their opponents by luring them deep into the hinterland. This was not going to happen to Sherman. The two commanders met in the little railroad depot of Durham Station in the home of James Bennett.[98] There now ensued a tangle of technicalities that threatened to derail the peace process. Sherman wanted to follow Lincoln's dictum, "Let em up easy." The Confederates were to repair to their homes, cease all armed resistance to Federal authority and obey local laws. In return, they were not to be disturbed by the government. The problem hinged on the political agreement. "Existing state governments were to be recognized . . . The political rights of all individuals were to be guaranteed . . ."[99] The status of the slaves was not addressed. This was not unconditional surrender.

Secretary of War Edwin Stanton

Secretary of War Edwin Stanton interpreted Sherman's agreement as one which would have preserved the political integrity of the Confederate government. He vehemently denounced it in the newspapers and insinuated that Sherman's conduct bordered on treason. Sherman was deeply hurt and angered by this and never fully forgave Stanton. The assassination of President Lincoln no doubt contributed to a panic mentality of clandestine plots and lurking assassins. This tempest was set against the backdrop of emerging post-war American politics dominated as they would become by the Republican Party fragmented into two parts: A radical branch intent upon punishing the South and relegating it to the status of conquered provinces and a moderate faction whose purpose was to bind up the nation's wounds as painlessly and quickly as possible.

Generals Sherman and Johnston discussing terms of surrender

Post War Trauma

This schism would result in the impeachment of President Andrew Johnson and his near removal, had it not been for the personal and political integrity of Edmund Ross, the junior senator from Kansas. He stood by his convictions by voting in favor of the President against the radical wing of his party thus narrowly preserving Johnson's presidency. The resurrection of war hatreds would characterize American post-war politics. Slogans like, "vote as you shot" echoed with reminders of the "bloody shirt," in spite of President Grant's call to "Let Us Have Peace."

Franklin Murphy became a loyal and dedicated Republican as most veterans of the Grand Army of the Republic would become, yet a moderate with liberal and progressive tendencies. He once de-scribed himself as "an old fashioned Whig" who had "marched as a boy with the Wide-a-Wakes in the Fremont campaign of Fifty-Six." The Wide-Awakes were also young men who had stood behind Lincoln in 1861 ". . . held gigantic rallies . . . in most northern cities, with the innumerable processions of young Republican 'Wide-Awakes' clad in black oil cloth capes and caps, bearing rails surmounted by torches . . . the Wide-Awake clubs, with their frequent meetings, organized drills, and processions, stimulated immense enthusiasm on the part of younger voters, many of whom cast their first ballots in this election."[100] Murphy's political star was yet to shine but shine it would in what Henry Clay had called his "state of beautiful villages."

Federal troops marching into Richmond, Va. on April 13, 1865

As for Sherman, he was dedicated to reconciliation. General Grant wrote Secretary of War Stanton from Raleigh, North Carolina, on April 26, 1865, "Sherman and Johnston had another interview today, and Johnston has surrendered on the same terms as Lee accepted. I think the great bulk of the army will start for Washington over and in a few days. I will be guided by circumstances in the absence of any instructions from you. I think we will hold on here for some time."[101] Terms of unconditional surrender signed by General Johnston satisfied the Washington officials and finally brought the war to a close. "The duty of receiving the arms of the late Confederates and of issuing the paroles was committed to General Schofield, and was performed at Greensboro, North Carolina. The Confederate general had declined the use of a house for his headquarters, and a few war-worn tents sheltered him and his staff. Johnston scrupulously distributed to each officer and man a coined dollar out of a small sum of money he had received from the Confederate treasury, and, with this token of the unpaid services they had given to the lost cause, the men in gray scattering on different routes, took up the journey homeward . . ."[102] The vanquished Confederate commander was touched by Sherman's magnanimity and wrote from Greensboro on April 29, 1865, the following letter:

Major Gen. W.T. Sherman
Commanding U.S. Forces

. . . The enlarged patriotism manifested in these papers reconciles me to what I had previously regarded as the misfortune of my life—that of having you to encounter in the field. The enlightened and humane policy you have adopted will certainly be successful.

I am General, &
J.E. Johnston[103]

Franklin Murphy and the New Jersey boys of the 13th Regiment remained in camp until April 29, 1865, when they were ordered to move out. Murphy's friends Captain A.M. Mathews, Captain C.H.

Bliven, and Lieutenant John R. Williams all survived with him. The war was over and they were on their way home. They marched north across the Neuse and Tar Rivers onward to the Roanoke and Meherin Rivers reaching Manchester opposite Richmond by May 9. On May 11 they crossed the James River and entered the Confederate capitol. They remained here a short time marveling at the points of interest amidst the destruction of burned out shells that had been once homes and places of business. Among these were Castle Thunder, Libby Prison, and Jefferson Davis's mansion on 21st street. The next morning they crossed the Chickahominy River and moved up the north side of the Pamunkey River crossing the Mat, Ta, and Po Rivers on to Spottsylvania Court House and Chancellorsville, finally crossing the Rappahannock River at United States Ford. On they marched past the Bull Run Battlefield with its memories of the first days of the conflict, arriving at Alexandria and camping at Fort Worth. They had "marched from Raleigh, a distance of about two hundred and seventy-five miles in twenty days." [104] As they arrived orders came down for a grand review of Federal forces in the city of Washington:

The Grand Washington Review

Special Orders,   Headquarters of the Army
   No. 239   Adjutant-General's Office

Washington, May 18, 1865.

. . . On Wednesday, the 24th instant, will be reviewed the Army of the Tennessee, Major General O.O. Howard commanding, and the Army of Georgia, Major General H.W. Slocum commanding, the whole under the command of Major General W.T. Sherman. The following will be the order of march: The head of column will each day rest on Maryland avenue at foot of Capitol Hill, moving at precisely 9 a.m., passing around the capitol to Pennsylvania avenue, thence up the avenue to the Aqueduct Bridge, and across to their camp. The troops will be without knapsacks, marching at company front, closed in mass, and at route step, except between Fifteenth street and New York avenue and Seventeenth street, where the cadence step will be observed. Each brigade will be accompanied by six ambulances passing three abreast . . . The review-

ing officer will be stationed in front of the President's house, where provisions will be made for members of the Cabinet, heads of military and civil departments, governors of States, members of Congress, and Corps Diplomatique . . .

By command of Lieutenant-General Grant:

E.D. Townsend,
Assistant Adjutant-General.[105]

It was a grand spectacle replete with the pomp and circumstance that came to typify nineteenth century pageantry. Although the event might have reminded one of the regal splendor of a grand European epic such as the coronation of Queen Victoria at Westminster Abbey twenty-seven years earlier, it had a decided American uniqueness. Throngs of people lined the avenues in awe of those who had saved the Union. The competitive American spirit rose to the occasion as each unit displayed the pride and self-respect earned after four long years of war. Citizens organized themselves into state groups and hailed their troops as

Grand Review of the 20th Corps in Washington D.C. on May 24, 1865

General Slocum and staff at the Grand Review

they passed. Schools were closed as were shops and businesses. The western troops vied with eastern troops as each strutted with the proud gait of battle-hardened veterans. Sherman worried about his troops. "Meade, I am afraid my poor tatter-demalion corps will make a poor appearance tomorrow when contrasted with yours." They did not. The troops, eastern and western, marched together down the streets of Washington past the reviewing stand of admiring officials, breaking step on occasion to sneak a glance at the celebrities. If they lacked the precision of the Coldstream Guards or the Grenadiers, weren't they entitled? After all, hadn't their sacrifices entitled them to bend military protocol after having left their homes and families for four long years to save the Union? If General Sherman thought so he did not comment. They were his boys and he was proud of them. One of Lieutenant Murphy's comrades in the 13ᵗʰ New Jersey Volunteers wrote,

Pennsylvania avenue was a compact mass of human beings from the Capitol to Seventh street. Flags, banners, handkerchiefs, scarfs, bouquets and wreaths of flowers were thrown up in the air and shouts and cheers broke forth from the assembled multitude from time to time. The scene down Pennsylvania avenue was magnificent . . . The flags of the Thirteenth Regiment, which had been worn to shreds by hard service, were frequently applauded by the enthusiastic multitude . . . We saw the names of Ohio, Massachusetts, and Connecticut, but when the banner of New Jersey, which was stretched over the walk, greeted our sight, a spontaneous cheer broke forth throughout the Regiment.[106]

Lieutenant Murphy recalled the splendor of this event. "Then came the grand review where for two whole days the victorious soldiers marched past their honored and respected commanders and gave them their final salutes. That magnificent review inspired . . . a poem by Bret Harte in memory of those who were not present . . . It is called the 'Second Review of the Grand Army.' "[107]

I read last night of the Grand Review
    In Washington's chiefest avenue—
Two hundred thousand men in blue,
    I think they said was the number,—
Till I seemed to hear their tramping feet,
The bugle blast and the drum's quick beat,
The clatter of hoofs in the stony street,
And the thousand details that to repeat
    Would only my verse encumber,—
Till I fell in a revery, sad and sweet,
    And then to a fitful slumber.

And I saw a phantom army come,
With never a sound of fife or drum,
But keeping time to a throbbing hum
    Of wailing and lamentation.
The martyred heroes of Malvern Hill,
Of Gettysburg and Chancellorsville,
The men whose wasted figures fill
    The patriot graves of the nation.

So all night long swept the strange array;
So all night long till the morning gray,
I watched for one who had passed away
    With a reverent awe and wonder.
Till a blue cap waved in the lengthening line,
And I knew that one who was kin of mine
Had come; and I spake, and lo! That sign
    Awakened me from my slumber.

A comrade of Franklin Murphy lamented that the Review resulted in needless loss after the long conflict was over. He wrote on June 10, 1865, from Baileys Cross Roads near Washington D.C.,

. . . and a soldier can get used to almost anything but fighting, that hardly ever came natural to me to tell the Truth if there was fun in it I saw it but seldom. But there was a stern reality, when a man was expecting every minute would be the next. The sun is coming out again. I guess the rain is nearly over. I suppose you have seen by this time the full account of yesterday's review in the New York papers. It was a big thing in the dust & hot sun & some of the Boys who have been through thick & thin for nearly three long years fell from the effects of the heat & dust which comprises the city of Washington . . .[108]

Yes it was sacrifice, sacrifice to preserve the Union that Murphy recalled when he wrote "the memory of those eventful days . . . a memory of long and weary march; of hunger and privation; of the smoke and danger of battle; of patriotic service gladly rendered that our country's flag might float unchallenged from the Potomac to the Gulf. It was a Civil War. The life of the Nation was at stake, and in many cases it was father against son and brother against brother . . ."[109]

Discharge at Long Last!

The Thirteenth Regiment New Jersey Volunteers moved about two miles down the Blandesburg Road and went into camp. They remained there several days receiving friends and neighbors who made the trip from Newark. Among these were Marcus L. Yard and John Y. Foster. Muster rolls were signed and the formalities of discharge papers were completed. On June 9, 1865, Murphy and his surviving comrades boarded the train and started for home. It must have been a gripping experience as the men passed through Philadelphia and arrived home at the Market Street station in Newark. Murphy had not been home in three years and eagerly anticipated an enthusiastic reception. Although rain showers prevented an overwhelming turnout the men were happy to be home. They marched on to Lockwood's Hotel and received a warm reception by Mayor Runyon. They were called into line at Ward U.S. Hospital near Centre Street, stacked arms and received their discharges. A dinner and parade would await them on June 15 that was a fitting testimonial by their city and state for all the sacrifices they endured.

The war was over and it was now a time to heal the nation's wounds. This would take years if not generations as the bitter memories of war would linger in the hearts of Northerners and Southerners alike. Some were able to put the past behind them while others would anguish with lingering memories of death and destruction. A young lady writing from Winchester, Virginia, on June 23rd, 1865, to James Grimstead in the U.S. Signal Corps caught the Unionist spirit as she wrote,

My Dear Friend Jimmie

I suppose you have been having a very pleasant time in camp or at least I hope so there are a great many of our friends coming to see us every day returning to their homes. I hope you will be fortunate enough to get home and accompany your sister from school. I think she will be pleased almost to death to see you coming after her or at least I would if I were her. I suppose you had a magnificent time at the Review. I would love to have been there very much, we want to see you very much and if you get discharged you must visit old Winchester once more before you return to your native state. You speaking about the different places you was at I suppose Richmond and Petersburg are very much dilapidated. Oh how much I would be delighted almost to death to travel through the South and see how the rebels are getting along since they got such a good whipping. I know they feel very

General Lee and two of his staff

sad but they brought it all on there selves and will have to put up with it all and live under our laws.

Your true friend,
Nellie[110]

To what extent each side in America's Civil War curried favor with the citizens of the other has always been a provocative question asked by students of the conflict. It is quite impossible to determine the exact number that did so but there is no question that the ideology that motivated one side found adherents on the other. It is also clear that this ideology contributed to the deep-seeded feelings that worked against reconciliation and contributed to the rancor that persisted well into the twentieth century. An outstanding example of this can be found in a letter written by E. Osbourn, raised and schooled in New Jersey before the war, who chose to link his destiny with that of the Confederacy. He wrote from Charleston, South Carolina, on January 9, 1866, to James Grimstead, his childhood schoolmate in Bonhamtown, New Jersey, a letter that expresses strong emotional sentiments for the righteousness of his cause while suggesting a subtle desire to move in the direction of what President Warren G. Harding would label a "Return to Normalcy" some fifty-five years later.

My dear old friend & Schoolmate

Now that the war is over & things settled down generally, I resume our correspondence where it was broken off, that is when we could not agree on politics. Now Jim, I went in the secession movement heart & hand. I tried my utmost to make Maryland move but she would not move. Howsomever I went to Richmond the same identical place so many Yankees found a little farm 3X6 feet, joined the First South Carolina Regt. as a private & I surrendered myself or Genl Lee, God bless his grey hairs, did it for me, as Senior Capt. Of the Regt. From the Ranks I rose & I am proud of it. I took part in all the actions my commands was in, & God in his infinite kept me from having as much as a scratch. But Jim, my dear fellow I am roaring, rabid, ultra secession as I ever was. We were not whipped, we were crushed by the rabble & jail birds of Europe combined. Jim, may be I am stepping on tender ground but my dear fellow I might much better speak openly, than play hypocrite.

Jim, after the surrender of our Army I went within 12 miles of Bonhamtown but my rebel proclivities were so prominent that I had to keep in the dark. I would have been up to see you, but the wounds so recently inflicted on both sides had not commenced to heal & we might have had instead of a cordial meeting one of the directly opposite. My eldest Bro. William doubtless you remember him, was killed in the Confederate Service, poor fellow . . . Just imagine our mental arithmetic class. It was a race & a well contested one who should have the lead . . . Then the boys must go out in the orchard opposite to get firewood then our good old games of ball, & the splendid skating on Colyers Mill Pond, then again hide & seek through your barn, then a slide down the hill on our sleigh. Jimmy my boy when I think over those times it makes the blood bound through my veins." [111]

So as men on both sides reminisced on old times they returned to their homes and families eager to start new lives as peace was restored to the nation.

Franklin Murphy returned to Newark, New Jersey, and eagerly began a new life. At nineteen years of age life loomed large to the young man who had endured so much. Memories of carnage and suffering remained with him as with all the soldiers North and South who had sacrificed for their cause. Murphy was able to forgive if not forget. There is not a single example in any of his letters, addresses, diary entries, etc. that harbors the least sentiment of rancor toward his former enemies. Perhaps his deep seeded religious convictions helped make this so. He was, after all, a devout Christian whose dogma called for forgiveness. So unlike Nellie or Osbourn, he put the war behind him quickly, and moved on with his life. As time went on he was able to reflect on his experiences, fine tune his memories in the context of a larger national picture, and draw remarkable conclusions. He had a brilliant analytical mind that poured over past events and evaluated them with the precision of a man who wore many hats. He was both an actuary-statistician, and humanitarian whose patriotic focus produced a remarkable analysis of the war years, long after it was over. Historians value accounts such as these which have endured the scrutiny of time. They have provided, among other things, a multiple perspective not possible among contemporaries of the time and the analysis of documents not yet accessible. Here are his observations contained in an address entitled "The Cost Of The War" delivered at St. Paul's Methodist Episcopal Church on May 27, 1894.

The Cost of the War

As long as the nation endures the story of personal prowess and thrilling incident of those days will be told to interest the coming generations. No War (of modern times at least) engaged so many men, in none were the issues so important. There are so many points of view from which any address on the War may be written that it is difficult to choose a single one from the many which present themselves. I have thought, however, that it might be interesting if we consider for a few moments the cost of the War. I must ask your patient attention to the statistics which I will make as brief as possible.

First let us consider the cost in dollars, and for this purpose I quote freely from an article that appeared a year or more ago in the New York Sun, *an article whose purpose was stated to be to put together some of the items of expenditure and loss, clearly and directly chargeable to the War account; in other words to establish a minimum estimate of the money cost of preserving the Union.*

If we were to go into the matter of consequential damages, such as the paralysis of certain branches of business, the suspension of trade with the Southern States, the extinction of a large part of our maritime commerce, the enormous loss resulting from the arrest of the normal increase of population, and the peaceful development of the nation's resources, we should pass at once from the domain of precise arithmetic to that of vague conjecture and unverified speculation. The figures presented come from the official records, or when the amount is estimated it is so stated and care is taken to keep the estimate well within bounds. The actual current War expenditure during the four fiscal years from June 30, 1861 to June 30, 1865, was:

For fiscal year 1862 $469,570,241
For fiscal year 1863 $718,734,276
For fiscal year 1864 $864,969,098
For fiscal year 1865 $1,295,099,289

Total $3,348,372,904

This, however, includes what the government would have spent if there had been no war. Taking this amount to be the same as the four years immediately preceding the War and offsetting the country's growth under normal circumstances by the restriction of the field of administration to the Northern States, we have a total for four years of

$272,872,181. Deduct this from the total for the War period and add the total paid by the Government in premiums for loans, an item not included in the statement of annual expenditure, and which amounted to $169,429,364 and we have a total actual current War expenditure of $3,144,975,087.

The totals of local bounties paid to the several States to fill quotas under the calls of '63-4-5, are obtained from the report of 1866 of Provost-Marshall General James B. Fry. We omit from consideration any account of the money paid by the States or towns or individuals over and above the amount refunded from the United States Treasury for the creditable equipment of the troops sent to the front. The total would be very large but it is practically undeterminable. The amount thus paid from the beginning to the end of the War in the loyal States amounted to $285,941,128.

Throughout the North during the War there were not less than seven thousand local associations of patriotic men and women contributing money, time, and articles of every description to promote the well-being of the soldiers fighting at the front, or to add to their comfort. Besides these local societies there were such organizations as the Sanitary Commission and the Christian Commission operating on a large scale and in the general field. The Sanitary Commission alone raised and expended more than $20,000,000. The aggregate of these contributions of associated or individual patriotism, from the society of little girls who sold rings and lockets for the benefit of the wounded soldiers, to the capitalist who equipped a regiment at his own expense or gave a steamship to Lincoln's Government, can never be computed. When set down at $50,000,000 for the purpose of this inquiry, it is a low estimate.

A large item properly belonging to the cost of the War is the loss to productive industry of the time and labor of the citizens who enlisted in the Army. This item is approximately ascertainable.

If we take 847,701 as the average number of men in the Union armies during the War (and tables show this to be the average number) and estimate the earning capacity of the average soldier at $300.00 a year above the cost of his own subsistence, the direct loss occasioned by the diversion from productive to unproductive labor would amount to $254,310,300 a year, or for the four years of the War period, to $1,017,241,200.

It would be the work of a lifetime to cipher out the whole amount paid since the War, under general or special acts of Congress, in compensation for the real or alleged destruction of property, or for War supplies seized or furnished, or for indemnity for loss of personal effects, or for back pay or bounty of volunteers, or for horses or mules lost, or for the reimbursements of States or minor civil divisions, or for expenditures necessitated by the War, or in any other of the countless ways in which the War still draws upon the Treasury. If we estimate that since 1865 the War claims allowed and paid by the Government have averaged only $5,000,000 a year, the total would be $140,000,000. If this sum were doubled we should still probably be well within the bounds of probability.

The interest on the War debt has been constantly growing less and has been reduced from $133,000,000 in 1866 to $20,000,000 in 1893. The total amount paid for this item since the War is $2,355,829,102.

The pension expenditure on the other hand has been as constantly increasing and it has grown from $15,000,000 in 1866 to $146,000,000 in 1893. The total since the War expended on this account has been $1,551,198,500, less an allowance for other pensions of $112,000,000, which leaves the amount to be charged to this item $1,431,198,500.

Recapitulating these several items of expense and omitting from consideration any of the other myriad sources of expenditure or loss properly or less properly chargeable to the Civil War, we obtain a fair minimum estimate of what it cost the North to preserve the Union.

Current War Expenses	$ 3,144,975,087
Bounties other than Federal	285,941,128
Estimated Private Contributions	50,000,000
Loss of Soldiers' Productive Labor	1,017,241,200
War Claims of Various Sorts	140,000,000
Interest on the War Debt	2,255,820,102
Pensions on account of the Civil War	1,431,198,500
Total	$ 8,425,185,017

These figures stagger the imagination. Like all symbols for quantities so stupendous as to be far beyond the accustomed range of thought, they go from the eye to the brain without producing immediately an effect adequate to their mathematical importance. One million conveys the idea of vastness. A thousand millions, eight thousand millions is appreciated slowly, and only by an indirect process. What does it mean when we say that the money cost of the War to the North alone was nearly eight and a half billions of dollars?

If the burden was distributed among the whole earth's population, every human being, man, woman, child, civilized or savage, living anywhere on the face of the earth, would be taxed about six dollars. If every gold or silver coin or piece of paper money now in circulation among the four hundred million people of this country and of England, France, Germany, Austria, Holland, Italy, Spain, and Russia, should be gathered in and counted, the total value reduced to United States money would cover only three quarters of our War cost. The amount of money indicated by the figures $8,425,185,017 is more than five times the aggregate of the deposits in all Savings Banks of the United States; more than eight times the aggregate of the deposits in all the State Banks, Trust companies and private banking concerns in the United States; almost double the aggregate of deposits in all of these institutions combined.

Put it another way. By the census of 1860, the estimated valuation—true valuation not assessed—of all property real and personal of the eleven rebellious States was $5,202,166,207. Thus it appears that in order to keep these eleven States under the flag, the Nation has paid at least $3,223,018,810

more than the entire valuation of all the property in those eleven States at the time when the War was fought.

Take another view of it. The slave and the right to own him was an important factor in causing the War; perhaps the most important. The census of 1860 shows that in the then slave holding States of Delaware, Maryland, District of Columbia, Virginia, North and South Carolina, Georgia, Florida, Alabama, Mississippi, Louisiana, Texas, Arkansas, Tennessee and Kentucky, there were 3,838,765 slaves owned by 347,525 slave holders. The average value of a slave, old and young, male and female, was about $400. If you charge upon the slaves the cost of the War, you must value them at over $2000 apiece.

There is another cost of the War much more important than the cost in money, and that is the cost in lives.

The total enrollment of the Union Armies, officers and men, not including three and six months men, was 2,864,272. Of this number there were killed in battle 67,058; died of wounds 43,012; died of disease 199,720; died of other causes 40,154, or a total number of deaths of 359,528. How the very statement of these enormous losses reminds one of Gettysburg, Spottsylvania, Wilderness, Antietam, Chancellorsville, Chickamauga, Cold Harbor and other bloody battles of the War. How they recall to us McPherson and Reynolds and Sedgwick and Kearney and Lyon and the many of less rank but not of less courage. How all of us who are old enough to remember those days, remember incident after incident of individual bravery, not less than those examples of regimental courage whose record makes immortal the history of our battlefields.

Fox's Regimental Losses in the Civil War gives a list of over sixty regiments, each one of which lost over fifty per cent of the men engaged in some single battle. In this list New Jersey is represented by two of

"All Quiet Along the Potomac Tonight," a popular Civil War ballard

her gallant regiments. The *Eleventh New Jersey* lost 55% of its men at Gettysburg and the *Fifteenth New Jersey* lost 63% at Spottsylvania. Let me quote from Fox. "Perhaps their significance will be better understood when compared with some extraordinary loss in foreign wars; some well known instance which may serve as a standard of measurement. Take the charge of the Light Brigade at Boclaklava. Its extraordinary loss has been made a familiar feature of heroic verse and story in every land, until the whole world has heard of the gallant six hundred and their ride into the Valley of Death. Now as the Light Brigade accomplished nothing in this action—merely executed an order which was a blunder—it must be that it was the danger and its attendant loss which inspired the interest in that historic ride. What was the loss? The Light Brigade took 673 officers and men into that charge; they lost 113 killed and 134 wounded; total 247, or 36.7%, a percentage, I may add, which don't permit them to be named in our list of famous regiments. The heaviest loss in the German army during the Franco-Prussian War occurred in the Sixteenth Infantry (Third Westphalian) at Mars La Tour and amounted to 49.4%."

I shall have accomplished something tonight if I impress upon you the fact that the American soldier, a soldier not by profession but by the highest call of patriotic duty, has left a record that for courage and heroism leads the world.

But no estimate of the cost of the War is complete until we add another factor. Many a wife saw her husband march off to the War, but never saw him return. Many a father and mother bid their boy farewell and God Speed, and read in the papers some morning after a battle that he had fought his last fight. Many a sister bid her brother as he marched away to the front, good-by forever.

Who shall put a value on a wife's affections? Who shall measure a mother's love? Who shall put a price on patriotism?

The men who bravely died at the front did not suffer it all. All over this land there are homes where the sun has gone out forever because of the husband or son or brother or lover who gave his life for the flag. The shot that killed them pierced other hearts far away. How many families are there reduced from comfort to poverty because the bread winner gave himself as a sacrifice? How much privation constantly and privately borne and that must be borne to the end, was caused by the War? Who shall estimate it?

There is not a city in all this land where the crutch or the empty sleeve are not present to remind us of those days of anxious trial. The maimed are everywhere. Corporal Tanner had his legs shot under him so that they had to be amputated above the knees. A few years afterward the old wounds opened and they had to be amputated again. Only recently the wounds again opened and a third amputation was made, this time near the body. Many a private soldier is hobbling along through life or confined to a bed of sickness, perhaps permanently, whose pension from the government barely suffices to pay for bandages and salve for his wounds. Let you and I who in reasonable health enjoy the blessings of a United Country, never forget how much we owe these brave men.

What did we get for all this expenditure of money and blood and grief? What did the War do? It killed secession forever. It freed the slaves. It put a new duty on every American citizen.

We have the fairest land the sun ever shone upon, but problems face us today only less serious than those which faced our brothers and our fathers in '61; problems of capital and labor, of immigration, of honest government-all made more serious as civilization grows more complex. Shall we be as equal to our duty as they were to theirs?

It is a legend of the dwellers by the Rhine that on a certain night in every year when the moon is at its full, the Imperial Charles leaves his tomb and revisits the scenes he loved. Walking upon an arch of light, he crosses the river, calling down a benediction upon the land, blessing fields and flocks, vineyards and cities, hamlets and sleeping people; then softly returns to his slumber in La Chapelle. So do the spirits of those of whom we speak tonight come to bless us with a benediction of patriotic love and inspire us with patriotic endeavor. You and I believe in God. I charge you as you love your God, to love your country only less. I beseech you by the memory of those who gave their lives to give you a country that you be true to that country with all the highest inspiration of your nature.

Aqueduct Bridge crossing the Potomac River at Georgetown

Franklin Murphy, now nineteen-years-old was a battle hardened veteran who had seen three long years of combat. He was seasoned beyond his years as anyone would be who survived the internecine carnage that took 620,000 American lives. Yet he exuded the optimism of youth with an unbroken spirit that remained with him as he grew older. He identified his spirit with that of the Union when he wrote, "It is this spirit that carried us through the War of the Rebellion for the extirpation of slavery. It is this spirit that will carry us through all our perils, as a Nation, and keep us secure, united and great. Let it be the mission of this society to kindle afresh from time to time the slumbering fires of patriotic love, so that our flag, which represents that which our fathers fought to establish, and some of us have fought to maintain, may remain forever the unsullied emblem of human freedom."[112]

4

Swords Into Plowshares

THE CIVIL WAR had brought great changes to America in four tumultuous years, and this growth pattern would assume geometric dimensions in the years that followed. Historians often refer to the period between 1865 and 1900 as those which transformed America from a primarily agricultural nation to a mighty industrial power with a glossy veneer of wealth that Mark Twain would label the "Gilded Age." The Industrial Revolution begun by Thomas Newcomen and James Hargreaves et al., had changed dramatically by the time of Thomas Edison and Henry Ford. This worldwide phenomenon progressed by leaps and bounds and would continue, as some would argue, to the present day.

Franklin Murphy displayed remarkable resiliency as he adapted to these changes of postwar America as a product of his times while contributing to and leaving his legacy on those times. He returned to Newark, New Jersey, and was mustered out of service with the Thirteenth New Jersey Volunteers. At nineteen he was still a very young man and had that wanderlust for adventure that was typical at that age. He received his back pay from the army and decided to see as much of that country that he had fought so hard to preserve. Along with his older brother William, the two set out. This was characteristic of Murphy when he wrote that "he never enjoyed anything alone."[1] They traveled to all of the major northern cities and as far west as Chicago in a quest to soak up as much of America as their time and money would allow. They returned home, contented at the end of their trip, "penniless and perfectly happy." Franklin said to his father, "Now that money's gone, I guess I'd better earn some more."[2] Several days passed as he searched for some way to "earn some more." He came home one evening and told his father that he could buy a 50 percent share of a small varnish industry for a few thousand dollars, although as he recalled, "I didn't know varnish from molasses but I could learn."[3] His father backed him, and his business career was off and running.

Franklin Murphy circa 1870

The New Idea In Business

He did learn as did his associate Thompson Price, although the two were soon to adopt different business philosophies. This ultimately resulted in Murphy buying out his partner. It happened like this: Murphy was on the road selling his goods shortly after buying the factory. Sales were good, so much so that in about two months Price telegrammed calling Murphy home. "Come home you've sold more varnish than we can deliver."[4] Price wanted to catch up with the orders while Murphy wanted to expand the operation to "enlarge the factory and also to change the entire policy of the business."[5] Murphy called this change "The New Idea In Business."[6] It began with understanding the problems that varnish manufacturers had in their production techniques. He concluded that false economies often led to shoddy results requiring refinishing products that had yet to leave the factory. "He settled it in his own mind that the best possible varnish, whatever the price per gallon, would be the cheapest varnish manufacturers could buy."[7] Price disagreed so Murphy convinced his father to buy out his partner and with additional money contributed by James G. Barnett formed the business which would eventually be incorporated as the Murphy Varnish Company in 1891.[8]

Marriage To Janet Colwell

Almost three years to the day after returning home from the Civil War, Franklin Murphy married Janet Colwell. She was a beautiful brunet, the daughter of Israel Day and Cathrine Cox Gale (Hoghland). He was twenty-two years old; she was twenty-six. The wedding took place on June 24th, 1868, at Saint Paul's Methodist Episcopal Church in Newark, New Jersey. She was born on December 30, 1842, in New York City and moved with her mother at an early age to Newark, New Jersey. It was there that she met the young erstwhile Union lieutenant turned entrepreneur. They were a handsome couple. He exuded the self-confidence and polish of education and experience, and she radiated dignity and grace "a demeanor and traits that unmistakably reflected her cultural inheritance."[9]

This inheritance included a thorough education in Newark's public schools. She completed advanced courses that prepared her for a career in teaching, and she became employed in the Newark public school system. Her love of children went beyond the classroom. She worked hard during the summers in the city's "fresh air fund," providing many unfortunate youngsters the rare opportunity of rural excursions into the pristine countryside. She became a manager of the Protestant Foster Home for orphaned youngsters and was chosen honorary vice-president of the Board of Managers of the Babies' Hospital in Newark. She also found time to work for women's causes on the Board of Managers of the Newark Exchange for Women's Work. It was no wonder then that Franklin Murphy, keenly intelligent in his own right, would be attracted to and choose for his spouse a woman with such intellectual, cultural, and sensitive proclivities.

Janet Murphy was widely acclaimed for her literary talent. A number of her poems were published as were some of her descriptive short stories, consisting primarily of the places she visited. Of particular interest were areas of the American South through which she traveled and, perhaps coincidently, were scenes that her husband witnessed during the war on his march to the sea with General Sherman. Her professional life came to an end with the birth of her children, Franklin Jr. in 1873 and Helen in 1877. She was totally devoted to her husband and children ". . . doing those little tasks that insure happiness to the family circle. This caring for her own was not carried on in any selfish spirit; indeed, it served only to broaden her sympathies and to make her a liberal supporter of all worthy efforts to bring happiness to others."[10] As Murphy's political star continued to rise, she rose with him, becoming the pivotal mainstay of the social events they hosted until, in good time, she became New Jersey's "first lady." "She presided with dignity and graciousness over the executive mansion at Trenton, over the family residence in Newark, and over the summer home at Elberon on the Jersey shore."[11]

Janet Murphy

Franklin Murphy papers

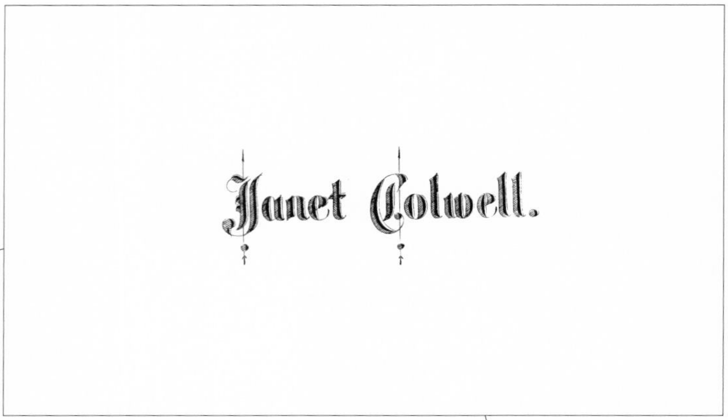

Janet Colwell.

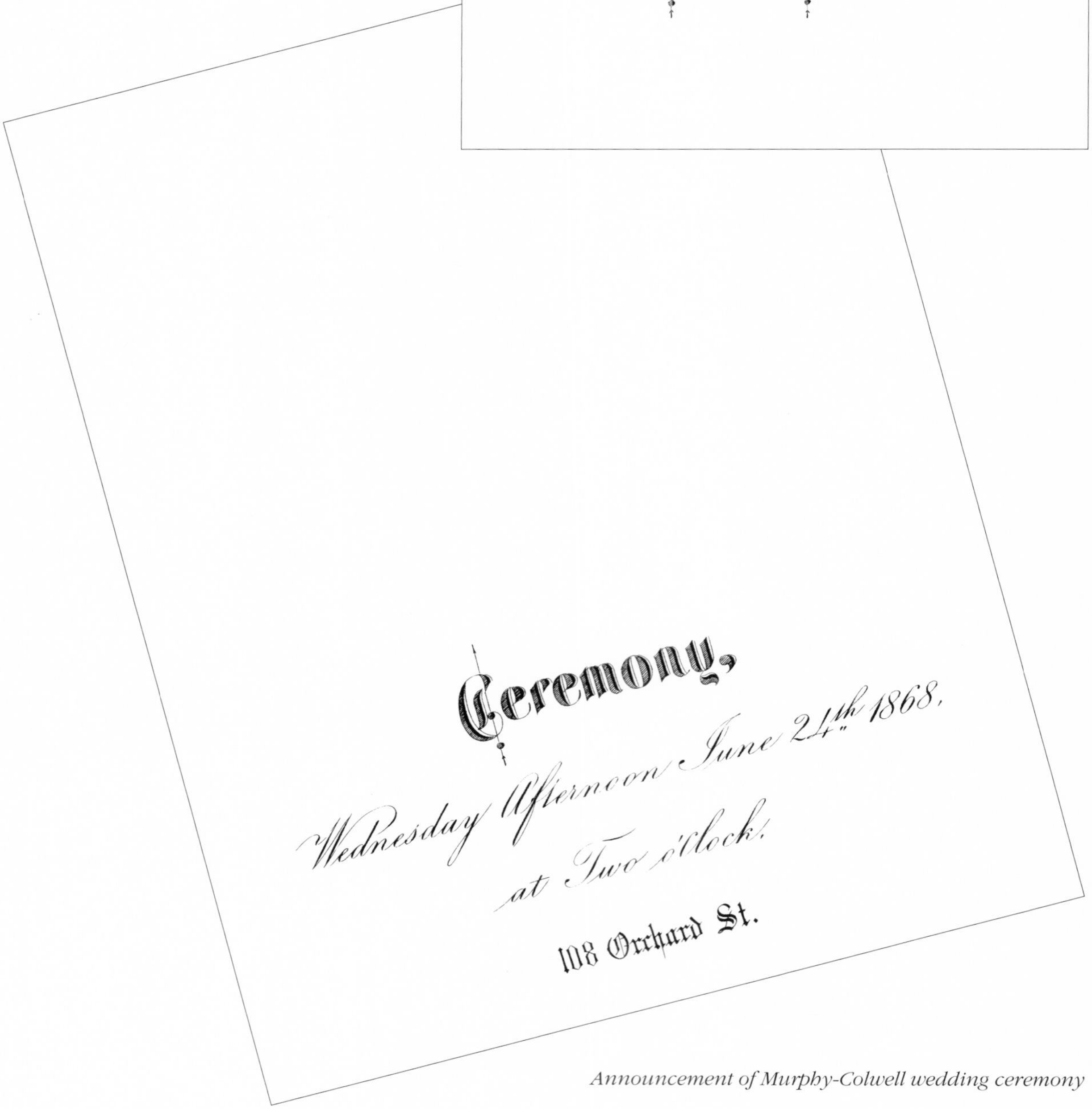

Ceremony,

Wednesday Afternoon June 24th 1868,

at Two o'clock,

108 Orchard St.

Announcement of Murphy-Colwell wedding ceremony

The Murphy Varnish Company

Meanwhile, Franklin Murphy's business flourished as did most of the varnish industry yet remained outside the realm of the combinations and trusts that came to dominate American industry in the days before the Sherman and Clayton Anti-Trust Acts. "The varnish industry thus far has refused to enter into the schemes of the promoter of combinations—an occupation which has created the word 'combinator'—and still remains in the hands of perhaps one hundred and fifty separate, independent concerns, who produce from fifteen to twenty million dollars' worth of varnish annually."[12] The demand for varnish during the Victorian Era was enormous in countless products ranging from yachts to pianos. This was furthered by the architecture of this period which typically sported intricately milled moldings with the beautiful luster of gloss or satin varnish finishes. There was decorative scroll work called arabesque, molded wood trim around doorways known as architrave, and bolection, a heavy curved molding bulging away from the wall. Today, this has vanished from all but the most expensive homes and offices. These were the times and peculiar circumstances in which Murphy found himself, but his talents in introducing uniformity to the industry assured his success. "His genius for systematizing everything with which he was connected showed very vividly and the users of varnish were quick to appreciate the advantages that reliable varnish gave to them."[13] New products were added as the business grew. The one small building fanned out down McWhorter Street in Newark, New Jersey, until it occupied fully four city blocks and employed one hundred and fifty people by 1915.[14] Factories were also built in Chicago, Cleveland, and Montreal as additional opportunities presented themselves in the burgeoning national and overseas markets. The dozen kinds of varnish grew to more than two hundred with about twelve hundred shades of color. In addition to varnish, there were Japans, shellacs, fillers, surfacers, Japan colors, oil colors, enamels, stains, konkreto, and varnish removers. The following is a sample list of some of the products offered by the company:

MURPHY VARNISH COMPANY PRODUCTS

Murphy Transparent Interior Varnish

Murphy No-gloss Varnish

Murphy Semi-gloss Varnish

Murphy Transparent Floor Varnish

Murphy Univarnish (for interior and exterior woodwork, including floors where waterproof varnish is desired).

Murphy Velvet Floor Varnish (for a final coat where a semi-gloss finish is desired without rubbing)

Murphy Shellacquer (White and orange)

Murphy Muronic Enamel Undercoating

Murphy Mineral Paste Filler
A-White
B-Light Red Brown
C-Medium shade Red
D-Dark Red Brown
E-Brown Black shade
F-Black

Murphy Muronic Enamel Gloss
Furnished in White, Gray and Ivory

Murphy Muronic Enamel Semi-gloss

Murphy Penetrating Oil Stains
Mahogany
Brown Mahogany
Dark Oak
Light Oak
Bog Oak
Gray

Murphy Oil Colors

Murphy Japan Colors[15]

Murphy Varnish Company logo

Murphy replied to a question as to what had been his business policy, "Every manufacturer must decide upon the kind of patronage to which he will appeal, and stick to that kind . . . I decided, at the beginning of the business to make varnish for those who required the best."[16] He believed that creating the best possible product regardless of the price would eventually become the least expensive for his customers. He combined three concepts which brought him success. First, he insisted on the best ingredients regardless of the cost. He passed these costs on to the customer in a more expensive varnish but one that was better, lasted longer, and was ultimately cheaper. Next, he streamlined plant operations to create the most ideal conditions of productivity, sparing no expense in searching for the best state-of-the-art capital facilities. For example, he employed chemists to work the wonders of science in modern laboratories. Finally, and most important of all these efforts was his concern and respect for his employees. Regardless of position, from the mailroom boy to the plant supervisor, there were no holds barred in his attempt to instill loyalty and devotion among his workers. He did this, of course, by paying them a good salary and including what would be considered today a "benefits package" of disability and life insurance and pensions. This was not a simple quid pro quo, however; it went beyond that. Money and profits were one thing, but they were subjected to the higher law of a quality of life for all. So it was not unusual for men who had started out in the stockroom to retire thirty years later in supervisory positions with comfortable pensions. A few examples will serve to illustrate these points. In an interview entitled "Personal Influence," Murphy was asked how he stood with his employees. Was there a labor problem in his business? He thought for a moment, then got up and went to a file and came back with an article from a magazine saying that

few businessmen appreciate the far-reaching power, good or bad, of their personal influence. They seem to forget that the mood of the head office is a bracing or a poisonous atmosphere which pervades the whole institution. Their attitude, at best, is here are the rules,—there are the work,—obey orders. At worst, it is the worst in them, exaggerated by egotism and worry. Let me read you one sentence from an article in the recent issue of a trade journal— "the head of a great business concern should be a man whom every employee is always glad to meet, regardless of weather or trade conditions; a man who never gets grouchy from an east wind of any sort,—a man whose sympathy and cheeriness and enthusiasm overflow the office and fill all the department and warm and inspire the entire force."[17]

Murphy sought to pay his people above and beyond the norm to make them happy. He believed happy employees would be enthusiastic about their work, and the resulting productivity would reflect that happiness and enthusiasm. It seems that Murphy was beyond his times in implementing concepts of profit sharing and incentive plans. He wrote, "The practical values of ability and training are doubled by enthusiasm. Given the very best that a manager, superintendent, laboratory man, process man, salesman, accountant or common laborer will do for good wages—then as an enthusiast for Murphy Varnish Company, he will double that best. Men are more likely to be enthusiastic when they are happy."[18]

Progressive Employee Relations

How did Franklin Murphy instill such loyalty into his work force? What made his workers happy and enthusiastic? In the first place, there was a great deal of personal care taken by the managers and supervisors in the training of every promising employee with an eye to his promotion. Ten-dollar-a-week workers were made to realize that a career position awaited them if they responded to the training. "Some of the ablest of the superintendents and managers were office boys or working in the process rooms not so many years ago," recalled Murphy ". . . Every member of the force knows that a good sound pension awaits him, when he grows

Engraving of the Murphy Varnish Company plant

old or is disabled in the service and no penny of his wage is taken for that fund either. This pension under certain conditions amounts to sixty percent of the best wages ever paid him."[19] Murphy wrote affectionately of one of his employees on June 26, 1903,

> *Mr. Ettinger . . . came up from Belmar . . . and informed me of his desire to retire at least from active service. I consented with a good deal of reluctance but I did so. He has been with us for about thirty years and was an upright, devoted and loyal officer of the Company. Of course, I greatly regret that he feels that the time has come when he must leave. He is about sixty years old and has an ample fortune and feels as though he was entitled to a rest. I made an arrangement with him which was very pleasing to him and he is to be relieved from all the detail of his work and is to have all the liberty he wants, but is to continue to look after the Pullman business for us and advise us from time to time as to how he finds things.*[20]

His factories shut down at 12 o'clock every Saturday in what he called the "half holiday." He made a special effort during the holidays to bring a spirit of joy and good tidings. At Thanksgiving, for example, a turkey was delivered at every employee kitchen door and bonus checks were distributed at Christmas. Murphy's diary entry on Christmas Eve 1904 states, "We had a half day at the office today and a very busy one it was. I excluded all visitors as much as possible, desiring to have a peaceful and quiet morning with the folks in the office. We concluded to close the business both office and factory at twelve o'clock in order to give the clerks a half holiday that they might be enabled to complete their Christmas purchases before night. This was enjoyed very much by them all, as was the present of five per cent on their salaries which we gave to every employee in the company everywhere, the sum so expended being something over $10,000."[21]

The "outing day" was a special summer event which might be compared to today's company picnics. Trains or boats were chartered to some special resort or picnic ground with free tickets for all including wives and sweethearts. This is quite remarkable put in historical perspective. After all, this was at a time of sweatshops and company stores when many workers eked out a miserable subsistence working fourteen-hour-days, six days, a week. Conditions were so bad in the tenement slums of the northeast cities and elsewhere that Karl Marx prophesied that capitalism had become so depraved that it was inevitable that the working proletariat would rise up in a glorious revolution and overthrow their capitalist masters. It was men like Murphy who prevented this from happening in America. He contrasted greatly with many of his fellow captains of industry who were intent on maximizing their profits by cutting the wages of their workers. For example, the railroad titans cut wages 20 percent in 1877 resulting in one of the worst strikes in American history.[22] Jay Gould would often "supplant old employees with inexperienced persons at much lower salaries" while Jim Hill boasted: "I will make one engine do the work of three and dispose of two crews."[23] Andrew Carnegie who sanctimoniously proclaimed "Thou shalt not take thy neighbor's job," arbitrarily fired his workers at the Edgar Thompson works in Pittsburgh during the brief depression between 1884-1885.[24] Perhaps the most egregious expression of contempt for the toiling masses by a mogul of industry came from Jay Gould when he said that he could "hire one-half of the working class to kill the other half," [25] while the disdain of other titans toward the populace was caught in William H. Vanderbilt's comment, "The public be damned."[26]

Franklin Murphy went on to establish his mark on the American capitalist system by establishing what eventually became the largest varnish manufacturing industry in the country. He joined with a growing number of talented entrepreneurs who implemented many of the principles of "scientific management" years before they were codified by Frederick W. Taylor. "The young men who were to form the new nobility of industry and banking had, most of them, reached their prime of youth or manhood when Lincoln issued his first call for volunteers. Jay Gould, Jim Fiske, J.P. Morgan, Philip Armour, Andrew Carnegie, James Hill and John D. Rockefeller were all in their early twenties . . ."[27]

None of them sacrificed in their country's service but instead took advantage of the opportunities the war presented to launch their personal fortunes. Murphy, on the other hand, chose to fight to preserve the Union. For him, there would be time to make money later. Although the others may have had a head start and their fortunes may have grown larger, few of them could compare their record with his. He was honest to a fault and succeeded by establishing the most efficient business methods possible while always looking to further the interests of those he employed. Machiavellian techniques of Social Darwinism that called for the destruction of the competition by a convoluted rationale of the survival of the fittest were not for him. He was too noble for that.

Ideals into Results

Franklin Murphy sincerely appreciated his life and times and often expressed these feelings to his friends and associates. "I think we have a great cause for thankfulness for the times in which we live. Never in all history has the mental and moral and material welfare of the people been so ministered to as today; never had there been placed within the reach of all so many opportunities for physical comfort and mental development as are within our reach."[28] It was Murphy's deep religious and moral convictions that brought him to the conclusion that wealth and material success were but part of a man's fulfillment. He developed a sense of "noblesse oblige" that had him look to public service as a measure of tangible contribution. The appreciation of one's good fortune and personal success was one thing; however, turning these into contributions to society, was something else. He expressed it this way: "The question to be asked us in the day of final account is not what you believe, but what have you done; and the same law will hold at the last day as at the first—By their fruits shall ye know them."[29] These noble values should not mask Murphy with the veil of a starry-eyed visionary. He was a pragmatic man, politically conservative and economically dedicated to free entrepreneurial capitalism. He believed in the intrinsic goodness of business when he wrote, "In breadth of view, in firmness of purpose, in moral and physical courage the great merchant is equal to the great general." He likened capitalism to a great crusade for the betterment of humanity ". . . be proud of your work . . . do the very best work you can." He considered money a means to an end. It could broaden life and bring power to do good by creating opportunities that brought with them responsibilities. "Be thankful if it [money] comes to you and don't abuse it."[30] The wonders of the industrial age where combinations could provide cheap and better products to America's consumers had a definite appeal to Murphy. He agreed with Theodore Roosevelt that bigness was not necessarily badness. Historian Irving Kull captured Murphy's belief in the benefits that big business could provide society. "Mr. Murphy had never disguised his sympathy with the larger business combinations which had been fruitful of wonderful business achievements that are beyond the reach of individual efforts."[31] A

representative of "The Cosmopolitan" happened to be present at the Murphy Varnish Works and questioned one of Murphy's business managers about what sort of person he was. His answer gives a first hand account of what his workers not only thought about Murphy personally but also professionally. Indeed, his business values were a bigger part of a philosophy that suggested capitalism was a service to humanity. The manager said, "Were it not for a habit of working out his ideals into results that are solidly and lastingly practical, you might call him a dreamer. He has that unshakable faith in the success of merit and that high conception of business as a service to humanity which we commonly associate with the enthusiasm of youth. He really thinks that his management of his business is a contribution to social progress, to the general betterment of the world, just as truly and perhaps as great as that of a university president or the editor of a first class magazine or the promoter of any great reform."[32]

5

By Their Fruits

FRANKLIN MURPHY became a dedicated public servant. By 1883 he was elected a member of the Newark Common Council and was a loyal Republican who was genuinely interested in the welfare of the city, not as he wrote to "work the city for the entrenchment of (his) party". . . "but to work the party for the improvement of the city."[1] He believed in the American political system and the inherent ability of government to improve itself in its service to the people. "As distinguished from the corporation moguls who had sought governmental control for selfish purposes, Murphy had gotten into politics because he liked it and wanted to make improvements in the government.[2] He was successful and believed that he should give something back to the community and society that made that possible. He called upon his fellow citizens to sacrifice for the common good, to give up the comforts of daily life and contribute to society by participating in public service. He echoed a clarion call ". . . We talk in these days of public spirit. What is public spirit? Have you ever tried to define it? If we say it is an unselfish interest in the affairs of the community we shall not be far wrong, but it must be an active and not a passive interest, the kind of an interest that leads a man to put on his coat and hat after dinner and attend some conference on public affairs rather than sit at home with his newspaper and his cigar. It has in it something of devotion. It often requires the sacrifice of our ease and comfort . . . Have you ever thought that a man may be a very good man and at the same time a very poor citizen? He may love his wife and children, and go to church and pay his debts, and conform to all the conventionalities, yet take little interest in public affairs and refuse to respond to a reasonable call for public service. The excuse is he hasn't time. In many cases he could find the time if he had a proper conception of the duty he owes his neighbors, his friends and his fellow citizens."[3]

The terms Republican and Democrat have been applied to a multiplicity of political factions during the history of the Republic. It is necessary, therefore, to clarify where Murphy stood politically and his political philosophy to the extent that generalizations are valid. He stood right of center in the post Civil War Grand Old Party, a party which was the activist political faction of the times according to historian Allan Lichtman. The Democrats tended to be the more passive.[4] He was exactly right for his times, a conservative who believed in party structure, sound money, and tariff protection. These were orthodox values of the Republican Party at the close of the nineteenth century. Yet Murphy was sensitive to the inequities of the time and believed that progress was only possible through the existing institutions. He had no faith in what Theodore Roosevelt would call the "lunatic fringe." He went on to establish a "long and distinguished public career . . . [which] gave some indications as to his character and the type of administration one might expect—a respectable, conservative, businesslike conduct."[5]

Active on the Newark Common Council

Franklin Murphy became particularly effective on the Finance Committee of Newark's Common Council. It was during the 1880s that Newark became financially unstable and had, in fact, been threatened with bankruptcy. His skill as a business administrator put the city's finances back on a sound footing and the city prospered. "His fine energy and ability together with his business-like attitude made him a public servant of the greatest value."[6] It was not surprising that he was made President of Newark's Common Council[7] and worked to modernize and beautify the city in what came to be known as the "City Beautiful Movement." He tore up the old cobblestones and re-paved the city streets. The somnolent gas lamps were replaced by new electric street lights and the city library was established. He was particularly proud of the accomplishments of the Park Commission that laid out and completed the parks of Essex County. He had been instrumental in getting the legislature to create the Park Commission in 1895. This was the first county park body in the country.[8] Branchbrook Park exemplified Murphy's vision. He wrote, "The purchase of between three thousand and four thousand acres in various tracts were quietly made at honest market rates and were so skillfully located as

Franklin Murphy circa 1880

to improve the quarters and build up new suburbs while giving an artistic redemption to the entire city and county for these tracts reach from the salt meadows to the Orange Mountains and include the famous Eagle Rock."[9] The other members of Newark's council who worked closely with Murphy during these years included James Smith Jr., James F. Connelly, Major Thomas O'Connor, Pierson G. Dodd, Charles M. Theberath, Joseph M. Riker, Alexander H. Johnson, and Elisa B. Gaddis.[10]

The "Larger Political Experiences"

In 1885 Franklin Murphy was elected to New Jersey's House Assembly. By 1892 he had become Chairman of the Republican State Committee after several requests by Republican gubernatorial candidate John Kean.[11] This marked the beginning of his "larger political experiences." Murphy detested Governor Leon Abbet (1883-86) (1889-92) whom he called a "shrewd, selfish, unprincipled man . . . who was obnoxious to Democrat and Republican alike"[12] and worked hard for Kean's election over what he called "Abbettism." Perhaps memories of the war lingered in Murphy's mind and contributed to his contempt of Abbett. Leon Abbett had been a staunch states' right advocate during the war, an outspoken Democratic Copperhead who opposed Lincoln's civil rights policies and supported George McClellan in the election of 1864.[13] After three months of hard campaigning, the Republicans in New Jersey and elsewhere across the country suffered the most overwhelming defeat in recent years. This was not a very good start for Murphy. He gained valuable experience, however, and became personally acquainted with many state and national leaders. Among these were William McKinley and Philip Sheridan. Murphy commented on the speaking styles of these men, "McKinley undertook to elaborate the principle of Protection [high tariffs] Sheridan showed its practical result."[14] He was not intimidated by the power and prestige of the great men of his times. He was too secure for that. In a letter to a Mr. William Nelson at Paterson, New Jersey, dated May 13th, 1895, he wrote ". . . When I was younger and supposed that great men were made of a special fine brand of clay reserved for their particular use, I used to think it quite an honor to have them enter my household, but since I have learned from a somewhat extended acquaintance that most of them are built on standard specifications of no especial quality of material . . ."[15]

He did not mince words or couch his opinions. For example, he considered Sheridan ". . . fat and dumpy and far from possessing an appearance, but for lucidity of style, aptness of illustration, vigor of argument . . . I have seldom heard his speech surpassed."[16] He wondered about the results of the election. Was Cleveland a stronger candidate than Harrison? Was the high tariff bill of McKinley too extreme? Those were questions that remained unanswered for Murphy but he concluded that "I may have done well enough for a new man, but politics is a profession. It requires both adaptability and experience."[17] He became determined to be adaptable and gain that experience and he did. He had a warm personality and made many friends.[18] He continued as Chairman of the State Republican Committee for many years as New Jersey gradually turned more and more toward the Republican Party. There were a number of issues that contributed to this change, and one, free silver, would dominate American politics in the last decades of the nineteenth century. The years following the Civil War were a period of deflation where more goods were produced relative to the money supply in circulation. This was particularly hard on the farmers who were often debtors and needed inflated currency to pay off their loans. While the farmers generally demanded inflated currency and free silver, city workers opposed higher prices for consumer goods. "The Free Silver issue tended to pull Democrats that opposed this into the Republican party in urban areas especially."[19]

New Jersey experienced significant political and economic change during the 1880s and 1890s. "By 1890 the state's 20th largest cities contained over half the population . . . In the three largest cities: Newark, Jersey City, Paterson seventy percent of the people were foreign or mixed native parentage."[20] The other factors tilting the state toward the GOP included the legalization of race track gambling, ballot box stuffing, the growth of conservative commuter suburbs, and the political impact of the depression between 1893-1896.[21]

Franklin Murphy's star continued to shine. He became a member of the Republican National Committee and attended the National Republican Conventions at Saint Louis in 1896 and at Philadelphia in 1900 where he voted for William McKinley.[22] In the 1890s Murphy organized North Jersey Republicans against the South Jersey Bosses who had solidified a disproportionate amount of power relative to their rural constituencies. It was during this polit-

Franklin Murphy, Franklin Murphy, Jr., and William H. Murphy circa 1890

ical baptism of fire that Murphy would prove his metal. His chief opponent was General William J. Sewell, the "iron-willed Bismark of the Republican Party"[23] whose power base was Camden and neighboring counties. The more populous northern counties had long resented the rural and non-progressive South. Murphy "resolved to make for them the opportunity that seemed too long a-coming."[24] He knew Sewell wanted the Senate seat and waited until the Republican Party had reached its zenith of power to challenge him for it. Murphy did not expect to beat Sewell, and didn't, but to serve notice that his monopoly on power was no longer to be left unchallenged. He "set the handwriting on the wall . . . [to] warn the conquering chieftan that the days of his dominion were numbered."[25] This open defiance of Sewell set in motion forces that had

Franklin Murphy circa 1885

supported Garrett Hobart's candidacy for Vice-President under William McKinley. McKinley and Hobard liked Murphy and appreciated his political support. Hobart wrote from the Vice-President's Chamber, Washington, to Murphy on June 14th, 1897, the following letter offering him the ambassadorship to the Czar's court at Saint Petersburg.

My dear Frank:

I have only a moment today to write to you and tell you the situation with regard to the Russian Ministership about which I cabled you. I cannot write all the details that led up to this subject and the agreement that I might cable you, given by the President, who emphatically had agreed to name you for the Russian Ministership. He wanted to do something handsome for New Jersey and in my opinion the only person through whom that should be manifested was yourself, in fact from my standpoint there was no one else in it. I talked with the President about it two or three times and finally, in my house, the President in the presence of Mr. Hanna and Mr. Bliss, told me that I might cable you. In the mean time General Sewell was very anxious to have Professor Powell named as Minister to Hayti, while the President knew that the General was not your personal friend; so to accomplish what we desired with as little friction as possible, he directed that Powell be named as Minister to Hayti in the morning, and I cabled you. I am sorry, more so than I can express, that you could not see your way clear to take the place, but you know best the state of your own health and your own business requirements. When you come back home I will give you an interesting story of its development. I will now have in mind the Paris Commissionership, but there are so many hundreds of applicants for that office that I cannot tell where we will come out. I talked yesterday with Mr. Hanna about the Dawes Commission, and he says that in no respect is that fit for you. He gave me some reason why, and I fully agreed with him.

Give my love to Mrs. Murphy and with great regard, I am, always,

Yours very sincerely,
Garret A. Hobart[29]

smoldered under the surface but would eventually erupt and "batter down the Camden Citadel."[26] Sewell never forgave Murphy and considered him a traitor to his party. This is not surprising as tyrants and despots have always considered their opponents traitors; so it was with Sewell. The political intrigues and machinations of the 1890s pitted many factions against one another. For example, in the contest over delegate selection to the Republican National Convention at Saint Louis, Murphy had beaten the Sewell and Allison forces in the Essex caucus which resulted in strengthening McKinley's candidacy. "Sewell had supported Iowa's Senator Allison."[27] The Hobart influence became important in the New Jersey Convention held in April 1896 which chose the national delegates.[28] These, in turn,

Hobart died suddenly in 1899. New Jersey turned to John D. Long who had been Secretary of the Navy during the Spanish American War to replace Hobart but "Easy Boss Platt" of New York forced it on Theodore Roosevelt.[30] Murphy succeeded Hobart as New Jersey's representative on the National Republican Committee and was appointed one of the members of the Executive Committee. By 1900 the Sewell forces were in decline. The General had become ill. He lost touch with many of his supporters who became increasingly independent of his party machine. For example, "his Hudson County lieutenant, Colonel Dickinson went over to Franklin Murphy." [31] Sewell died in the spring of 1902. Murphy set aside any feelings of rancor and attended his memorial as a gesture of respect to his old nemesis. This showed he was a man of character with high standards of personal integrity. He confided to his diary on March 24, 1902 ". . . Today was the day set apart for memorial exercises in memory of the late General Sewell. The address was delivered by his old friend and admirer, Senator E.C. Stokes, and was in every way worthy of the orator and the occasion."[32] Meanwhile, Murphy's popularity continued to grow and there was talk about running him for governor. A series of judicial vacancies filled by other likely contenders placed Murphy out front and cleared the way for his candidacy in 1901. "For the first time in a quarter century Sewell was absent . . . Senator McCarter of Essex named Mr. Murphy to the delegates as George L. Record seconded the nomination." Ironically, it was this same Record who would cause Murphy problems later in his term. There was no opposition as Murphy was unanimously nominated by acclamation in September, 1901.[33]

The Gubernatorial Campaign

Fate struck a terrible blow on September 6, 1901, as Franklin Murphy opened his campaign for the governorship of New Jersey. A young anarchist named Leon Czolgosz, concealing a pistol in a bandaged right hand, approached President William McKinley in Buffalo's Temple of Music. He shot the President in the chest and abdomen, mortally wounding him.[34] This tragedy cast a pall over the gubernatorial election in New Jersey as people quickly dubbed it the "handkerchief campaign." The guests at Murphy's banquet quickly lost their festive spirit. They sent their food to local charities and quietly returned home. The assassination produced startling results, however, as the somber news wafted across the land bringing Republicans who had deserted the party back into the ranks. "It would kindle the flame of loyalty flickering in Republican hearts. The pistol shot that rang through the world, would be as a clarion call to the wandering to come back to the fold."[35] The third assassination of an American President brought with it the usual condemnations. Fingers were pointed at the Democrats who were, of course, not involved any more than the Confederate leaders had been in the murder of President Lincoln. The melancholia gave way in some circles to a ballyhoo exemplified at the Republican State Convention with the singing of McKinley's favorite hymn "Lead Kindly Light."[36] It is difficult to ascertain with any degree of certainty the results of the assassination of President McKinley on Franklin Murphy's bid for Governor. It seems that McKinley was a political asset to Murphy and vice-versa. What is certain is that when the smoke cleared Murphy defeated Newark's Mayor James M. Seymour. The vote stood at 183,814 for Murphy to 166,681 for Seymour.[37] Murphy's election had given the Republicans control of the executive branch for the third consecutive time.[38] Shortly before his election, Franklin Murphy addressed the party faithful with these words which gave insight into his perception of the political party structure and his responsibility of placing its interests ahead of his own.

I am here tonight as the candidate of the Republican Party for Governor of the State of New Jersey. The experiences of a candidate are unique. For a few brief days or weeks he lives in the limelight; he heads the procession—when he appears the band plays "Hail to the Chief," and the applause of the multitude greets him where ever he goes. And then the light is turned out and he disappears. It makes little difference who he is or what his name is.

The Joint Committee of the
Senate and General Assembly
on Inauguration
requests the honor of your presence, at the
Inauguration
of
Honorable Franklin Murphy
as
Governor of the State of New Jersey,
on Tuesday, January the twenty-first, 1902,
at twelve o'clock, noon,
Taylor Opera House,
Trenton.

DEMPSEY & CARROLL, N.Y.

Invitation to the inauguration of Franklin Murphy as Governor

For the time being he is not himself but the magnet which draws the hope and ambition and purpose of the Party he leads. And he represents not himself but the principles of his Party. Then election day comes and if his Party is successful, the attraction of his office is not equal to the glamour of his candidacy.[39]

A new epic was dawning on America which called for reform. It was labeled the Progressive Era and was led by the middle class which demanded reform of the excesses and inequities created by the changes brought forth by rapid industrialization. "From the national government at Washington down to the smallest municipalities, political life was stirred by the problems which increasing industrialization, concentration of wealth, and the disappearance of the frontier were bringing in their train . . . its leadership and philosophy . . . were those of the enlightened and socially conscious bourgeoisie."[40] Franklin Murphy, a conservative Republican whom his enemies called an "Old Bourbon" was indeed, an enlightened and socially conscious member of the bourgeoisie.[41] He was the first businessman and non-lawyer to become Governor of New Jersey in fifty years with the single exception of General George B. McClellan 1878-1881. He was exactly right for his times bringing the experience of a Captain of Industry to the problems that industry created. He knew the system and how to work within it; he knew how to address the issues of the day within the confines of the existing order and how to allow status quo institutions to grapple with the problems and find pragmatic solutions. "There has been a tendency on the part of historians interested in the progressive era to overlook the fact that New Jersey had a series of sound Republican governors between 1896 and 1910. At least three of them, Foster M. Voorhees, Franklin Murphy, and John Franklin Fort, helped establish the liberal base on which Woodrow Wilson operated so effectively."[42] Walter Evans Edge, a young aspiring politician and future New Jersey governor, while serving as Secretary of the Senate wrote of the first decade of the twentieth century as one being marked by "significant developments in New Jersey politics." He was referring, in part, to the progressive reforms of Governor Murphy. He contin-

Governor Franklin Murphy

ued, "It was during this period that the groundwork was laid for most of the accomplishments which many historians today over-generously credit to Woodrow Wilson."[43]

Governor Franklin Murphy

Murphy was inaugurated at 12 o'clock on January 21, 1902, in the Taylor Opera House in Trenton. It was an elaborate ceremony in keeping with the pomp and circumstance of the Victorian Age which included the entire National Guard and many county societies. The Essex Troop escorted the new Governor. Seated in the carriage with the Governor-elect were Governor Voorhees, Governor Gripps, and Senator Kean. They were followed by the carriages of the Committee of the Legislature. The procession wound its way up State Street to Broad and on to the Opera House which was filled to capacity by throngs of enthusiastic well-wishers. Murphy recalled the details of that day when he wrote, "The opening prayer was by Reverend Henry R. Robinson. The administration of the oath was by Chief Justice Gummere, immediately after which a salute of seventeen guns was fired from the state house grounds. The delivery of the Great Seal of the State by Governor Voorhees then followed, accepted in a brief speech by me. Governor Voorhees then formally introduced me to C.A. Francis, President of the Senate, who then formally presented me to the Senate and General Assembly, who were seated on the stage. I then read my inaugural address, after which the benediction was pronounced by the Reverend Judson Conklin, and the ceremonies were over."[44] Lunch was then served to several hundred persons at the Trenton House before Murphy was taken to the reviewing stand in front of the State House for the grand parade. Units of the state's militia filed past, dressed in splendid regalia. Major General Wanser and staff were followed by General Cambell and staff to include the First Brigade. The First Regiment, Colonel Brientnall, commanding, came next and so on down the line. The new governor was visibly moved by what he saw next and wrote in his diary ". . . Then came the survivors of the old 13th Regiment, to the number of about sixty. This detachment of my old regiment impressed me more than any other feature of the entire parade. Many of the men were well advanced in years, but they exhibited great enthusiasm as they passed the reviewing stand."[45] After the military came the civic part of the parade consisting of about 2500 men including the employees of the Murphy Varnish Company and the various state associations. It was a damp overcast day which threatened rain, that as it turned out "held off until after the procession was over." Reception followed reception at the Executive Chamber. Then it was on to dinner at General Oliphant's and back to the Chamber for yet another reception. This one was for the general public and was mercifully ended by torrents of rain "which sent the people home." Murphy was understandably exhausted and retired with a new sense of the enormous task that lay ahead. "I went to bed very tired, but with a distinct sense of my new responsibilities."[46] He retired reflecting on his closing comments of his inaugural address.

You [members of the Legislature] in your province, I in mine, are entrusted with a high responsibility by the State we love. The history of New Jersey, the patriotism and sacrifices of her sons in the days that are gone, give us all just cause for pride in the past of our State. Let us dedicate ourselves fully to her service. Such at least is my determination, and in my work I ask the assistance of my associates, the considerate judgment of my fellow-citizens and the favor of Almighty God.[47]

One of Murphy's first priorities concerned the accountability of state department heads. It had become common practice for state officials such as Secretary of State H.C. Kelsey, Clerk in Chancery H.S. Little, and Clerk in the Supreme Court B.F. Lee to be conspicuously absent from their Trenton offices four of the five days of the working week.[48] They and others would leave the day-to-day tasks to their subordinates, reminiscent of British colonial custom during the mid-eighteenth century. New Jersey officials would come to their offices on Tuesday of each week following a practice attributed to Governor Abbet, which became known as "Governor's Day."[49] It was at these " cabinet meetings" that reports would be presented of what, if anything, had been accomplished and schedules for the coming week were roughed out. By contrast, Governor Murphy expected state supervisors to be on the job and intended to, if necessary, to "shame the department heads into efficiency."[50] He wouldn't tolerate absentee salons getting fat at the public trough. It was his business sense which demanded a fair day's work for a fair day's pay that required the bureaucrats to be at their posts. This applied to everyone including his personal friends and acquaintances. An example of this can be seen in a visit by Secretary John Swayze on October 19, 1902. He called on the Governor at about 2:00 o'clock that Sunday afternoon requesting permission to establish his law office in Newark ". . . to work up a little legal business that would add to his income."[51] Murphy had already interceded with the legislature to increase the Secretary's pay and categorically denied Swayze's request. Murphy wrote ". . . that I felt bound by the bargain made with the legislature . . . saying that when they increased the salary of his office it was done at my request, with the understanding that the Secretary was to be at the Executive Office six days in the week."[52] Murphy had a firm yet gentle way of logically presenting his rationale to his subordinate. He was not a confrontational man. "I assured him (Swayze) of my desire to help him in any way I could, but insisted that he should remain in the office at Trenton. He went away seemingly relieved by the interview."[53]

Obtaining a Governor's Residence

Franklin Murphy was a man who led by example. He wanted an executive mansion in Trenton. There had not been one there since the old "Governor's House" on State Street which had been turned into a hotel.[54] Moore Furman had originally sold this property to the state in 1798 for a Governor's residence, and it functioned in this capacity until about 1845. It was on the northeast corner of West State Street and Chancery Lane. About 1845 as a result of lack of interest in it by the State's chief executives, it became the Hotel Sterling and was commonly known as the State Street House.[55] A bill

appropriating twenty-five thousand dollars to expand the state grounds on either side of the state building and granting the State House Commission authority to acquire an executive mansion was perceived by many in the media to be in the selfish interests of the Governor. He skillfully deflected this criticism by pointing out the benefits of such a residence.

Concerning the Executive Mansion, I think this may be said: It is brought to the attention of the Legislature because of the opinion I hold that the time has come when the State should provide a suitable residence for its Governor. A number of States do this already, and I think the citizens of this state are willing to dignify the office to this extent. It has not been the custom of former Governors, with few exceptions, to live in Trenton during the session of the Legislature and at other times. They have come to the State House in the morning and gone away in the afternoon or evening as their work was finished or about finished. Citizens from every part of the State have their interviews with him in his office or on his way to or from the train, and his habit of life has of necessity been lacking in comfort and dignity. It is desirable, also, that the Governor should have a house where he may entertain visitors from abroad as well as to have a suitable gathering place for important occasions in the current life of the State. If the State were poor, the question of expense might be raised, but the State is rich.[56]

The administration was unsuccessful in getting a new permanent residence despite an effort to obtain the property adjoining the state house grounds. It was owned by a Mrs. Green. She successfully appealed to the legislature and they refused to dispossess her.[57] Murphy yielded to the will of the legislature and rented the Scudder Home on West State Street.[58] He rented other homes during his tenure as well, including the Stryker mansion. He wrote on Tuesday September 23, 1902, "I called at noon on Mrs. General Stryker, who showed me through her house, and I accepted her proposition to rent it during the session of the Legislature."[59] Franklin Murphy's dream of an executive mansion would come to fruition years later. The Stockton family built a beautiful two-story brick home in Princeton at the turn of the eighteenth century. Succeeding generations expanded the residence and Annis Boudinot Stockton named it "Morven" after "the home of Fingal, a legendary Scottish chieftain."[60] A future governor, Walter E. Edge, who had been friends with the Murphy family, would acquire Morven and turn it over to the state in 1954. It became the official Governor's mansion in 1955 and remained so for nearly three decades. Yielding to the growth of the state and the need for more room in the executive residence, "Drumthwacket," a new governor's mansion, was established in Princeton in 1983. Morven, however, continued to be used by the State Historical Society. Drumthwacket, also a turn of the eighteenth-century home, was named by Moses Taylor Pyne. It is a Celtic term that means "wooded hill."[61] It was originally the home of the Olden family, prominent among whom was Charles Olden, the State's Chief Executive during the first years of the Civil War. It is interesting to speculate what Civil War veteran Franklin Murphy might have thought of these future events as he had to content himself as a tenant Governor, a product of the temper of his times.

Getting the Job Done

Governor Murphy's inaugural address reflected his down to business approach. It "was a brief, direct crisp speech which outlined the things he hoped to see done."[62] They called for many progressive reforms. These included stopping pollution of the Passaic River which "has destroyed the use and beauty of a noble stream."[63] The secret ballot should be implemented to assure the end of "extraneous influence" and to guarantee the voter that "his ballot may be the expression of his own conclusions and wishes."[64] He proposed either the Massachusetts practice of ballots obtained only by election officers or the use of voting machines. A primary election law would replace the "agents selected by the dominant organization within the

party under which the primary is held."[65] He insisted that New Jersey's finances by overhauled so that interest be earned on the surplus which amounted to $2,351,683 as of October 31st, 1901. Murphy predicted that the state would net $45,000 a year. It turned out to be more. He called on the "disposition of a portion of the large surplus" for public education, state institutions, and public roads. He believed the National Guard should be increased to five regiments of infantry ". . . I regard it as a high importance that the militia of the state should be maintained in reasonable numbers and at the highest point of efficiency."[66] Finally, the new Governor called on the legislature to create a hospital for those stricken by tuberculosis, an insidious disease that particularly affected the poor. Murphy concluded that "if the grip of the white scourge ever takes hold . . . however gentle may be its first touch, it strengthens its hold month by month, never relaxing, never weakening, until the final end . . . At least this is so with the poor."[67]

It was the squalid conditions in which the poor eked out their wretched livings that became the subject of muckraking journalists. Jacob Riis in his book, *How The Other Half Lives,* exposed the unhealthy conditions of the tenement slums. In it he wrote, "Suppose we look into one? [a tenement] . . . The hall is dark and you might stumble over the children pitching pennies back there. Not that it would hurt them; kicks and cuffs are their daily diet. They have little else . . . Here is a door. Listen! That short hacking cough, that tiny, helpless wail—what do they mean? They mean that the soiled bow of white you saw on the door downstairs will have another story to tell-oh! A sadly familiar story—before the day is at an end. The child is dying with measles. With half a chance it might have lived; but it had none. The dark bedroom killed it."[68] These stories touched Murphy's sensibilities and compelled him to action.

Governor Murphy succeeded in achieving many of his goals outlined in his inaugural address. The Passaic River, "the haven of artists and the pride of river clubs," started its long journey back to the pristine beauty of pre-industrial days. This was done by the disposal of sewage by "authority" with the aid of the federal government over local financial interests "for the public good." For example, jurisdictional disputes between Newark and Paterson were solved by the Passaic Trunk Sewer Authority.[69] Election reform became a pivotal focus of progressive legislation because the polls had become so blatantly fraudulent. The direct primary had been tried by George Record and Governor George T. Werts but was not successful until Governor Murphy in 1902.[70] He used his influence to encourage the party independents to check the influence of the bosses who had made ". . . mockeries of the franchise . . . the committeemen who fixed the times and places for taking of the ballots and sent their own satellites to receive them and count them and announce the results."[71] The quintessential symbol of shoddy electioneering became the cigar box which doubled for the ballot box. Murphy became convinced that the state's election process should follow legal and decent guidelines. "He was a strong believer in respectability; direct nominations never appealed to him, but he did feel that the election of convention delegates should be conducted in a decent, orderly fashion."[72]

Accordingly, the legislature called for a commission to examine the question of a direct primary. It consisted of E.C. Stokes, George Record, and Joseph L. Munn.[73] This, of course, took time for a law to pass which became the foundation of later legislation. The American art of political compromise followed and came up with something between a "full direct primary and some regulation of the election of convention delegates"[74] Despite the opposition from machine politicians and political bosses, the legislature passed the reform law in 1903 which was essentially what the commission had presented ". . . Primaries were to be held at fixed days and hours, the regular election of each major party was to conduct the primary of that party, publicly printed ballots were to be furnished. A provision was included to guard against cross voting."[75] Murphy brought a businessman's approach of checks and balances to the nominating process of both parties. The primaries became subject to the safeguards of the regular elections as he provided the people with an open primary system "surrounded by all the safeguards of a regular election, and supplemented it with the voting machine as a foil to ballot-box stuffers and other election booth cheats."[76] Walter Evans Edge, Senate Secretary, wrote that "this was a step in the right direction. It gave every qualified citizen an opportunity to become a candidate for nomination provided a regular primary day on which supervision of the election would be assured."[77] Murphy wrote in his diary, "I regard this (primary election) as a very great victory in the cause of good government . . . (it) will give the people of the state a chance to express their opinion at the polls, in an independent way."[78]

The issue of surplus money in government is one that is rarely applicable today. One merely has to glance at the digital progression of the national debt at New York's Times Square to become amazed that huge surpluses were stockpiled a century ago. There were surpluses on the state levels as well and New Jersey had followed a practice of depositing these funds in various statewide bank accounts that earned no interest whatsoever. The Governor wrote that (this practice) was "pleasant for the institutions, but loose business for the state" and brought "nothing but party favors."[79] It was reminiscent of the "pet banks" during the Age of Andrew Jackson. Governor Murphy was appalled at this practice and withdrew the state funds and deposited these moneys in interest-bearing accounts which earned an astonishing $60,000 the first year.[80] In his message to the Legislature he said, "The financial prosperity of the State has been so great in recent years that the amount of extraordinary disbursements has become relatively large; but notwithstanding this the surplus has increased until it has reached the sum of $3,000,000. I have on former occasions expressed my opinion that this surplus should be used for the present needs of the State."[81] He tied the various state departments, boards, and commissions to the attorney general's office and eliminated duplicated legal council. He required the accounts of the various departments to be audited and wondered "how a manufacturing concern would keep out of the receiver's hands if everybody were allowed to spend its money and nobody were obliged to show a voucher."[82] Murphy wrote that it was "quite astonishing after that how many things were not needed and how many needed things cost less money—not at all astonishing, however, that a number of party whips and leaders complained."[83]

The Governor stood above party on another issue as well—public education. To address technicalities which made the Public School Law unconstitutional required an additional session of the legislature. The Republican Party leaders became alarmed that this extra forum would give the Democrats an opportunity to strengthen their support. Murphy defied political pressure and insisted on the extra session. "It will throw the election to the Democrats next fall," Republican Party leaders complained. "I hope it will not," replied the Governor, "but if I knew that it would I could not shirk this plain and simple duty. If worst comes to worst the people can get along better with the Democrats in than with the school teachers out." The extra session was called, the schools provided for, and the state went Republican.[84] On October 22, 1903, Murphy wrote, "On Thursday I went to Trenton to be present at the opening of the special session of the legislature, which I called to consider the passage of a new school law, the old law having been declared unconstitutional by the Court of Errors. I sent a message to the legislature recommending it . . . The papers throughout the state rather endorsed my position."[85] Murphy went on to support a law that established the independence of local school boards from local government. The power of the state board of education increased, teachers were assured their salaries, and mandatory school attendance was required.[86]

Taxation became an important focus of reformers during the post Civil War period. Prominent among these was Henry George, a social critic and philosopher of the Gilded Age who believed that justice could be achieved through taxation . . . "who would by taxation take all land from railroads and speculators and place it in cultivation, that is, in use, seemed to attack the ground rent evil at its root and won thousands of supporters after 1881."[87] In his epochal study entitled *Progress and Poverty*, George clamored for an across the board levy which he termed the "single tax." This would eliminate the disparity between the fabulously wealthy and the dismally poor. He did not believe that "social evils resulted from the working of fixed laws, inevitable and eternal but came from a rationalization of greed."[88] Although most Americans rejected these extremes, they did not ignore the increasing costs of providing services to the growing municipalities and the resulting increases in taxation. The tax burden was rarely shared by the large corporations such as the public utilities and the railroads. They often enjoyed special rates below those assessed the general public. "Because of political connections and a reputation for indispensability the railroads and utilities secured preferential tax treatment and immunity from close governmental regulation or prosecution."[89] This prompted grass-roots movements to demand more equitable taxation. This issue arose in New Jersey during the administration of Franklin Murphy. Its chief sponsors were Jersey City's Mayor Mark Fagan and attorney George L. Record. Both men were followers of Henry George and were committed to use the "power of taxation to break up the trusts and regulate the utilities.[90]

This movement came to be called the "New Idea." New Jersey's legislature was dominated during these years by conservatives often called the "Old Guard" or simply the "interests." In fact, "many of the railroad directors and attorneys were both party members and state officials."[91] There was little perception during these years of what later would be considered conflict of interests. When the Republican state legislature ignored the progressive demands for equal taxation, Fagan and Record sought alliances with Democratic machines in other New Jersey cities. They formed what became known as the "Mayors' Equal Taxation League."[92] The utilities responded by forming the Public Service Corporation, a combination of the Prudential Insurance company, the Fidelity Trust, and the United Gas Improvement Company.[93] By 1903 the battle lines were drawn. Murphy took no active part in the squabble but probably sympathized with the corporations reflecting his conservative business philosophy. He otherwise left the legislature to its own devices. Fagan and Record's reform bills were ignored by the conservative Republicans, many of the bills remaining locked up in committee or denied a hearing on the floor of the legislature. Little was achieved after months of turmoil. "Neither the press or the public, the legislature nor the judiciary supported Record's radical fight."[94]

America was torn between the forces of reform and those intent on preserving the status quo. The latter believed the Republic had been built upon the sacrosanct pillar of laissez-faire. There was a conspicuous fear and distrust of foreign "isms," movements afoot that undermined the wonders and benefits of capitalism and threatened the foundations of the Republic. At least these became the perceptions of many as a result of occasional outbursts of violence such as the Haymarket Square Riot in Chicago on May 4, 1886. It was there that a labor demonstration turned violent. A bomb was thrown, killing a number of policemen. To this day the identity of the assailant remains unknown. The impact discredited the labor movement and spread fear and anger across the nation. The Governor was concerned about the threat of anarchism to the nation. He made a special trip to New York City on October 13, 1902, to address the issue. He wrote ". . . I [went] to New York to meet General Anderson, which I did about eleven o'clock at the Albemarle Hotel, and spent an hour or two with him discussing his proposition to prevent anarchism in the United States-rather a large contract."[95] The specifics of the meeting were never known but the Governor's concern was apparent. Murphy didn't necessarily equate organized labor with "foreign isms" although he was, no doubt, suspicious of the motivation of some of its leadership. Murphy was dedicated to his workers and proved time and time again that he had their interests at heart but he would not be bullied and intimidated by strong arm tactics.

An example of this can be seen in an incident which occurred in late August 1903. Murphy wrote of this episode,

We have been very much annoyed this week by the fact that we have been boycotted by the local Painters Union. The trouble occurred not because of anything the company had done, but because the decorator I had employed to do some work at the house, and who I suppose employed union men and who, as a matter of fact, usually does employ union *men, had, without my knowledge, sent two non-union men to the house. The union declared the boycott without giving me any chance to explain, or indeed notifying me that they were to do so, and the goods of the company, which really had nothing to do whatever with the matter, are put on the unfair list because of an alleged action of mine. Two delegates from the union came down to the office and talked the matter over with Bissell, admitted that they had been hasty, and after discussing the matter, agreed to straighten the affair out . . . It is only one of many instances we are having these days of the tyranny of organized labor.*[96]

Mayor Hinchliffe of Paterson had asked the Governor to send troops to that beleaguered city on June 28, 1902, to quell possible labor violence. There was no strike-breaking or violence of any kind. The presence of the troops was enough to assure the peace and tranquility of the city, and they were removed on July 2nd. Murphy mentioned this incident to the legislature in his annual message applauding the conduct of the state militia. He said in part, "The discretion of the officers and the excellent bearing and conduct of the troops prevented bloodshed, and they are entitled to the thanks of the State for the creditable manner in which they performed a disagreeable duty."[97] This showed his resolve to act decisively in what he believed to be the public interest.

In the meantime Fagan and Record, although down, were not out. Thwarted by the legislature, they decided to go directly to the people by publishing an open letter to Governor Murphy. This would become the classic tactic of Woodrow Wilson some two decades later in both his domestic and foreign policies, i.e., appealing over the heads of the legislators directly to the people. Perhaps Wilson studied the actions of Fagan and Record. Although there is some evidence that the letter was initially intended to be sent directly to Murphy, for some reason it found its way to the press before it reached the Governor.[98] It was a stinging rebuke that threatened to split the Republican Party of New

Jersey wide open. It openly questioned why the railroad tax question was denied a hearing on the floor of the legislature and why franchise legislation was ignored. It read in part

> . . . what is the meaning of all this? . . . The answer is plain. The Republican legislature is controlled by the railroad, trolley, and water corporations, and the interests of the people are being betrayed . . . While I charge no man with personal corruption I do not hesitate to say that this condition of affairs which is essentially corrupt, and which, if unchecked, means the virtual control of our state and our party by corporations. As a citizen, I say that this condition is dangerous and demoralizing. As a public official, I protest against the injustice done to Jersey City. As a member of the Republican Party, I deplore its subserviency to corporate greed and injustice. No political party can long receive the support of the people with such a record as this Republican legislature is making.[99]

This letter shook the Republican Party to its foundations. Murphy's response was calm and deliberate. "It speaks for itself." He formed a special committee to make recommendations to the legislature. "A conference was immediately called, a plan adopted to refer the whole matter of taxation to an investigating commission, and a resolution to that effect put through both houses."[100] It consisted of Chief Justice W.S. Gummere, Associate Justice Charles G. Garrison, Associate Justice Chandler W. Riker and State Board of Taxation member Charles C. Black.[101] The prominence of the committee indicates the priority the Governor gave to this problem although there was little decisive action. "The reports reflected the difference of views . . . embracing one scheme or the other."[102] The final result was that the number of corporate properties known as second-class properties became subject to local taxation.[103] The activity of Fagan, Record, Everett Colby, (the aristocratic leader of the progressives), and the

one-armed Civil War veteran, Carl Lentz forced the Republican "Old Guard" to become more progressive. This in turn undermined the "New Idea" and to some extent satisfied the public's clamor for reform.[104] The Governor succinctly expressed his position on this issue in his message to the Legislative Session of 1905.

> The subject of the proper taxation of railroad property should receive the earnest attention of the Legislature. Many people sincerely believe that the property of these companies is not bearing its full burden of taxation, and, in response to a general demand, I appointed at the last session of the Legislature a commission to consider the subject of the taxation of all classes of property . . . Meantime, both political parties in their platforms have demanded a change . . . Important interests are involved, however, and must not be overlooked, and the first duty of the Legislature is to protect the income of the State. The State's revenue, for which the money annually received from railroads has been the chief reliance; the rights of property themselves, and the burdens of the municipalities, must all be kept in mind. In my opinion nothing should be done which will decrease the revenue now received by the State from this source, or divert any of that revenue to the local municipalities.[105]

Serious Welfare Concerns

If Governor Murphy could be somewhat conservative on the issue of corporation taxation he waxed aggressively progressive when it came to the welfare of the people, particularly children. His Irish spirit rose in indignation when he became aware of the child labor conditions in New Jersey in the opening years of the twentieth century. This was part of a national outcry for curbing the abuses and exploitation of children in the work place. There had been laws on the books in New Jersey that hadn't changed in over twenty years at the time Murphy took office. "In New Jersey, the beginnings of this reform antedated the New Idea, and the first big step was taken during the administration of Governor Murphy."[106] These laws had generally set a minimum of twelve years of age for boys and fourteen for girls for employment in mining or manufacturing but were often ignored by legal loopholes.[107] Responding to appeals from various labor organizations, Murphy sought to close these loopholes.

He did this by improving the state system of supervision. This brought the Governor in direct conflict with the state's chief factory inspector, the "elephantine ex-Senator J.C. Ward of Salem County."[108] Stories of underage workers in the New Jersey glass factories abounded. The Governor, however, did not rely on hearsay. He wrote on March 6, 1903, "I also had Fuller's agency send over a detective for the purpose of investigating the employment of child labor in the southern part of the state."[109] Conditions in these plants had deteriorated to the point where the workers had become virtual slaves of their employers. They were paid in company scrip and forced to buy their groceries at company stores at higher prices than local retail establishments. In the case of a rare surplus, where credits exceeded the debits, they had to take "store orders" against subsequent purchases.[110] "Families had told the Senate Committee that all their labor had not brought in a single dollar in cash from year's beginning to year's end."[111] These deplorable conditions and others were brought to the attention of Inspector Ward who ignored them and failed to take any action whatsoever. In desperation, they turned to the Governor who ordered Ward to take action to end the abuses. Ward had the temerity to respond that, "it was none of the Governor's business."[112] This, of course, incensed Murphy. But what angered him more was when he found out that there was no law enabling him to admonish Ward. Well, if there had been no statute before, there would be one now.

He prevailed upon Assemblyman Lord of Essex County to draw up legislation granting the executive the power of removal. As soon as this bill was approved by the Legislature, Ward was promptly fired, and the entire state supervision system was revamped. Colonel Lewis T. Bryant of Atlantic City was named the new Chief Inspector and was given fifteen assistants.[113] They went after what Theodore Roosevelt would call the "malefactors of great wealth" with a vengeance. Bryant became so renowned for his efficiency and that of his department that he was re-appointed by Democrat

Woodrow Wilson in 1913.[114] On January 7, 1903, Bryant visited the Governor. Murphy wrote in his diary the next day that "Colonel Bryant came up last night with us, and accepted the position of Chief of the Department of Factories and Workshops, which I tendered him. I hope he will prove a popular appointment, as I am sure it will be a good one."[115] And a good appointment he became, so much so that labor reform became a combination of improving the statutes and appointing personnel who were dedicated to their jobs. "The better laws make lengthy and detailed provisions regarding inspections . . . how often inspections shall be made; when and to whom their reports shall be made . . ." "The kind of person appointed to see that the provisions of the law are enforced is of especial importance."[116]

Inspection positions were also open to women. This is significant because most positions of supervision in turn of the century America were open only to men. Perhaps the activities of the feminists and the suffragettes had made headway in New Jersey. In any event, traditional roles and societal norms did not dissuade the Governor from including women in his progressive administration. He wrote on January 8, 1904, "Miss Van Leer called at the office on Wednesday afternoon to discuss the question of her accepting the position of Factory Inspectress."[117] Presumably she worked well with Bryant. Murphy was especially proud of creating an environment in New Jersey that protected youngsters from exploitation. He wanted them to grow up healthy and happy and enjoy the fruits of education in this land of opportunity. He was the right man for these times, guiding New Jersey through a tumultuous era. He applauded Secretary Bryant and his department in his message to the Legislature although he didn't mention him by name. His words capture his sensitivities and his deep sense of pride at what had been accomplished.

Especial attention was given to that feature of the law concerning child labor, so that its provisions might be enforced. I was fortunate in securing the services of the present head of the department, [Colonel Lewis T. Bryant] and the results of his administration under the new law are such that the inspectors under him report fully as to their work; that the general factory conditions throughout the State, so far as they affect the operatives, have been greatly improved; that what is technically known as child labor has practically disappeared, and to such an extent that I am told in some sections of the State night schools have been abolished. The children who formerly attended them now go to day school, because the law does not permit them to work . . . the present law . . . is a credit to the State, and it gives a relief and a benefit to the working classes that is most gratifying.[118]

Murphy stepped up to this challenge presented by the exigencies of the times having the gumption to come down on the side of right. He would have it no other way.

Close on the heels of the issue of child labor were the conditions of the tenements. In many ways these were intertwined as the poor and destitute sought shelter in the only housing they could afford: wretched stifling slums void of light, heat, and ventilation—the harbingers of disease such as tuberculosis, the dreaded "white scourge." The northeastern cities had become fouled by overcrowding that belied Jefferson's perspective that America would have land enough for a thousand generations. There may have been justification for Jefferson's abhorrence of urbanization with the passing of a mere five generations. In New York City there were 500,000 people living in 90,000 tenements in 1898 with 747 people living on every acre of ground.[119] New Jersey was not far behind. Evert Colby, one of the few progressive Republicans in the New Jersey Senate, painted the dismal condition "of the perils to life and health that lurked in fifteen thousand of these humble homes

that sheltered more than sixty thousand families representing a sixth of the state's population and where more than eighty percent of the deaths from tuberculosis were occurring."[120] Governor Murphy was truly concerned. He created a Tenement House Commission and had a bill drawn up which "outlined an efficient system of supervision as to heating, lighting, ventilation and safety appliances."[121]

The priority of this issue with the Governor can be seen in his diary entry of May 28, 1903, when he invited the Commission members to his home to discuss the situation. "The newly appointed Tenement House Commission met in my home this afternoon at two o'clock for the purpose of obtaining my views as to their work. All the members were present with the Secretary and we discussed the tenement house question for upwards of an hour."[122] Murphy was intent on having proper supervision and wrote on November 21, 1903, of a meeting he had with several officials including a Mr. Gray and Secretary Allen. They wanted to know if the regulations were to apply to the major urban areas or to the entire state. The entire state it would be. Murphy was happy with their work and noted the thoroughness of their reports.

I had a meeting this morning of the Tenement House Commission . . . The conversation was along the line of their report . . . Many instances were cited by each of them showing the deplorable condition in which tenement houses existed in the various parts of the State, and it was agreed finally that an attempt should be made to organize a new State Bureau with an official at the head, who should have supervision of the tenement house regulations. The commission has been very zealous in the work of investigation and have evidently given to it a great deal of work and care.[123]

There lingered in Murphy's mind the memories of an earlier time when open spaces were the norm and not the exception. He had an aesthetic appreciation of nature which perhaps explains his devotion to the park system in the earlier part of his career. This continued throughout his life and the beauty of natural settings always made deep impressions on his mind. This nostalgia surfaced now and then as exemplified in a visit to the home of his friends, the Kean family of Elizabeth. "The Kean family owns several hundred acres. The house is located in the center of a large park that was planned before landscape architects were invented, and the old trees, sycamores, magnolias, as well as elms, oaks, and maples and right in the center of the lawn a real old-fashioned apple tree, full of fruit, making the place unusually attractive. There is something about it which reminds me of my boyhood days, when places of this general type could be seen everywhere, but which in the progress of the times have mostly disappeared."[124]

Murphy even dared to trespass on the railroad interests when it came to preserving the beauty of the state's countryside. He hated the billboards that cluttered the railroad right-of ways and even went so far as to count them on one of the major lines from Jersey City to Trenton. "By actual count, 1601 signs . . . They are of all kinds and sizes. They are disfigured by all sorts of effigies of impossible men and women, and they advertise remedies for all the ills that human flesh is heir to, as well as all sorts of foods and drinks, and the various contrivances born to human ingenuity. If they continue to increase, it is not difficult to imagine the day near at hand when the traveler will have the beautiful hills and vales and trees and flowers shut completely from view."[125] The billboards became a permanent mode of advertisement although regulations were imposed over the years as to their number, size, and location. As for the tenements, they were here to stay as well, a permanent product of industrialization. Loopholes continued to allow unscrupulous landlords to take advantage of the working class. It was sometimes cheaper, for example, to pay the fines than to right the conditions. This does not diminish the accomplishment of far-sighted statesmen like Franklin Murphy, who recognized wrong and worked hard to right it. The question was not whether the goal was accomplished one hundred percent but what would have been the conditions had no effort been made at all. Murphy was a pragmatist who realized that tenements could not be made to disappear but could be regulated by what today would be called zoning laws and building codes.

As our state grows in population an increasing number of the people are compelled to live in tenements. Fortunately the percentage now compelled to live in them is not large, but, as the number increases, it is important, from a moral and physical point of view, that tenement houses should be constructed under the latest approved standards. Sufficient space should be provided for each occupant, each room should be lighted from without, the plumbing should be approved in character, and generally the health and welfare of the inmates should be considered. The experience of our sister state of New York shows that this can be accomplished and a reasonable return on the investment obtained by the owner. The question is comparatively a new one in our State, and now is the time to consider it.[126]

Coping with the Automobile

The Governor's next big challenge came not from a political rival or the conditions created by rapid industrialization but from an invention—the automobile. Perhaps nothing ushered in the new century with more glamour and fanfare than the invention of the automobile. As historian Harold F. Wilson writes in his book *The Story of the Jersey Shore*, "The people received their first introduction to the horseless carriage today when a family came slowly into town mounted on an automobile . . . The vehicle was driven by a small gasoline engine and made unsteady progress . . . If this is a fair sample of the machine that many writers prophesy will soon supersede the horse, then all we can have to say is that noble animal has a long call on the auto."[127] This journalist's statement could not have been further from the truth. Many of the first automobiles were powered by electric batteries and were called "electrics." They had a limited range which was their chief liability, but they attracted notable personalities of the times such as the flamboyant "Diamond Jim Brady" who was often seen riding along the ocean with the beautiful Lillian Russell."[128] The "electrics" were replaced by gasoline powered automobiles which made their debut, according to historian John Cunningham, in the Jersey back country. It was there that Thomas A. Edison Jr. and Edward R. Hewitt introduced what were called "locomobiles."[129] Hewitt proved without doubt that the automobile was here to stay when he and his wife successfully completed a trip from his home in Ringwood to Morristown and then on to New York City.[130] These feats were soon eclipsed by sensational speed records set on the hard sand of Cape May County. In July and August of 1905, for example, races were held which included all the famous automobile personalities including Henry Ford in his six-cylinder "Wonder."[131] Protests abounded against what was perceived to be excessive speed which was reminiscent of the complaints lodged against the railroads seventy years earlier. Governor Murphy recognized the challenges that these new machines presented to the state of New Jersey. As an enthusiastic motorist himself and with a "motoring" legislature, he put through a motor bill which was the best in the country ". . . which made New Jersey's fine roads entirely safe and which brought a motor car tax that made good the wear and tear of the roads by motor cars."[132] This wasn't easy and was not accomplished overnight. In his First Annual Message to the Legislature, Murphy called on the legislature to pass a law regulating the use of automobiles.

They are machines which, as everyone knows, may go anywhere. If a man is to drive a locomotive engine, must serve years of apprenticeship as a fireman and undergo successfully a rigid examination as to his duties. And the locomotive engine is confined to a carefully built track, from which it is never able to move very far. An automobile, with its power to run wild, is now allowed to be driven by men, women and children, who, in the majority of cases, have little knowledge of machinery, and when the thing goes wrong, as it frequently and suddenly does, they are helpless. A record of the accidents of the past year would be a long and sad one. In the in- *terest of the lives and comfort of the community, I ask the Legislature to pass a law that will require a suitable examination to be passed before any one may be allowed to drive an automobile, and that no automobile shall be allowed in this state that is geared to run at a higher speed than fifteen miles an hour.*[133]

Gasoline powered engines followed the "electrics." State-of-the-art models at the turn of the century such as the one-cylinder Wintons with a top speed of ten miles per hour gave way five years later to larger faster models such as the two-cylinder Ford whose top speed was thirty miles per hour. The *Asbury Park Press* of July 18, 1904, advertised this latter model.[134] The automobile changed the economy of America gradually but persistently as filling stations and repair "garages" replaced livery stables and blacksmith shops. New Jersey, the corridor between New York and Philadelphia, became the hub of automobile activity. The "shore," always the destination of the rich and famous, became increasingly accessible as "touring" became a favorite past-time. These joy-riding excursions also became known as "tally-ho" parties. An August 1904 issue of the *Asbury Park Press* caught a glimpse of this activity. "One couple brought their famous 'yale' automobile with them and 'toured' over the 'beautiful drives and retreats' surrounding the city."[135] Touring was soon accompanied by organized racing. Long Branch, for example, introduced racing at Elkwood Park in 1908.[136]

Governor Murphy supported public funding of the state's road system. The "Road Law" as he called it appropriated $250,000 a year over several years for the construction of macadam roads. The term macadam to describe the surfacing of roads came from "a Scot, John McAdam, [who] worked out a new way of building roads. First came a roadbed of large stones, then layers of carefully selected smaller stones."[137] By 1904 about one thousand miles had been constructed, and New Jersey had some of the finest roads in the country. The Governor hesitated, however, to support increasing state funding to $400,000 which had been proposed by some members of the state legislature. Perhaps he was aware of the excessive funding of roads and canals that led to the financial panic sixty-seven years earlier. He took the position that if any county chose not to use its allocated share of state money for road construction, then it should revert back to the treasury and not be passed on to other counties.

As cars rapidly increased in numbers, size, and power, it became clear that enforced regulations were needed. Constables and police officers were authorized to arrest offenders. Murphy, in his Third Annual Message in January 1905 called on the Legislature to curb the speed limit to twenty miles per hour on country roads and eight miles per hour within city limits.

There seems to be an infatuation in the running of a machine that incites the driver to get the best possible out of it whenever he thinks he can do so with safely, and, notwithstanding a certain element of danger, the exhilaration of the sport is such that it seems to be impossible for him to resist the temptation to send his machine along at its utmost speed whenever he may do so without being arrested for violation of the law . . . It seems to me therefore, to be clearly the duty of the Legislature to provide for the strict enforcement of the law, which limits the speed to twenty miles per hour.[138]

The state acted on Murphy's advice the next year and passed a law "limiting the speed to ten miles per hour on curves and twenty miles per hour on the open road."[139] It was necessary since speeding would continue to be a permanent danger to modern society.

"Not only did automobiles cause accidents but frightened horses . . ."[140] The Governor's horse was no exception. Murphy recorded in his diary that, "I have been taking up my horseback rides during the last week and have been out three or four times. The difficulty seems to be to secure a satisfactory horse that is safe. The one I am now using is very much afraid of automobiles."[141]

Early fees were simply collected by the town clerk and passed on to Trenton. "No license plates were used. The state issued a license card, and the owner furnished his own tag . . . In 1906 the legislature created the Motor Vehicle Department, and in that year 13,759 automobiles were registered in New Jersey, and $67,973 in fees were collected."[142]

Automobiles continued to interest and become a part of Franklin Murphy's life as they did most Americans at the turn of the century. The following excerpts from his diary illustrate the impact the automobile had on his life and the lives of many Americans.

July 18, 1904

"Friday evening I went to New York with Frank to visit the automobile show, which was most interesting. We afterwards dined at Delmonicos"

July 7, 1904

"Today I spent in Elberon. In the morning I took a ride to the Indian Spring Farm, four or five miles from the cottage, almost due west from Deal. Helen & Billy going in the 'rockaway' [A rockaway was an expensive horse-drawn carriage]."

September 6, 1904

"Frank (Murphy's son) had an accident in Long Branch and had to leave the machine and come home on the stage."

September 7, 1902

"A rainy morning. It cleared up in the afternoon so that Janet and I took the Rumson Neck drive for the first time together this summer. The road never looked more beautiful."

September 22, 1904

"I rode from Elberon to Newark with Frank in his machine . . . It was a beautiful trip on a perfect day. The country looked fine. The roads were good and the machine behaved itself. I think it was the finest automobile ride I have had yet . . ."[143]

Death of Janet Murphy

Tragedy struck abruptly at twenty minutes to twelve o'clock on Wednesday February 10, 1904, with the death of Murphy's beloved wife Janet. She died suddenly of an apoplectic stroke. She had been complaining for some time of her rheumatism and some other troubles, but there had been no signs of major health problems, although the Governor felt that "she was far from well and had been failing for six months." She had been under the care of Dr. Hewlett who had prescribed a number of medications for her maladies. The Murphys had planned on going together to Hot Springs, Arkansas, where it was hoped the warm baths would alleviate her rheumatism. The Governor conducted some last minute business with Mr. Kissam and other members from the Military Board in Philadelphia and was on his way back to Trenton to meet Janet. He was intercepted by Jimmy Dale who informed him that his wife had collapsed; they both raced home in Dr. Clark's carriage. "I arrived at the house about six o'clock. Mr. and Mrs. Briggs were down stairs with John Swayze and another. Upstairs in the bedroom was Dr. Clark and a trained nurse and Ellen. Dr. Oliphant had been present in consultation. Janet's breathing was deep labored. Dr. Clark almost gave me no encouragement from the beginning. Dr. Hewlett had been telegraphed for and he arrived about 6:30. Frank arrived about 7:30 and Helen and Billy with baby Janet, from Atlantic City, arrived about eleven. Everything was done that could be done but nothing was of any avail and at twenty minutes to twelve the end came."[144]

Murphy endured the funeral in a daze supported by his closest friends and family. Among the former was Thomas and Robert McCarter and Robert Ballantine. John Swayze went "and practically took charge of things at home and was most efficient in every way until after the funeral." The funeral was held at St. Paul's Methodist Episcopal Church in Newark and was very simple by the standards of the time. The public was not allowed to look upon her at the funeral, and it was requested that no flowers be sent. The only flowers came directly from the family. There was one exception, however; several white flowers were sent from two "little poor children" from Trenton who Mrs. Murphy had befriended. The casket lay in the drawing room during the funeral where it was placed upon its arrival from Trenton and where the friends sat during the service. Murphy received about eight hundred letters of sympathy from notable personalities across the country and from around the world. A family scrap book has survived filled with examples of these letters and Western Union telegrams expressing the sorrow and grief of friends and acquaintances. There are three that stand out most and serve to exemplify the prominence of the Murphy family and the lofty reputation that they had attained on both the state and national level.

Princeton Feb. 15, 1904

My Dear Governor Murphy

I hope it will not be deemed intrusive for me to assure you that I deeply and sincerely sympathize with you in your recent bereavement.

Yours Very Sincerely

Grover Cleveland

Hon Franklin Murphy
Governor of New Jersey
Trenton[145]

Princeton University
Princeton N.J.
President's Room

20 February, 1904

My dear Governor Murphy:

The news of Mrs. Murphy's death came to me as a most grievous shock. I have hesitated to write to you sooner, because I deem it almost a presumption to intrude upon any one while such a grief is fresh upon him. Even now I feel almost like apologizing for writing; but my esteem for you is so genuine that it would be a positive pain to me were I not to give my sympathy at least this imperfect expression.

I deem it a privilege to have known Mrs. Murphy, and I pray most earnestly that God may in His mercy support and comfort you in the irreparable loss which you have sustained.

Always,
Cordially and faithfully yours,
Woodrow Wilson
Governor Franklin Murphy.[146]

The White House
Washington
February 12, 1904

My Dear Governor Murphy:

I have just seen in the paper the news of the death of Mrs. Murphy. I hope you will not deem it intrusive of me to send you a line to express my profound sympathy with you in your great grief. There is no word I can say to lighten your load; I wish there were.

Faithfully yours,

Theodore Roosevelt

Theodore Roosevelt

Hon. Franklin Murphy
Governor of New Jersey
Trenton, N.J.[147]

Murphy had been a devoted husband and the sense of loss and grief penetrated his soul as time passed. He found himself feeling that emptiness that accompanies the loss of a partner and friend and the despair and hopelessness that often grips the survivor. It surfaced in those quiet moments, in the evening when the activity of the day had passed. It is said that time heals all wounds yet for Murphy there would always be that part of his life that was shared with his beloved Janet who bore his children and shared his success and failures. Indeed, her demise cast a pall of emptiness that no one could ever fill again. He kept a stiff upper lip and with the support of his son Frank, he got through each day. He wrote on March 4, 1904, "Frank came down each night to Trenton to spend the night with me. I have had three or four to dinner and lunch each day and have got through the days pretty well. My loneliness is felt mostly at night."[148] The holidays have always been a difficult time for those who have lost loved ones. The Governor confided to his diary on December 31st, 1904, "I had a sad, but upon the whole, as agreeable a Christmas as was to be expected this year. I could not get my sorrow out of my mind and the joyousness of the occasion seemed to intensify my own grief . . . Santa Claus was good to all of us, certainly to me and the day seemed to be as happy as could be."[149] He gradually recovered and pushed on with his life although he never got over the loss of Janet.

State Camp at Sea Girt

Governor Murphy looked back over his administration with a certain pride and sense of accomplishment. He had truly come to grips with the social and economic problems that his times presented. He accepted those things that he could not change and pursued those which he could. He never read too much into an issue but rather sized up a problem and adopted a pragmatic approach which often led to a successful solution. He had a particular fondness for a number of events and episodes which occurred during his administration. Perhaps his role as commander-in-chief of the state militia was his favorite duty. He enjoyed the two weeks he spent each year at the National Guard camp at Sea Girt. This was no doubt a result of his experience with the 13th New Jersey Volunteers during the Civil War. Some say that the experience of the military remains with a person; this seems to have been the case with the Governor. He confided to his diary his experience at the camp during July of 1902.

The State Camp opened today at Sea Girt, General Gillmore of the Second Brigade in command. The Second Regiment from Camden, Colonel Shinn, arrived at the camp about noon and is to spend the week, when they will be succeeded on Saturday next by the Third Regiment. I went down from Elberon with Janet and Frank, arriving about 3:15, and was met at the station by General Gillmore, the Adjutant General and various members of my official and personal staff. Upon arriving at the Governor's cottage I received the usual salute of seventeen guns and the State flag was run up at the flag pole in front of the cottage and the Governor's personal flag displayed from the front porch . . . Dress parade occurred at 5:15 . . . In the evening the band came to the cottage to serenade us, and played for a couple of hours very well indeed. The electric lights about the trees, the music and the moon light all conspired to make a rather fine occasion.[150]

Governor Murphy and his staff at Sea Girt in 1902

He recalled how delightful the divine service was the following day and how the entire band was present accompanying the regiment as they sang "Nearer My God To Thee," "Lead Kindly Light," and the "National Hymn." The afternoons were usually spent receiving visitors and dignitaries such as Chief Justice and Mrs. Gummere. The Governor stayed in camp with few exceptions for the entire two weeks. "I have taken interest in the routine of camp life. Each day began with a bang as the morning gun was fired, and from then until taps the regimental and company drills, the guard mount, evening parade, the occasional review and the almost constant coming and going of visitors to the cottage have kept my interest in the life alert."[151]

The most exciting day at camp that summer was the visit of President Theodore Roosevelt. Murphy had requested Senator Kean extend an invitation to the President who immediately accepted. Perhaps Roosevelt, too, waxed nostalgic as he looked back to his past and his days with the Rough Riders at San Juan Hill during the Spanish American War. The camp was bustling with the news of the visit of the President. The New Jersey Central Railroad volunteered a special train, consisting of three Pullman cars, a day coach, and the private car "Atlas" for the occasion. Murphy recalled and wrote in his diary the events of that exciting day.

I requested Senators Kean and Dryden and the general and personal staff to accompany me on the train from Sea Girt to Atlantic Highlands to meet the President . . . On arriving at the Highlands we found the Mayflower, *on which the President came*

Governor Murphy and Lieutenant Edge leaving Murphy's home in Elberon, N.J. for Sea Girt

from Oyster Bay, in sight . . . I sent Frank out in a launch to the ship, giving instructions where to land, etc. and after a delay of an hour and a half the Presidential party arrived in the launch of the May-flower. It consisted of the President, Mrs. Roosevelt, Miss Roosevelt, Mr. and Mrs. Emlin Roosevelt and daughter, Assistant Secretary Loeb and several secret service men and newspaper people.[152]

The Governor was welcomed to the High-lands by the mayor and town council who intro-duced him to several thousand citizens who had

Lieutenant Edge winning the revolver match

Awaiting the arrival of President Roosevelt at Atlantic Highlands in 1902

The President's party approaching the landing

congregated on the pier and along the shore. It was not long before President Roosevelt came ashore. He was promptly escorted to the train which took him, Governor Murphy, and their parties on to Sea Girt. The engineer was deliberately instructed to run slowly through the towns so that the officials might greet the people. Every station was decorated with flags and bunting, and thousands of people turned out to see the train pass by. The President stood on the rear platform, accompanied by the Governor, the two senators, and Generals Wasner and Campbell. President Roosevelt bowed continuously as the train passed through the crowds. The largest crowd by far was at Asbury Park. A band

Governor Murphy escorting the President to the train

The President and Governor with their entourage before the review

had been assembled on a boat on Deal Lake near the railroad which struck up "Hail to the Chief" amidst the cheering crowds. The scene was truly one of the ballyhoo that came to typify nineteenth century American politics. This fanfare produced unpredicted delays which resulted in the train arriving about an hour and a half late. President Roosevelt's schedule did not allow for adjustments in his planned departure which necessitated the omission of a number of scheduled activities. Governor Murphy worked around these obstacles and extended the President every courtesy possible.

The President and Governor before the review at Sea Girt

He [President Roosevelt] was received by the Color Battalion at the station, and then driven to the cottage, passing the two other battalions, who were lined up in front of the cottage and who presented arms as he passed. As he alighted the Presidential salute of twenty-one guns was fired, and the regiment marched to the parade ground for review. We were accompanied on the review by the general

Reviewing the troops

and personal staff, and everything passed off suc-cessfully. After the review, the President occupied a stand erected for the purpose and made a speech to the troops, who were massed about the stand, and immediately near them was the crowd to the num-ber of anywhere from ten to fifteen thousand . . . We were compelled, much to Mrs. Murphy's regret, to send him away without his partaking of the lunch which she had prepared for him and his party.[153]

The trip back to the Highlands was quiet and uneventful, and Murphy had the opportunity to dis-cuss the political events of the day in private with the President. It was during the return trip that Roosevelt confided to Murphy his desire to gain nomination in his own right. Murphy wrote, "On the way down I had a very close talk with him [President Roosevelt] on the political situation, and discovered then, if I did not know before, how earnestly he desires to be renominated."[154] The en-campment closed with the usual ceremonies. The regiment formed in line of battle and marched to the Brigade Headquarters as the band played the

national anthem. The flags were lowered and a twenty-one gun salute was fired. Franklin Murphy would long remember these events and wrote of them that 26th of July 1902. "The regiment marched past the Governor's cottage to the train, giving me a marching salute as it passed. This was the ringing down of the curtain on a very enjoyable experi-ence."[155]

There were other military duties associated with being the Governor of the state of New Jer-sey. Some of these were serious matters concerning the state's military preparedness while others were purely ceremonial. In both instances the Governor devoted his undivided attention and seemed to rel-ish their importance. For instance, on Monday, Sep-tember 15th, 1902, Franklin Murphy inspected the fortifications protecting New York Harbor on Sandy Hook. He went by water on the yacht *Vixen* and

The President and Governor reach "left of the line"

was met at the landing by Lieutenant Colonel Stewart commanding Fort Hancock and Captain Black who was in charge of the proving grounds. None but an army veteran would have had the understanding and interest displayed by the Governor. He recalled the events in his diary. " I was received with the Governor's salute on entering each post. We were very much interested in the work that is being done by the Government, and noticed with much interest the method of testing powder and guns in use in the proving grounds."[156]

Three days later Murphy left for Gettysburg to join in the dedication of a new bronze monument to General Slocum. This became part of the larger annual meeting of the Society of the Army of the Potomac. The town was filled with old soldiers and their families and friends. Recalling the events of those awesome days thirty-nine years before, Murphy toured the battlefield in a carriage provided by General Sickles. He went over the entire line of the second and third day's fighting stopping at the extreme right on Culp's Hill. It was here that he, with his 13th New Jersey Volunteers, engaged the Confederates and no doubt the memories of his experience with the southern prisoners became vivid once again. The years might have dimmed his memory, but he could never fully forget. He was visibly touched by the events of this day and wrote in his diary,

Secretary of State Elihu Root and Governor Murphy at the review

We spent half an hour at this portion of the field [Culp's Hill] recalling the exciting events of the battle and listening to a number of incidents related by some of those who were present. We attended the ceremonies of the unveiling of the statue of General Slocum at three o'clock. General Sickles presided and there were on the platform General Howard and General Webb and many other old generals of the war; Governor Odell of New York, Governor Stone of Pennsylvania and a large number of prominent men. General Sickles opened the ceremonies by giving an interesting story of the battle, paying tribute to the personal and soldiery qualities of General Slocum. Addresses were also delivered by General Rogers and Colonel Archibald Baxter, and after that I spoke . . . In the evening I attended a meeting of the Army of the Potomac . . . It was a very interesting occasion.

Lunch with the President

Wednesday, October 26th, 1903, was a special day for Governor Murphy. He left with Senators Kean and Dryden on a yacht for Oyster Bay, where he had been invited for lunch with President Theodore Roosevelt. The purpose of his trip was to discuss the President's plans for a visit to the Civil War Battlefield at Antietam, Maryland. The trip did not go smoothly as a strong tide delayed the Governor, and he did not arrive at Sagamore Hill until

Antietam Battlefield, 1902

nearly 3:00 o'clock. He missed lunch, of course, but the President understood. After all, he had been in many similar situations as a public figure. The President regretted, ". . . that the three empty chairs at his lunch table were not filled." Murphy prevailed upon the President to attend the ceremony dedicating the monument. Roosevelt agreed with a "great good spirit" and Murphy recalled, "we were of course very happy at receiving his consent, as it will give a dignity and importance . . . which it could not otherwise have." Murphy's description of President Roosevelt is a priceless recollection that catches the real man in all his pugnacious exterior which in some ways concealed a warm and gentle side. Murphy described the meeting.

> *He met us in the library . . . He looked like a prize fighter. He was dressed in a cheap sack coat, an unstarched plain shirt with a limp turn-over collar, and a little string tie, poorly tied, a pair of cocky*

knickerbockers, no vest, yellow leather leggings and russet shoes, with spurs screwed into the heels, and as he stood before us with his eyes gleaming through his glasses and the mouth drawn up in the manner peculiar to himself, giving his face an expression of fierceness, he looked as if he was ready to take us all by the throat, and entirely equal to the job, instead of being one of the most attractive men in his own house that I know of. I think his appearance was rather a surprise to all of us . . . Senator Dryden is a man who is in perfect form; always kindly and gentle, always modestly dressed, but perfectly dressed. Senator Kean, with very little taste but a good tailor, always looks presentable, and I, for the time being, dressed with some reference to the occasion, were distinctly in contrast to the muscular, brawny, vigorous, aggressive man who met us. In the hour we spent with him he showed his gentle side—hospitable, genial, versatile, kindly. I have known him for twenty years and in the hour he seemed to exhibit all the pleasant traits that in my former experiences were exhibited singly and at long intervals . . .[157]

Dedication of the Antietam Monument

The New Jersey Legislature appropriated $10,000 dollars in 1902 for the erection of a monument to the state's Civil War veterans who fought at Antietam, Maryland, in September 1862. It authorized Governor Franklin Murphy to appoint a commission of three to superintend its erection. He chose three old veterans, two from his regiment, J.O. Smith of Newark, and J.E. Crowell of Paterson, and Colonel John J. Toffey of Jersey City. They were instructed to receive designs and bids for the construction. Their work resulted in the completion of a beautiful monument situated on that part of the battlefield where the 13th Regiment of New Jersey Volunteers was most actively engaged. The next year additional funds were appropriated to cover the cost of formally dedicating the monument. The date was set for September 17th, the forty-first anniversary of the battle. The commissioners arranged for the transportation of all the veterans who were interested in attending. The itinerary included an excursion to Hagerstown on Wednesday; Thursday was to be spent on the battlefield; and the veterans returned to Gettysbury Thursday night, having time to visit the Gettysburg Battlefield Friday morning and returning home that evening. There were about four-hundred-and-sixty veterans who took advantage of the free transportation while many others arranged to attend at their own expense. President Theodore Roosevelt accepted Governor Murphy's invitation "on the part of the nation." It was a gala event with all the ceremonial fanfare typical of the times. There was a special train arranged to convey the leading men of the state. It consisted of three, twelve-section drawing room and sleeping cars, one dining car, and a combination Pullman smoking and baggage car. Murphy captured the events of this day in his diary entry on Saturday, September 19th, 1903.

[the train is] a superior train in every way. It was made ready in the station at ten o'clock, and just about that hour the President and his party arrived. This took us a little by surprise, for I thought he would land from his yacht at 10:30, and I was just

President Roosevelt inspects the Antietam Monument

on my way to receive him thinking I had abundance of time to reach the wharf, when he put in an appearance. I spent a few minutes with him and presented a few of the staff to him, and then he retired to his room to do a little work before going to bed. I breakfasted with him in the morning in company with the two senators, at his invitation. The train arrived at Antietam about nine o'clock, and we found there awaiting us Commissioner Smith and General Carman [my old Colonel] and a detachment of the regular battery that was to fire the salute, under the command of Captain Foote, the detachment having appeared in response to my request to furnish a mounted escort for the President. We waited an hour for the train from Hagerstown to bring the veterans, and then proceeded in carriages to the site of the monument, passing through the old village of Sharpsburg on the way. A severe rain occurred in

President Roosevelt and Governor Murphy at the Antietam Monument dedication, September 17, 1903

Burnside Bridge, Antietam, Md., September 17, 1903

the early morning that drenched everything and prevented the attendance of a large number of citizens of the neighborhood who otherwise would have been present. I should say that about twenty-five hundred or three thousand persons were present. Mr. Smith made the report of the Commission, I responded in a speech of half an hour, accepting it on the part of the State and turning it over to the nation, and President Roosevelt followed, accepting it (on part of the nation). We, in company with the President and his friends, drove over the battlefield under the pilotage of General Carman, who has been the Governmental officer in charge of the laying out of the work done there. It was a most interesting ride. The important scenes of the field were all visited. Bloody Lane, Burnside Bridge and Observation Tower, to the top of which we all went, and we returned to the train . . . The President dined with us in our dining car. I felt that the members of our party would be very much pleased to have him . . .[158]

The old veterans dispersed after the close of the ceremonies no doubt gripped with the heart wrenching emotions of the memories of long ago. Perhaps the words of a comrade in arms echoed in their minds, those words of Private Murphy or was it Governor Murphy whose speech ended, "The Republic has need today, as then, of men of high and lofty patriotism. Our country is as dear to the men of 1903 as it was to the men of 1861, and the State of New Jersey, in grateful commemoration of the highest sacrifice of her patriotic sons, has erected this monument to her dead on this field. In her name I present it to the nation through you."[159]

Christening the U.S.S. New Jersey

The voyage of the U.S.S. *Oregon* around Cape Horn during the Spanish American War demonstrated dramatically the need for an isthmian canal and the expansion of a two ocean navy. It was, in part, a reflection of the foreign policy of President Theodore Roosevelt that called for military preparedness and the expansion of what came to be known as the "Great White Fleet." Alfred Thayer Mahon's book, *The Influence of Sea Power Upon History 1660-1783,* influenced the leaders of the world and encouraged the naval arms build-up. The

Reception to Governor Murphy.

Admit bearer to Steamer "Sea Gull." The Steamer will leave Adams Express Pier, Pennsylvania Station, Jersey City, at 10 A.M., on Saturday, June 4, 1904. You are requested to be on the Steamer promptly. Lunch will be served on the boat.

Committee.

Invitations to a reception for Governor Murphy aboard the Sea Gull *in June, 1904*

battle cruisers of the turn of the century were the precursors of the mighty dreadnoughts of later times, both of which would come to occupy respected pages in the annals of naval history. So it was that the state of New Jersey lent its name alongside the names of her sister states to a new fleet of warships which carried the flag to the far recesses of the globe, as America took her place among the mighty powers of the earth. Franklin Murphy was proud and honored that the task of officiating over New Jersey's contribution to the battle fleet occurred, in large part, when he was Governor. The U.S.S. *New Jersey BB 16,* was a magnificent ship. Commanded by Captain W.W. Kimbel, she was the sister ship of the *Virginia, Nebraska,* and *Georgia,* and was authorized on February 4, 1902. Her displacement was 14,948 tons; length, 435 feet; beam, 76 feet 2 1/2 inches; mean draft, 23 feet 9 inches, and speed, 19.18 knots. She was armed with 4-12" 40 caliber, 8-8" 45 caliber, and 12-6" 50 caliber guns. The ship's company consisted of 40 officers and 772 enlisted men.[160] November 10, 1904, was the day set for the launching of the U.S.S. *New Jersey.* Governor Franklin Murphy with his staff and a number of State officials and representative citizens of New Jersey left Jersey City in the afternoon of

November 9, and arrived in Boston later that evening, where they went to the Hotel Somerset as guests of the Fore River Ship Building Company.

Accompanying the Governor were his daughter Helen, who was to christen the ship and her husband William. In addition to his staff which included Brigadier General R. Heber Breintnall, Adjutant General; Colonel Franklin Murphy, Jr.; Colonel Charles W. Parker; Colonel Lewis T. Bryant; Captain Arther H. MacKie; and Captain Walter E. Edge were the Honorable John Kean, R. Wayne Parker, and William H. Wiley.

The next morning, November 10, the party together with Governor Bates of Massachusetts, his staff, Brigadier General Frederick Carpenter, Attorney General Parker, and a large number of officials and prominent citizens of Massachusetts, went to the Fore River shipyards on a special train, where they were met by Rear Admiral Francis T. Bolles and other officials of the company. The U.S.S. *New Jersey,* decked with red, white, and blue bunting from stem to stern, presented an imposing picture as the launching party gathered on the platform at

The U.S.S. New Jersey

*Governor Murphy's daughter Helen christens the U.S.S.
New Jersey at the launching*

*Governor Murphy, his staff, and naval officers at the
launching of the U.S.S.* New Jersey

Governor Murphy, his daughter Helen, and dignitaries at the launching of the U.S.S. New Jersey

Part of the U.S.S. New Jersey *'s silver service*

Snapshot of the U.S.S. New Jersey *after launching, probably taken by the Governor or his daughter*

12:45 P.M. The tide was not at its height until 1.02 P.M., but it was decided not to wait until that hour. At the given signal, the great ship started down the ways, and Murphy's daughter Helen smashed the bottle of champagne christening her "New Jersey" as the band of the Battleship *Missouri* played the "Star Spangled Banner."[161] Governor Murphy recalled these historic events in his diary entry of November 13, 1904.

On Wednesday, the 9ʰ (November) . . . I started with a party of twenty-four to Boston to attend the launching of the Battleship "New Jersey" at the Fore River Ship Yards. Helen (Helen Kinney-Franklin Murphy's daughter) was to do the christening . . . My personal staff went, together with Messrs. Hunt, Scudder, Rappelyea, Miss A., Dr. Jacobson and a few others. We had a private car by courtesy of the New Haven Road to take us over and back, through Mr. Brooker, and the Fore River Works looked after our comfort at the Hotel Touraine. [Note: apparently some of the party were put up in the Hotel Somerset while others including the Governor stayed at the Hotel Touraine.] We arrived safely at 8:30 and went to our hotel and to bed. The next morning, Thursday the 10th, we took a special train to Quincy, where the shipyards are located. It was bright and clear and everything incident to the occasion passed off successfully. Helen very much smashed the bottle as she christened the ship, being determined that the failure at the launching of the Connecticut should not be repeated by her. There were present beside Admiral Bowles, Secretary Long and Governor Bates, with his staff, and their friends . . . The trip upon the whole was delightful in every way and all who went seemed to enjoy it very much.

Murphy's army orientation yielded at least on this and one other occasion to the splendor and pomp and circumstance of the navy. Eight months earlier, on a visit to Captain Bronson at the Naval Academy at Annapolis, Maryland, he had occasion to observe the midshipmen on parade. "A company of marines were drawn up, with a band of music, who presented arms, and the battery fired the usual seventeen guns . . . The entire battalion was marched on the parade ground in front of his (Captain Bronson's quarters). I was surprised and gratified to see how well these young men marched and drilled as soldiers."[162]

New Jersey at the World's Fair

October 6, 1904, was designated as New Jersey Day at the Saint Louis World's Fair. It was a particularly fond memory for Franklin Murphy as he glanced back over his tenure as Governor. It was an exciting time, as all world's fairs tend to be. The international community displayed its wares in a competitive and peaceful open forum. It was not all as easy as that, however. A bill was originally passed appropriating $25,000 to the Governor for the expenses of a celebration of New Jersey Day at the Fair. These funds were to pay for the attendance of a detachment of the National Guard, members of the legislature who wished to attend, as well as the

Governor's general and personal staff. Murphy politely declined the legislative stipend when he realized that the public would consider this sum excessive. He chose instead, to pare down the contingent to a modest party and found, upon inquiry, that there was a considerable balance of money in the hands of the World's Fair Commissioners. He suggested that they pay the expense "of a modest party to St. Louis, which they agreed to do." He wrote on October 10, 1904, "I invited the United States Senators and ten members of Congress, the heads of the various departments, two or three of the more important boards and half a dozen newspaper men, all told to the number of sixty-five or seventy."[163] Only about forty-five people finally attended.

The Pennsylvania Railroad provided a special train consisting of three Pullman cars, a dining car, and a baggage car. It was the second section of the Saint Louis Limited which left New York at ten o'-clock, whisking Murphy and his New Jersey delegation off to Saint Louis. It was a beautiful day, and everyone seemed to be in good spirits as the train sped along, arriving in Saint Louis shortly after noon on Wednesday, October 5. Immediately upon arrival, they took three "tally-ho" coaches out to the fair grounds. Murphy recalled the details. "I stopped at the cottage with the Adjutant General and Frank and the two United States Senators. The rest of the party were quartered at the Inside Inn."[164] Murphy's arrival coincided with the celebration of Rhode Island Day so "immediately after our arrival I called on the Governor of Rhode Island at the Rhode Island building, with the staff."[165] After paying his respects, Murphy was off to the Philippine exhibit which fascinated him above all others. This is interesting inasmuch as the archipelago had only recently been acquired from Spain at the Treaty of Paris which ended the Spanish American War. Just prior to the conflict, President McKinley admitted he could not have located it on a map. This proved conclusively that Murphy kept up with the times and adapted to his rapidly changing world. A Doctor Wilson was in charge of the Philippine exhibits and showed Murphy around. There were a half dozen different villages which displayed the products of the Islands and the articles that were manufactured there. Murphy recalled, "It was so interesting that we remained until dark. I think upon the whole the

"New Jersey Day" at the Saint Louis Exposition, October 6, 1904

Philippine exhibit is the most interesting and instructive of all the exhibits at the great fair."[166]

They dined at the Tyrolean Alps on the Pike for dinner. It was extremely overcrowded despite its immense size, but this was balanced with a magnificent orchestra of some sixty pieces that "furnished delightful music." The evening ended with some displays of "eastern dancing" and the party retired happily exhausted, awaiting the events of the morrow. The dawn ushered in a magnificently beautiful fall day as if Providence arranged that New Jersey would truly have its day in the sun. Governor Francis greeted Murphy's entourage of some twenty-two carriages at the administration building. Various military units were mustered in formation and two bands escorted the Governor and his party to the New Jersey Building which was a beautiful replica of a Revolutionary War tavern. There were several thousand people gathered on the lawn and in and around the building. The first order of protocol was the review of the troops. Governor Francis followed with a speech of welcome and then the main address from Governor Murphy. It was a moving tribute to the accomplishments of the state, its people, and its past with a vision of optimism for the future.

New Jersey Day At Saint Louis October 6, 1904

We are gathered together today in these surroundings in accordance with a custom, which was wisely established in the Exposition at Chicago, and continued at Buffalo, and now in Saint Louis, to join in celebrating what is known as a "State Day."

We come as Jerseymen to celebrate "New Jersey Day," and we have come a long journey to pay our respect and appreciation, not only to the great event which this marvelous Exposition commemorates, and to the able men who have organized and carried to successful completion this wonderful enterprise, but especially to join with those citizens of New Jersey, who may be here, in paying tribute to the skill, energy and enterprise of our State as shown in the wide range of attractive exhibits, which are here displayed to the gaze of the world.

World's Fairs come and go, and in the memory of many, who have not yet passed middle life, they have been held at such frequent intervals as in a sense to have lost their novelty. When a new one is suggested, the question arises almost at once, "Will it pay?" And coming so soon after the great Paris Exposition, that question very naturally arose as to this Fair, the greatest in many respects, if not in all respects, that the world has ever seen, and it is difficult to imagine how it can be surpassed. Whether it will pay dividends to those who have furnished the money for its cost I do not know, and I fancy it does not make much difference. That is the smallest consideration in an enterprise of this kind. From every point of view an Exposition like this pays immensely. In the first place, it presents to the people of the world examples of its progress in every line of human endeavor: it broadens the horizon of every man and woman that comes here to see it. No visitor to this great Exhibition can spend any time, however brief, without seeing something and learning something that more than compensates him or her for the time given. This Exposition is so vast that any mere statement of its statistics fails to convey a conception of what it really is.

When I heard a year ago that it was proposed to have an Exposition that would be nearly twice as large as the Chicago Exposition, which was the greatest the world at that time had ever seen, I said, "it is impossible." But when I came here a month or two ago and saw with my own eyes the wonders that had been accomplished, I said, "the half had not been told."

To this great Exposition New Jersey has contributed her share. Here may be seen intelligently displayed its public school system from the time the child begins to learn its A B C's until the mature student gets his or her diploma at the Normal School. I think it is not going too far to say that the Educational Exhibit of the State of New Jersey surpasses in completeness that of any other State, and it shows what may be done in developing a public school system in a State, where the cause of education, like the cause of justice, is taken absolutely out of politics. The State also presents an exhibit of its methods of road building and shows samples of its stone and shell and clay roads. Ours was the first among the States to furnish State aid in the construction of public roads, and we have today more than twelve hundred miles of roads, samples of which are here shown, extending all over the State, which have been of almost incalculable advantage to the people, and especially to the farmers. By common consent New Jersey stands at the front in the development of its road system and for many years has been the example from which our neighboring States have taken pattern.

The geological formation of our State is shown and our agricultural experiment station makes an exhibition of dairy management as well as methods of soil investigation, which are full of interest and value.

Our individual exhibitions, while not equaling the number of those of the larger States, do not in any way fall short in interest. It is not going too far to say that the statistical exhibition on the subject of life insurance made by the Prudential Insurance Company of which Senator Dryden is the founder and President, displays the facts and history and conditions of that business, in which the great majority of our people are interested, with a clearness and completeness that has never been equaled. Our manufacturers present the latest developments of mechanical ingenuity. New Jersey is the home of Edison. In our State most of his wonderful inventions have been brought into practical service are here exhibited. I must not weary you with a further recital, nor go more into detail of what is here to be seen. They are to be seen and not talked about, and you must see them for yourselves.

I must not, however, omit to call your attention to the fact that the beautiful building, which the State has erected for its use on these grounds, is a reproduction of the Old Ford Tavern at Morristown, which was used during the winter of '79 and '80. Here in those dark days of the Revolutionary War the great leader, with his little army poorly fed and poorly clothed but never poor in patriotic spirit, spent the long and cold winter. Here Alexander Hamilton made his home, and here he met the daughter of General Schuyler, whom he afterwards married.

Here came Greene and Knox, and Steuben, and Light Horse Harry Lee, and Old Israel Putman, and Mad Anthony Wayne. This building carries us back in our memories to those days of struggle, and privation and sacrifice.

Nor should I fail on an occasion like this to recall the important part that New Jersey has always taken in the affairs of the Nation. On her soil were fought the battles of Trenton and Princeton, and Monmouth and from the beginning of the Revolutionary struggle until today her sons have not been surpassed by any in their patriotic devotion to the State and the Nation, and at all times and under all circumstances the State has stood ever ready to respond to the Nation's call for any service however great, or for any sacrifice however severe.

Few States have grown relatively as has our State and no State of its size is of more importance today; and no one shares in a higher degree all those qualities of energy, of high purpose, and of courage that have made the State and Nation what they are.

The farms of New Jersey are worth more per acre than in any other State in the Nation. The products of those farms bring more per acre than any other State in the Nation. Her industries are more varied than those of any other State, and in her chief city no less than three thousand various industries find their home: so that whether in those material resources that make a State great in times of peace or those higher and more unselfish ideals that lead to sacrifices in times of peril, the State we represent is one that may claim and justly claim, the affection and pride of its citizens.[167]

The next two days were spent enjoying the many exciting exhibits of the Fair. Murphy was particularly fond of German food. He thoroughly enjoyed a dinner given him by a Colonel Bryant that Saturday evening at the German Restaurant. Afterwards, they rode in the electric launches over the lagoon and had the opportunity to see the cascades and a brilliant electric illumination that Murphy called, "the most wonderful . . . that can be imagined . . . a most beautiful and impressive conclusion to three or four days of unalloyed enjoyment." They were taken by automobiles to the train station and left Saint Louis at 11:30, arriving at Newark at 6:30 Monday morning "thoroughly tired out, but full of satisfaction with our visit."[168]

Honorary Degree from Princeton University

His governorship now ended, Franklin Murphy would reflect upon memorable events, events that were of significance to him though not spectacular to others: Woodrow Wilson's inauguration as President of Princeton University was a day that would forever occupy a cherished place in Murphy's memory as Wilson's day of honor became one of his own. It was on Saturday, October 25, 1902, that Governor Murphy traveled to Princeton, there to receive an honorary L.D. degree similar to the one he had received from Lafayette College the previous June. He had only been informed two days before and was asked to be in the Trustees' Room by 10 o'clock that Saturday morning. Accompanying him, as always, was his devoted son Frank Jr. and Chief Justice W. S. Gummere. Upon arrival they went to the Nassau Hotel where rooms had been reserved for the Governor's staff to put on their dress uniforms. Murphy met a large number of members at the Trustees' Room and was formally presented by Dr. Wilson who made a very complimentary speech; Dr. Carver conferred the degree on behalf of the Board. Murphy then signed the oath of the University as one of the trustees and

Society of the Cincinnati insignia

walked with ex-President Grover Cleveland in the procession from the library to Alexander Hall. Murphy recalled, "the day was a great one for Princeton. Presidents of the leading colleges were there and men distinguished in all walks of life-letters and business as well as politics."[169] As crowds filled Alexander Hall, Murphy introduced the speakers-Dr. Patton the retiring President, Mr. Cleveland, who spoke for the Board of Trustees, and Dr. Wilson, who read his inaugural before turning over the sod for the dormitory his class pledged to erect. Murphy went on, "I afterward went to lunch at the President's house and found a spacious mansion admirably fitted for its intended use. There were twenty-four that sat down to lunch, which was very elaborate—Mr. Cleveland on one side of Dr. Wilson and I on the other and President Hadley of Yale on the other side of me, altogether a very enjoyable affair."[170] It was a beautiful fall day which focused later that afternoon, as fall days would in future years, on football. Princeton won the game over Columbia by a score of twenty-one to nothing. Murphy was well-pleased and came home on a special train arriving back in Newark a little before seven P.M.

Society of Cincinnati

The Society of Cincinnati was an organization of Revolutionary War officers formed on May 10, 1783, in the Newburg and Fishkill area of New York "to preserve inviolate those exalted rights and liberties of human nature for which they had fought and bled."[171] It was, coincidentally, on this same date eight years earlier that Benedict Arnold and Ethan Allen had taken Fort Ticonderoga and its precious artillery that Henry Knox would use to force the British out of Boston. The Society's chief organizer was this same Henry Knox who helped name it after the Roman General Lucius Quintius Cincinnati.[172] It was an exclusive fraternal organization of veteran commissioned officers who had served a minimum of thirty months during the Revolutionary War. Membership was hereditary-based and passed on from father to eldest son. George Washington and Alexander Hamilton were early leaders. The rigid requirements were relaxed somewhat as years passed and Franklin Murphy became eligible for honorary membership through his lineage.

Josiah Crane, "Eastern Battalion Morris," of the Continental Army had been an ancestor of the Governor and it was this connection that led to his investiture into the Society in 1899. He was also a proud member of the Sons of the American Revolution. These affiliations were important to Murphy as they provided a continuity of sacrifice of the Civil War era with that of the nation's struggle for independence. Civil War veterans had a particular sensitivity and keen awareness of the torch that had been passed on to them by their Revolutionary forebears. It was the former who had created the Union through revolution, and it had been the latter who had been entrusted to preserve it from dissolution through Civil War. He was proud of his role and destiny in the great struggle; from his perspective he had been right for his times. His writings are filled with references to the patriotic sacrifices of fellow Americans at places like Saratoga, Yorktown, and Valley Forge. He rarely missed an opportunity to commemorate these anniversaries. So when it came to the 125th anniversary of the Battle of Monmouth, he enthusiastically traveled to Freehold to participate in the activities.

The Battle of Monmouth Celebrated

June 27, 1903, was a beautiful summer day in Freehold, New Jersey, perfect to commemorate the anniversary of the Battle of Monmouth that had been fought one hundred and twenty-five years earlier. It was then that British General Sir Henry Clinton left Philadelphia en route to New York and marched his columns northward through New Jersey. Washington's ragtag Continental Army and local militia pursued the British and Hessian troops, catching up with them near Monmouth Court House later renamed Freehold. The resulting engagement in the scorching sun proved indecisive as the Americans traded blow for blow with Europe's finest. Some historians hold American General Charles Lee responsible for preventing a decisive American victory. He had ordered an unauthorized retreat at a moment when victory might have been possible. Notwithstanding these lost opportunities, American arms emerged with renewed credibility; the Continental Line stood toe-to-toe with the British regulars. This was the result of the training at

Valley Forge under Baron Friedrich Von Steuben, the relentless task master whose frustrations were caught in a remark to a subordinate, "Come here and swear for me, these fellows won't do what I bid them."

The local committee had procured an appropriation from the legislature which provided for the presence of the Second Regiment, the Camden Battery, and the Red Bank Troop.[173] The Governor and a Mr. Sheppard among others took a car from Elberon and were met at Freehold by the staff in full dress uniform. They were taken to the house of Mr. Dancer for a reception and "collation" before joining the procession that marched through the town and on to Monmouth Park where the services were held. The town of Freehold was superbly decorated, and the whole community turned out for the festivities. Franklin Murphy recalled how "every house was covered with flags and bunting, every one desirous of using as many flags as possible evidently evincing a great interest in the day . . . the ladies and children could appear in their summer dresses and from beginning to end the celebration was a decided success."[174] The services were opened with a prayer by Bishop Scarborough and there were a number of speakers including Senator Charles Fairbanks of Indianapolis and Governor Murphy. He called the people's attention to the events of 125 years earlier, the impact on this day and thoughts for the future.

The following are excerpts from Governor Murphy's Address delivered at Freehold, New Jersey, on the One Hundred and Twenty-Fifth Anniversary of the Battle of Monmouth held June 27, 1903:

We are met on this historic field to refresh our memories of the eventful day a century and a quarter ago when a battle for liberty was fought on the very ground upon which we stand. The results of that battle perhaps no man may measure. The numbers engaged on each side are known. The individual acts of heroism displayed on that occasion have enriched the pages which tell the story to inspire and inflame the hearts of young and old with patriotic fever. These incidents illumine a brilliant page in

The Essex Troop

Governor Murphy at Governor Stokes' inaugural review

the history of the memorable struggle of the Revolution, but they are after all the incidents of a day and an occasion. The results of the battle may be seen in part and imagined only in part. The contestants on the one side were the well-appointed and well-cared-for troops under Sir Henry Clinton, and on the other the poorly fed and poorly clothed band of Continental patriots from Valley Forge under the immortal Washington. The story of the engagement has been eloquently told in detail . . . in the brief time I shall speak to you, suggest some of the results of that struggle of which the battle of Monmouth was such an important part.

A powerful and resourceful nation on one side, a few weak and poor colonies on the other and the issue civil liberty. Eight years of what at times seemed a hopeless struggle and then the surrender at Yorktown and final victory. In all that struggle the sons of New Jersey took an honorable part and on her soil were fought the battles of Trenton, Princeton, Monmouth, Red Bank, and Springfield; these names with Morristown make New Jersey's share in the contest altogether creditable.

Today as we stand here upon this field, the

A Billy Yank Governor / 174

grandsons and great-grandsons of those who here fought, our thoughts return with affectionate pride to the early times when our forefathers thought no sacrifice too great for the cause in which they had pledged "their lives, their fortunes and their sacred honor." As from this distance we consider the unlimited resources of Great Britain and the feebleness of the colonies, we see that few if any wars in history have been waged by more unequal combatants. But there was something more than visible resources to be taken into account. It was a war of right against wrong, of principle against selfishness, of freedom against tyranny . . . What was the result of that struggle? In the first place liberty throughout the world received an uplift. The divine right of kings received a shock from which it will never recover and the stability and prosperity of any government was seen to rest upon a consideration of the rights of the governed. In a broad and lasting way that principle was established by the success of the American Revolution as it never had been before and the history of the world since the surrender of Cornwallis at Yorktown shows that that principle in government has come to stay . . .

We have grown from a handful to eighty millions. Our thirteen feeble colonies have expanded into many mighty states, and our broken and uncertain western boundary of Revolutionary days has pushed onto the Pacific . . . No State has a brighter history. Contributing its full share of men and means in the Revolution, it has never failed to respond with alert and vivid patriotism to every call made upon it. We are proud of our State and the long line of patriotic men who have given their service to its development. The schoolhouse and the church are seen on every hilltop and our people are an intelligent and God-fearing people. We care for the poor, we provide for the sick in mind and body, and we love the flag. May the inspiration of this day fill our hearts with still greater devotion to our State and our Land.

At the close of the ceremonies, Bishop MacFall said a final prayer and people returned to their homes. Congressman Hemmenway of Indiana returned with the Governor for dinner at Elberon and stayed for the night. They left the next morning as Murphy recalled, "our guests, Senator and Mrs. Fair-

The Murphy home on Broad Street in Newark

banks and Congressman Hemmenway left us this morning about ten o'clock after a very agreeable visit. They seemed to enjoy their stay as much as we enjoyed having them."[175]

Passing the Torch

Franklin Murphy's three years as Governor had passed quickly. It was hard for him to imagine, as he sat with Governor-Elect Stokes, how fast the time had passed. It was he who had been Governor-Elect for what seemed a mere blink of the eye ago. He welcomed with a sense of relief that the time had come for him to step down and pass the reins to his successor, but his mind was full of memories of the events of three years earlier, of how he and Janet had had dinner with General and Mrs. Oliphant and how gracious they had been to him. In the ensuing years, the General had died and Janet had died and the world had lost much of its luster. He was anxious to spend one last evening with Mrs. Oliphant before his official time ended and made arrangements on Monday, January 14, 1905, to have dinner with her. Of course, Frank Jr. would attend to assure the proper Victorian decorum. It turned out to be a very nice time "as she is a very beautiful character."[176]

The inauguration of Governor Stokes "passed off in a very pleasant manner."[177] There was, of course, a large crowd of people gathered for the event consisting of several civic delegations from Cumberland, Camden, and Hudson counties as well as local citizens. The Essex Troop was there as a personal escort for the Governor. The proceedings were very formal and followed traditional protocol. At 11:55 A.M. Governor Murphy with his full staff in splendid regalia called upon Governor-Elect Stokes. They entered the carriages prepared for them and proceeded to the Taylor Opera House where the ceremonies were held. It was a bit of dejavu for Murphy. "The carriage in which the Governor and myself rode, together with the Attorney General and Colonel Murphy, was driven by four horses and was followed by the rest of the procession."[178] The ceremonies were typical of the occasion, and the place was packed with throngs of enthusiastic well-wishers. Murphy's role was limited as was that of his predecessors to passing on the state seal to the new governor. Governor Stokes delivered a spirited inaugural address which focused on the controversial issue of taxation. Murphy considered it "an exceptionally strong document . . . of . . . great force and vigor."[179] At the conclusion of the address, they returned to the stand in front of the capitol to review the procession which took about forty minutes. It was then on to lunch at the Trenton House. Later that afternoon, Murphy stopped in to bid Mrs. Oliphant good-buy and left Trenton at 4:07 P.M., thus ending his term as Governor.[180] He was accompanied as always by his ever loyal son Frank, Jr. who buoyed up his father and helped soothe the anxiety of a very emotional day. He confided his inner feelings to his diary that evening, reflecting on his experience as Governor and the trauma of the loss of his beloved Janet.

For the three years I have felt as keenly I think as most people the responsibilities of the office and I have tried to serve the state with my best service. I have minded no sacrifices and I have spared myself in no instance. I would like to have accomplished more during my administration than I have, but I have accomplished much and most of the laws that are now on the statute books will, I hope, be a permanent benefit to the people. I have in a certain way enjoyed the office. The people have been considerate and kind. Yet the death of my wife took away all its pleasure and for two or three months it has been an almost unbearable burden, and I have looked forward to this relief with unexpressable satisfaction. Just how I shall adjust myself to the new mode of life without the official cares and the lonesomeness of my condition remains to be seen. Fortunately I have some devoted friends upon whose loyal and unfailing friendship I can always count, but I feel a relief from the office beyond the power of words to express.[181]

He had forged many friendships with his staff which would endure for the rest of his life. Murphy loved to entertain them for dinner and recalled an evening at his home at 1027 Broad Street, Newark: "I gave a dinner to the full staff . . . The table looked very nice and sixteen sat down. I gave them a home dinner, some roast turkey and some roast Virginia ham and the things that go with them, as well as some champagne and 1792 port. The whole affair was characterized by the pleasantest of good feeling. I think that the affection of the staff for me is thoroughly genuine and it has been one of the pleasantest features of my administration."[182]

6

The Twilight Years

FRANKLIN MURPHY returned to his home in Newark, New Jersey, that he affectionately referred to as "1027" and adopted the genteel life of an accomplished business and political leader. He distanced himself from politics as was the custom of a retired governor at that time and remained on the sidelines as an interested observer. He continued his work for the Essex Park System and was appointed a Park Commissioner by Chief Justice Gummere. In 1905 President Theodore Roosevelt appointed him a member of the Board of Visitors of the Military Academy at West Point and a year later he was appointed in a similar capacity to the Naval Academy at Annapolis. These Presidential appointments were highly honorable positions, dating back to the efforts of Slyvanus Thayer who worked to improve the quality of West Point as early as 1819. A Board of Visitors was a type of civilian review panel charged with overseeing the service academies in all facets of their endeavors. He was also a member of the McKinley Memorial Commission and Chairman of its Building Committee. On September 30, 1907, the dedication of the McKinley Monument took place at Canton, Ohio. Murphy was proud of his part in this homage to the slain president. He had chosen Mr. Magonigle of New York, a distinguished architect from a number of promising candidates, to design the structure. Murphy left New York City on September 30, 1907, on a private railroad car called the "Sunset," with a small party which included Cornelius N. Bliss, John G. Milburn, Dr. Leslie D. Ward, and General Joseph W. Plume. They arrived at the city of Canton and found it beautifully decorated with "bunting and flags in every street and almost on every house."[1] President Roosevelt arrived about 10:00 A.M. and the procession that followed included soldiers from the Ohio militia, members of the Knights Templar, and delegations from many different societies. Thousands listened to a speech by President Roosevelt, poetry by James Whitcomb Riley, and prayers by Bishop Spaulding. Then followed the unveiling of the monument that "profoundly impressed [the people] with its beauty and its appropriateness."[2] Murphy returned to Newark satisfied that President William McKinley's legacy had been properly enshrined.

Perhaps the ex-Governor's favorite daily pastime during these years was his work as a member of the Board of Managers of the National Home for Disabled Volunteer Soldiers. This was located at Hampton, Virginia, where the chapel had been named in his honor. He made frequent trips there for official and unofficial inspections. He wrote, "This work has been full of interest and I have enjoyed it greatly."[3] Memories of the Civil War continued to occupy his mind as he visited nearby places of interest that had played a part in that great conflict. On January 14, 1908, for example, while on a trip to the Disabled Volunteers, he visited Fortress Monroe where Confederate President Jefferson Davis had been incarcerated after the war. Three weeks earlier, on Christmas Day 1907, he had been pleasantly surprised by a gift from his son Frank Jr. He wrote, "Santa Claus was very good to everyone . . . of all my presents, the most appreciated was my old sword that I carried as a Lieutenant in the 13th New Jersey Regiment during the Civil War. I missed it some years ago and had scoured the house for it on more than one occasion, but in vain. In some way it disappeared, and a stranger who had it wrote to Frank some months ago, informing him that he had the sword, and Frank at once purchased it, keeping it until now for one of my Christmas presents."[4] As devoted as Murphy was to his prior service, he was adamantly opposed to pensions or other compensation to Union veterans. This issue permeated the "Gilded Age" as the Grand Army of the Republic had become an important political constituency of the Grand Old Republican Party. Factions within that party curried support from veteran groups in return for the promise of pork barrel rewards in the form of patronage or pension stipends. Murphy steadfastly resisted all attempts to join those who wished to ladle out the spoils. An example of this occurred on January 18th, 1908. Murphy wrote,

I had a call this morning from my old friend and comrade in the 13th Regiment, Mr. John R. Williams . . . He called to enlist my public interest

in a Bill which has been introduced in Congress providing for the retirement of Volunteer Officers in the War of the Rebellion with half pay. I told him frankly what my position was—that I have never been at all in sympathy with the raids on the Treasury made by the Grand Army of the Republic, that I thought the cry for increased pensions was wrong, that the Government had discharged its duty to the men who served it, that, if men enlisted in the War from patriotic motives, as some of us did, they received their reward in the consciousness of duty performed. If, upon the other hand, they enlisted because of the pay offered by the Government, the obligations of the Government were fully discharged when that pay was received. I told him that I thought the general motive of these moves for increasing pensions was plunder, and it was fostered on the part of the Legislators and Presidents by demagogism-that I had never stood for it and I never would.[5]

In June 1910 President Taft appointed Murphy as a civil member of the commission to represent the United States at the celebration of the First Centennial of the Republic of Mexico. The millionaire varnish manufacturer may have been an unofficial ambassador for the President's business-orientated foreign policy, what historians have dubbed his "Dollar Diplomacy." The event commemorated the heroic struggle of Father Miguel Hidalgo who initiated Mexico's march towards independence on September 15, 1810, at the little town of Dolores. It was there that this priest summoned the faithful calling on "Mexicans . . . long live . . . Mexico." This was called "Groito de Dolores" or the "Declaration of Dolores," and has been celebrated on September 16th ever since.[6] These festivities were overshadowed by domestic strife and political instability as one Mexican faction vied with another for influence and control. These were to ultimately place the United States in an awkward position; on the one hand the American government stood for respect of national sovereignty and self-determination, while on the other, it had the responsibility of protecting its nationals and their property. This was set against the backdrop of a series of colorful desperadoes such as the notorious Poncho Villa. As Murphy returned home eager to re-enter politics, these problems would escalate into a full scale international crisis. War with America's southern neighbor was avoided, in large part, by the ominous events in Europe as the clouds of World War I began to loom on the horizon.

Almost Chosen Vice President

Good fortune did not always smile on Franklin Murphy in the game of American politics. He did not always receive a strong hand in what Theodore Roosevelt would symbolically label the Square Deal. For example, in 1908 he became New Jersey's choice for Vice-President preceding the Chicago Convention. Although he received seventy-seven votes, these were not enough to place him on the national ticket. It is generally believed that political obligations required concessions to the New York Republicans, which resulted in the selection of James Sherman from Utica, New York; such were the peculiarities of American politics in the years preceding World War I. Murphy was a tempered politician who dealt with adversity remarkably well, perhaps in the British tradition of the "stiff upper lip." This was, nevertheless, a natural disappointment for him after being led to believe that he was the likely choice. An hour long interview with Senators Kean and Aldrich on the impending Vice-Presidential situation encouraged Murphy. He wrote, "He (Aldrich) wrote of my career, my wide acquaintance, the favorable way in which I was known, and the general attitude of friendliness and confidence which the leading men of the Party shared concerning me . . . (I) was pleased to find that his opinion of me was so favorable . . . I later had a talk with Senator Lodge, who found me in the Vice-President's room, and inquired in a smiling way, if I had come to look over my future quarters."[7] This would not come to pass, but the outcome did not dampen his enthusiasm for his party and his determination to continue his contributions. "Ex-Governor Murphy's defeat for the Vice-Presidential nomination in Chicago did not impair his devotion to the Taft fortunes in the campaign that followed. He was persuaded to resume the chairmanship of the State Committee, and his generalship soon turned the tide overwhelmingly in Taft's favor."[8] The Republicans won by 82,876 votes.[9] Murphy

attended the inauguration of President Taft and recorded the events in his diary.

I returned last night from a trip to the Inauguration of President Taft, where I went on Tuesday afternoon with Frank and Harriet. We were unable to get rooms at the Willard, and so went to the Raleigh, where we had very nice quarters—better, indeed, than we had ever had at the Willard, and I found the people and service quite as good although it is not quite as much the center of all things . . . After dinner, Tuesday night, we took a walk about the City, going as far as the White House to see the preparations made for the decoration of the streets and their illumination at night . . . Wednesday proved to be a very busy day. I found a number of the Members of the National Committee at the Willard . . . Wednesday was not a very pleasant day-rather raw and Marchy, but the Weather Bureau promised fair weather for Thursday. When I woke up on Thursday I found the snowiest, coldest, dampest, most disagreeable day that one can imagine, one or two or three of the worst days for storms I ever saw. The slush was deeper than I ever knew it, the snow retaining the water in such a way as to make a slush of about ten inches. It seemed impossible to have a parade, and it was the general feeling that it ought to be postponed. Such, however, was not to be the case. We tried to get a carriage or an automobile to take us to the Capitol, where through the kindness of Senator Kean, I had secured three good seats. After waiting for some time, we finally found a broken-down horse and broken-down trap and a broken-down driver, who consented to take us to the Capitol. We got along pretty well until we were half way to Capitol Hill. Then the horse absolutely refused to go any further. He did not balk, and there was no excitement about it. He simply stood still and no amount of urging or whipping could induce him to move on. As consequence, we all had to get out in the slush and get to the Capitol as best we could. We arrived in time to see the last acts of the Senate and witness the inauguration, first of the Vice-President and then of the President. It was interesting to observe the arrangement on the floor of the Senate. The Senate itself was seated in small chairs on one side of the small chamber, a portion of the other side reserved for the House of Representatives. First appeared the Foreign Ambassadors, duly announced, and the Foreign Ministers, all in their diplomatic gold lace. Then came the Cabinet, then the Justices of the Supreme Court, and then the House of Representatives, and finally the President and President-Elect. In view of the inclement weather it was decided to have the Inauguration ceremonies in the Senate Chamber, instead of at the East front of the Capitol, where they are usually held.[10]

A Loyal Republican

Murphy had other disappointments as well, such as his loss in the Senate race to Joseph Frelinghuysen in 1916. Despite these setbacks, his twilight years were filled with energy and enthusiasm as he vigorously pursued many diverse activities. He would "hit the line hard" but in his own quiet and reserved manner, setting an example to others without lambasting what T.R. would call the "flub-dubs and mollycoddles." He believed in working within the system and to him that meant within the Republican Party. Perhaps his concept of loyalty grew out of his Civil War experience, when survival often depended on the reliability of a comrade; this was an important quality in the character of Franklin Murphy. In a speech delivered at the Dollar Dinner of the Orange Republican Club on May 26, 1910, Murphy expressed his faith in his party. "We meet tonight as Republicans of the old-fashioned, Simon-pure, 100 percent variety. We believe in party and party organization, and we believe in the Republican Party. We glory in what it has done, we are satisfied with what it is trying to do, and we have confidence that it will satisfy the people in what it will do."[11] He openly agreed with President Taft in the direction he was leading the Republican Party and called on the party faithful to support its leadership.

We are not Progressives, although we believe in progress. We are not professional reformers, although we believe in reform, and we are not Insurgents. . . . My friends, the Government is a government by party. Whatever we do for the land we love must be done through the agency of parties. No party has ever served any nation as the Republican Party has served this Nation. Let us purify it when needed; let us strengthen it always. Let us remember all that it has done, and let us believe-as we do believe- that through it may be accomplished the hopes and aspirations of a great and free people.[12]

President Taft was quick to recognize the accomplishments of his predecessor but had a decidedly more conservative approach. He was initially inclined to applaud Roosevelt and said so publicly. "The administration of President Roosevelt, like a great crusade, had awakened the people of the United States, and accomplished great advances in the operations and powers of the Federal Government. It was the business of the administration following his [Taft's business] to make these permanent in the form of law."[13] Murphy had the good fortune of knowing each man personally and his objective perspective is valuable in understanding the two men. He wrote,

Someone has well said that Taft, after Roosevelt, is like the day after the Fourth of July, and because we do not have the noise and the shouting many think little is being accomplished. I wish every man and woman in this country would read Mr. Taft's interview. Their criticism would speedily cease. They would understand the great things that have already been accomplished; they would learn in detail of the intentions of the present administration, and they would come to feel that we have a President who is in sympathy with what the people desire . . .[14]

In June 1912 Murphy went to Chicago to attend the Republican Convention as a member of the National Committee. He supported the conservative side of incumbent President Taft against the "insurgent" forces of Theodore Roosevelt, labeled the Progressive or Bull Moose faction. Roosevelt's aggressive approach, illustrated by his announcement, "My hat is in the ring, I am stripped to the

Franklin Murphy and William Howard Taft circa 1910

waist and I am ready for the fray," alienated many groups that had supported him earlier. As early as 1908 sizable numbers of African-Americans had become disenchanted with their perception of Roosevelt's high-handed approach and were not afraid to say so. Franklin Murphy's diary entry on Tuesday, June 9, 1908, caught the spirit of their sentiments. "It was a hot and wearing day at the Committee. [National Republican] We had more Southern cases and more negro oratory. Some of it was excellent. The negroes appeared to be having a great time, and we listened to them with interest until one of them began to speak of the 'kingly rule at Washington' and the 'high-handed domination of Theodore the First.'"[15] Taft won renomination but the schism resulted in rupturing the Republican Party which led to the election of Democrat Woodrow Wilson. The break between Taft and Roosevelt, once good friends, took place against the backdrop of a complicated scenario of differences both real and perceived. Issues surrounding disputes between

subordinates over conservation, i.e., the Ballinger-Pinchot quarrel, the merits of the Payne-Aldrich Tariff, and the complex power struggle between Speaker of the House "Uncle Joe Cannon" and the progressive members of the House of Representatives all combined to destroy a beautiful friendship and the Republican's hope for victory in 1912.

Lobbying for the Varnish Industry

President Taft had run for President committed to lowering the Dingley Tariff. High tariff rates had raised the prices of consumer goods. In addition, foreign interests were discouraged from selling their wares on the American market, earning American dollars which might have been spent buying

American agricultural surpluses. This potential foreign purchasing power was commonly known as the "Iowa Idea." Accordingly, one of his first acts was to call a special session of Congress to revise the tariff. Lower rates were adopted by the House of Representatives and sent on to the Senate for approval. The "Old Guard" resisted downward revision by tacking on amendments which actually raised some rates. The resulting Payne-Aldrich Tariff Bill was perceived by the progressives on the one hand as a sell-out of Taft's campaign promises, and by the President on the other, to be one of the

When Taft was running for President this group posed on the lawn of Governor Murphy's home. Seated (from left) are: Senator John Keen, Taft, and Senator Frank Briggs. Standing (from left) are: Representative R. Wayne Parker, William H. Wiley, Frank Hitchcock, and Governor Murphy.

best bills ever passed by the Republican Party. Franklin Murphy supported President Taft and believed in the policy of protection for the good of the country. In a speech delivered at the Dollar Dinner of the Orange Republican Club on May 26, 1910, he voiced his opinion on this subject.

The Payne Tariff Bill is criticized with unusual bitterness. It is true this criticism comes mostly from the Free-Traders who do not believe in any tariff, and who apparently would prefer free trade even at the cost of putting hundreds of thousands of

Americans out of employment, with all the untold suffering that would involve. This criticism should be vigorously met by all of us whenever we hear it, not only on public occasions or in formal discussion, but whenever we meet it- in our shops or in our offices or on the streets- for the Payne Bill, passed by a Republican Congress and signed by a Republican President, is precisely what Mr. Taft says it is. It is the best tariff bill ever passed by any Congress. It has generally reduced the duties on necessaries, and the advances, when made, have been generally on luxuries, and it provides, as no bill has done before, for the interests of the people as a whole, for the protection of the American workingman and the necessary revenues of the Government.

He had a legitimate viewpoint as a businessman and was not afraid of acting in his self-interest. For example, he lobbied with the party regulars to keep nut oil off the protection list, an integral ingredient of varnish. Murphy wrote,

I went to Washington this afternoon to see some members of the Senate concerning the proposed Tariff Legislation as it affects the Varnish Industry. The Aldrich Bill proposes a duty of eight cents a gallon on Nut Oil, which has heretofore been free."[16] *"I saw Senators Kean and Briggs, and afterwards Senator Burrows and Mr. Denby, the member of Congress from the Detroit District. I afterward saw Senator Burton, and met the Vice-President . . . Senator Kean brought me favorable news from Senator Aldrich, and I had . . . what was a satisfactory interview with Mr. Smoot. The proposition was to try and get the Finance Committee to make a Committee Amendment eliminating the proposed tariff on Nut Oil.*[17]

The Speaker of the House of Representatives, Joseph Cannon of Illinois, was an arch-conservative who wielded near-dictatorial power over that body. He was the head of the powerful Rules Committee which determined which bills were sent on for consideration by the House. Affectionately dubbed "Uncle Joe," Cannon did not endear himself to the progressives or "insurgents" who wanted progressive legislation pushed through the Congress. George Norris of Nebraska, among others, appealed

to President Taft in their struggle with Cannon. They received an icy reception as "Big Bill" sided with the Speaker. There is some evidence that cooperation between Taft and Cannon was an expedient political arrangement, i.e., a "quid pro quo," but the results bore the bitter fruit of further dividing the Republican Party. Ex-Governor Franklin Murphy stood on the side-lines and supported his friends. His loyalty would have it no other way. There has been much criticism levied at Cannon and his high-handed manner, much of which is no doubt deserved. There was a noble and democratic side to him, however, which often escapes the pen of the historian. Franklin Murphy wrote in his diary recalling a trip he had made to Washington after a visit to the Veterans Home.

. . . we went to the Speaker's Room (Cannon's), and the Speaker was kind enough to leave the chair and come into his room to see us. We had a pleasant half hour with him-partly devoted to Soldiers' Home matters, but more largely to the political outlook and the discussion of the chances of the various candidates for the Presidential nomination. Uncle Joe took a very strong and unselfish view of the situation, recognizing the honor it would be to him, but recognizing also that the interests of the country are superior to the interests of any man. His general talk was that the Delegates should go unpledged, and the nominations decided in the Convention, according to the opinions of the majority as to who might be most available at the time, and in this view I fully shared. Indeed, it is one I have held from the beginning.[18]

Murphy recalled meeting the Speaker on another occasion on the first day of the Republican Convention on June 16, 1908.

. . . that evening Tom McCarter, Senator Briggs, and Frank and I dined together at the Union League Club. As we were coming down in the elevator after dinner, we met "Uncle Joe" Cannon, whom we were very desirous of seeing, to enlist his interest against

a proposed Anti-Injunction plank that was slated for the platform. We went to one side of the great assembly room to talk, but were only fairly started when the Missouri Delegation, headed by Dick Kerens, appeared to pay their respects to the Speaker . . . after the Missouri people departed, we went up to his room in the Club that we might have a little privacy and for about an hour we discussed the situation [political] with great earnestness. To me it was an occasion full of interest, and one that I am not likely soon to forget.[19]

The progressives, allied with the Democrats, finally stripped "Uncle Joe" of most of his power but not before ex-President Roosevelt became convinced that his hand-picked successor had betrayed his legacy.

Richard Ballinger was President Taft's choice for Secretary of the Interior. With the President's approval he had reopened millions of acres of land for private exploitation that former President Roosevelt had set aside for conservation. Chief Forester Gifford Pinchot protested Ballinger's actions and was promptly fired for insubordination. Taft supported his Secretary of the Interior which made him appear, at least in the eyes of Theodore Roosevelt, as a turncoat and enemy of conservation. This was probably the last straw holding together any semblance of friendship between Taft and Roosevelt. Their relationship took a sharp turn for the worse as both men turned to personally attacking the other. Franklin Murphy stood above this quarrel, yet his open association with Taft left little doubt on which side he stood. It wasn't so much a question of conservation for Taft and Murphy but rather, the issue of fidelity and loyalty, qualities expected of subordinates.

The Committee of One Hundred

Franklin Murphy was elected for a final time on May 31, 1916, to the Republican National Committee and attended the convention which was held in Chicago. The Grand Old Party couldn't countenance Roosevelt for what he had done to the party in 1912, and turned instead, to Supreme Court Justice Charles Evans Hughes. Incumbent Woodrow Wilson narrowly defeated the Justice and ex-New York Governor and went on to control the White House for another term. Franklin Murphy served on the Republican National Committee for another two years before resigning in 1918 due to advancing years. He had developed health problems as well, such as a serious knee injury that had left him partially crippled. He remained active for a time in state and local politics. His last important public service contribution to his city was to chair the Committee of One Hundred, to prepare the celebration of the 250th anniversary of the founding of the City of Newark. Fittingly, it was the apogee of a long and distinguished public career in the city that he loved. He addressed his fellow citizens with enthusiasm and optimism on May 17, 1916. "We have arranged what we hope our fellow citizens will regard as a great celebration . . . I happen, by the grace of Mayor Haussling, to be chairman of the full committee . . . with a heart overflowing with your kindness . . . an occasion in which we can take each other by the hand, look each other in the eye, and with a smile in our voice, say: 'Hail and well done.'"[20] Murphy went on to extol the virtues of the nation, the state, and his City of Newark, citing important historical events and individuals who had left their mark. "This is the city in which we live. The city of our grandfathers to many of us, the city of our boyhood to most of us, the city of our affection to all of us . . . We can instill in the hearts of our people the spirit of service, a spirit that when it takes possession of us makes no journey too far and no day too long to accomplish its purpose. A spirit that will lift our city above the material and into the spiritual."[21] Perhaps his closing remarks quoted from an address by Murray Butler, President of Columbia University to the Associated Press, sum up his values best. "Shall we catch sight of that something higher than selfishness, higher than material gain, higher than the triumph of brute force, which alone can lead a nation up to those high places that become sacred in history, and from which influence descends in a mighty torrent, to refresh, to vivify and inspire all mankind?"[22] Murphy believed that Butler's words to the nation applied to his beloved City of Newark and the state of New Jersey.

SECTION 10 SECTION 11 SECTION 44

MASSACHUSETTS ILLINOIS OHIO NEW YORK

MARYLAND NEW JERSEY

TENNESSEE MONTANA VIRGINIA CALIFORNIA

LOUISIANA

The Republican Convention in Chicago, June 7, 1916

Enjoying Retirement

Franklin Murphy's twilight years were filled with diversity. He remained keenly interested in people, cultural activities, and travel. He had cherished friendships acquired over the years and his interest in life never permitted him to tire of new relationships and fresh acquaintances. It would be quite impossible to attempt a list of the many prominent individuals that crossed his path, yet a casual glance at a few of these will serve to illustrate the diversity of his many relationships. Perhaps the most unusual meeting of important New Jersey statesmen took place after the inauguration of Governor Franklin Fort in January 1908. The luncheon that followed was attended by five governors. Murphy remembered the occasion and wrote in his diary,

"After the Inauguration Frank and I went with the invited crowd to the Trenton House, and had lunch with the Statesmen of the day. One of the unusual features of the occasion was the meeting in the same room of five of the Ex-Governors- I think all that are alive- Werts, Griggs, Voorhees, myself and Stokes. We were all photographed, with the new Governor in the center, and the picture appeared in the New York and Newark papers."[23]

He was good friends with Secretary of State Elihu Root and had met Baron Takahira from Japan several months before the two men signed the epochal executive agreement guaranteeing the status quo in the Pacific. He was on pleasant terms with

Franklin Murphy's country home in Mendham, N.J.

George Cortelyou, who was a prominent political figure and served as Secretary to Presidents McKinley and Roosevelt and would become Secretary of Commerce and Labor, Postmaster General, and Secretary of the Treasury in later years. In addition, he was friendly with Senator Henry Cabot Lodge of Massachusetts, Cecil Lyon of Texas and Senator Penrose of Pennsylvania. On a trip to Illinois in June 1908 Murphy had occasion to dine with Senator and Mrs. Scott, Robert Lincoln, Charles G. Dawes, and Colonel Lowden . . . "I found Mr. Lincoln, whom I had never met before, a very interesting man, who seems to carry very well the position naturally given him as the son of his immortal father."[24] On a similar occasion four months later, he would write of Vice-President Charles Fairbanks,

Vice-President Fairbanks arrived this afternoon from Wilmington, at 4:37. I met him at the station and after arriving at the house and a little talk, I took him on an automobile ride through the Parks and Montclair, coming home by the way of Orange and Irvington. Chief Justice Gummere and Doctor Kip joined Frank and me at dinner with the Vice-President. He was most delightful company, as he always is, and the evening after dinner in the library was mostly given up to Army stories told by the Doctor and myself.[25]

On yet another occasion, at a dinner at the Lotos Club in March of 1909, he enjoyed the company of Andrew Carnegie and Mark Twain. "I went down to the Lotos Club tonight to a dinner given by the Club to Andrew Carnegie, as a guest of Colonel Fuller of Jersey City. I had an interesting time, meeting a number of people that I knew, and listening with interest to the speeches of Mr. Carnegie and

The music room of Murphy's Broad Street home in Newark

The library in the Broad Street home, Newark

Mark Twain. It was the first dinner in the Club House."[26]

In the meantime, Murphy had acquired a large rural estate in Mendham, New Jersey, and had employed the famous landscape architect Frederick Law Olmsted, designer of New York's Central Park, with "his partner, Mr. Gallagher and Mr. Rogers of New York, the Engineer, in looking over the Mendham property, and considering the improvements to be made."[27] There were times when Murphy's life seemed linked by destiny to significant future events. He had gone, for example, to New York to

bid his friends the Florences off on their trip to Europe in May of 1909. They had booked passage on the Cunard liner, *Lusitania*. It was this very ship that the German submarine U-20 would sink six years later off the coast of Ireland in May 1915 pulling America closer toward the maelstrom of World War I. "Frank and I went down to New York on the eight o'clock train to see the Florences off. They sailed on the *Lusitania* at ten o'clock. We went over the ship and admired its magnificence, and spent a pleasant hour before the gong sounded for visitors to go ashore.[28]

Franklin Murphy turned his attention increasingly toward cultural interests in his later life. He added a beautiful music room to his home at 1027

Franklin Murphy's study, Newark

Broad Street, Newark, furnishing it exquisitely with the finest amenities of the period. He loved the organ and commissioned the Art Organ Company to build one in his home in April of 1908. He recalled these initial arrangements, "A report recently reached me that the people who are making the new organ for my music room are not responsible, and there is some doubt about the organ being satisfactory. I had ordered it from the Art Organ Company on the endorsement of Steinway. I found that the Art Organ Company were really the representatives of a firm in Ohio named Wirsching. I asked Frank to go out to look the concern over, and he went tonight, with a young man by the name of Ulicsneck, who was formerly employed by them,

and who brought me the reports referred to."[29] Murphy's initial anxiety proved unfounded as the company made good their promise to deliver a quality instrument. It took time, however, and it was not until the following November that the new organ was finished. "The new organ is finished. Mr. Wirsching, the builder, has been here for the last two weeks or more, superintending its erection, and it appears to be all that I expected. Its tone is exquisite, and in volume it is quite all the room will stand. We have tried it several times, and it apparently fulfills all our expectations . . . the furniture is successful, and the family are pleased with it."[30]

Following the custom of the patricians of his time, he commissioned an artist to paint his portrait.

I devoted today to Mr. Smedley. I am having my portrait painted, and after much investigation selected William T. Smedley, a New York Artist of high standing, to do it for me. I desire to get something that will replace the portraits that now hang in the State House and in the dining room. As it was impossible for me to go to Mr. Smedley in New York, I invited him to come over to the house, which he consented to do. He came first on Wednesday, March 25ᵗʰ and worked that day and Thursday and Friday, then again on Monday and Tuesday of this week, and Friday and today, Saturday. He seems likely to get a satisfactory portrait. I am pleased with the man personally, but it is slow work and hard work for me to stand two hours in the morning, and two in the afternoon each day, and, although I have given him what is equivalent to eleven sittings, I fear the portrait is not half completed. I shall not regret it, however, if it turns out all right.[31]

Murphy became increasingly fascinated with the opera and the theater and attended performances whenever the opportunity presented itself. He often mixed business with pleasure as seen in his trip to his varnish factories in Cleveland and Chicago in January 1908. "On Friday night we all dined together at the Auditorium, and in the evening, as Mr. Van Woert's guests, went to see "The Man from Home." It is not often that I attend a theater where I so thoroughly enjoy the play as I did on this occasion. It has been running for many months, and has crowded houses. It is one of the best that I have seen in a long while."[32] His cultural lifestyle that preoccupied his time during his twilight years is illustrated by the schedule he kept between December 10, 1908 and January 23, 1909. In this period of little over a month, Murphy enjoyed performances such as John Drew in *Jack Straw*, Mary Garden in *Pelleas and Mesalinde*, and *Traviata*. He was particularly fond of Ethel Barrymore. He also enjoyed his city's cultural functions such as Newark's Halloween Parade. "This evening is Hallow E'en. Newark appears to be taking up the celebration of this old anniversary, and this year made unusual preparations for it. The parade formed just below the house, and in company with some of the family I saw the procession go by, but it was so dark I could not see some of its more interesting features."[33]

A New England Tour

Murphy delighted in traveling throughout the country both by rail and by automobile and he was constantly on the "go." He often planned trips of a week or more duration, carefully setting an itinerary that brought him to the popular resorts of an area. Although primitive by modern standards, automobile travel had become quite reliable on the eve of World War I, at least during the dry seasons of summer and fall. He was off on one such trip from July 3-13ᵗʰ, 1909.

I started today with some friends on an automobile trip through New England, with the idea of going to Boston by way of New Haven and Springfield, and then to Portland; from there into the White Mountains and over the Green Mountains, and home through the Berkshire Hills. The ostensible purpose of the trip was to attend the July Meeting of the Board of Managers of the Soldiers' Home. The real purpose was to have a week in the open air, with some agreeable companions in the automobile.[34]

He had planned the trip carefully, as he did all his travel excursions. He brought ample spare tires, what he called "rubber shoes and tubes" as well as rain gear "rubber clothing" and heavy blankets for the cool northern climate. His companions included Major Wadsworth and Major Harris of the Home Board, his friend William T. Hunt of Newark, and off course, his faithful driver, Bentley. The group was off at 2:10 P.M. of July 3ʳᵈ, traveling through the Bronx to New Rochelle and the various places of interest on Long Island Sound to New Haven. While crossing the Bronx River, one of the party had his hat blown off. Bentley backed up to retrieve it and bent a strut rod. Murphy thought they were in trouble but his reliable chauffeur fixed it, "Bentley is an

Franklin Murphy circa 1908

The Mount Washington House, another of the White Mountains' major attractions

optimist, and we got along all right." They enjoyed beautiful weather as they traveled all the way to Stamford, impressed with the scenery and the beautiful residences. There were quite a number of newly build roadside inns, built to accommodate the increase in automobile travel. They reached the New Haven Inn about 6:20 P.M. and obtained comfortable rooms and an excellent supper before touring the Yale College buildings. Wadsworth and Hunt were both Yale alumni. Later that evening they enjoyed a Wild West show and "saw some good examples of horsemanship, as well as marksmanship." The next morning they traveled up the Connecticut Valley to Springfield, through Wallingford, Meriden, New Britain and Hartford, where they crossed "the river on one of the finest bridges I know of. It is made of reinforced concrete, has extremely good lines, and is broad and substantial," recalled Murphy.[35] They reached Springfield later that afternoon and had dinner at the Massasoit House. "Wadsworth gave evidence of his simple bringing up on the Farm by eating cold pig's feet, -no wry face about it, either," mused Murphy.[36] They met Governor Long and his family who were also on an automobile trip. After a brief visit, Murphy and his friends continued on, traveling through Palmer, Warren, Worcester and Shrewsbury. They were impressed with the growth of the city of Worcester and the "beauty of the country about Shrewsbury- a small village ten miles east of Worcester."[37] On they went to Boston reaching the Hotel Touraine in time for supper. Murphy brought along his own refreshments and was not about to be caught short. He recalled, "I had some whiskey taken up to the room from the car, as my former experience in Boston led me to believe it would be impossible to get any stimulant that day, as it had always been refused. I was a little surprised, on talking with the bell-boy, to find that there had been a letting-down in the enforcement of the law."[38]

Fabyan House

The next morning (Monday, July 5ᵗʰ) they made their way to the Hotel Wentworth over the Charlestown Bridge to Revere Beach to Lynn, Salem, Newburyport and over the Merrimac River through Salisbury, to Newcastle. That afternoon they drove over the Piscataqua River and visited the navy yard and Fort Stark—"a small fortification, but equipped with modern guns . . . we were surprised to find this important work in charge of a corporal and six men . . . a good dinner and a good cigar finished an enjoyable day."³⁹ July 6ᵗʰ saw the party on their way to Kennebunkport by way of Salisbury Beach, York Beach and Rye Beach. They enjoyed the beauty of the coast of Maine and the well-kept homes which exemplified the Yankee life-styles.

There are two or three moderate sized hotels, but a number of handsome cottages—not especially large or pretentious, but attractive and comfortable, and evidently occupied by people who enjoy the finer side of living . . . It was really a beautiful ride over the rolling country of Maine, down the *Kennebec Valley . . . we found . . . a restaurant, furnishing what in that locality is known as the 'shore dinner', consists principally of a dinner of shell-fish . . . lobster soup . . . broiled chicken . . . then a broiled chicken lobster-a whole one served to each diner.*⁴⁰

Their next destination was Portland and then on to Poland Springs where they enjoyed the accommodations of what Murphy considered to be one of the finest hotels in the world. The capitalist varnish manufacturer admired other entrepreneurial endeavors and wrote of the famous spring. "The next morning after breakfast we went down to see the famous Spring, and found they had "done it proud," just as they should. I was told a year or two ago that the profits of the Rickers on the sale of Poland Water was equivalent to a dividend of six per cent on a capital of fifteen millions. The Spring

The Twin-Mountain House

itself, I was told, flows eight gallons a minute. They bottle most of it, and, large as the sale is, it is as yet not quite sufficient to take it all . . . and the atmosphere of the place does much to increase one's confidence in Poland Spring Water."[41] Their next destination was the Mt. Washington Hotel. They drove through Naples, Bridgeton, Fryeburg and Intervale and on through Crawford Notch to Bretton Woods. Murphy was disappointed by the dense woods which impaired his view of the countryside. This indicates how thoroughly he paid attention to every detail of the landscape and man-made structures. He wrote,

I felt we were losing because we did not have an opportunity to admire the beautiful scenery that was all around us . . . The Mt. Washington (Hotel) is one of the finest of the summer hotels in the United States. It has rooms for about six hundred, but it has accommodations on the first floor for many more than that. In addition to the ordinary equipment of an American plan hotel, it has a restaurant, a palm room, a bathing pool, a bowling alley, a squash court, and a cave grill-which is a sort of a rathskeller down underneath the piazza. We had good rooms and met a number of friends.[42]

By Sunday, July 11 they were off once more driving past the Fabyans and the Twin Mountain House, the Profile House and Flume House, and on through Woodstock where they had a minor break-down. Fortunately, Bentley had an emergency "spring-iron" and fixed the problem. They contin-

A Billy Yank Governor / 194

The Profile House

ued their journey to Sunapee Lake and around the west shore past Granliden and through Newport to the thriving town of Claremont on the Connecticut River where they spent the night in a "comfortable hotel." From there they made their way through Bellows Falls, Brattleboro and Greenfield,

> *down the beautiful Valley of the Connecticut river, through these prosperous places, over excellent roads . . . it was indeed a joy to strike the excellent roads of the latter part of our journey . . . In the evening on the porch (of the Aspinwall Hotel), Major Harris and I had a good old-fashioned visit together, where we discussed pretty nearly every subject under the sun, from the incongruity of Henry the Eighth establishing the Episcopal Church, to the cleanliness, or the want of cleanliness, of the American Indian,—but it was a nice old-fashioned visit, just the same.*[43]

Murphy returned home on July 13th on the Harlem Road by way of Stockbridge, Great Barrington, South Egremont, and on through Mt. Kisco. As they went "gaily along" through White Plains to Mount Vernon they were stopped for speeding as an "all too inquisitive cop on a motor cycle rode up to the machine and inquired if we knew how fast we were going. I left a fifty dollar bill as bail and Bentley's promise to appear next night in court."[44] Murphy paid the fine proving that he was not above a law which he had so strongly advocated when he was Governor. He returned home in time for dinner and considered "the trip, upon the whole, was distinctly enjoyable . . . the party congenial, and the weather without a flaw."[45]

195 / *The Twilight Years*

Hotel Royal Poinciana

The Royal Poinciana Tea Garden

Florida Vacations

The years took their toll and Murphy's health and stamina began to wane. He sought relief from the rigors of his business and the harsh winter climate of New Jersey by traveling by train to Palm Beach, Florida. "I had not been feeling quite up to standard for a month or two, and had thought more or less of a vacation" [46] He left Newark's Market Street Station on the Pullman car "Rover" with his daughter, Helen, her husband Billy, and their three children. He approved of the changes that had been recently made to the Pullman cars. They had been divided into staterooms and a large "observation end," which served as both a dining room and living room during the day. Murphy considered this a significant improvement over the cars which had the dining room in the center and a much smaller observation room at the end. They were off, going south over the "Southern Road" through Lynchburg, Charlotte, Columbia, Savannah and Jacksonville. The train stopped for a half hour at Columbia, South Carolina. The memories of the devastation of the city must have crystallized in Murphy's mind. He could not help but recall the fires that had engulfed the buildings as he marched with Sherman's army forty three years before. In some ways the city still bore the scares, at least it seemed so to Murphy, as he considered it to be "a dreadful looking town . . . I assume, as a matter of course, that we saw the worst of it."[47] He was happy to be on his way and his spirits rose with the warm weather as they reached the Florida line. The countryside was adorned with peach and cherry blossoms. They spent about three hours in Jacksonville taking in the sites, noticing particularly how the city had become a metropolis and was no longer a winter resort. Murphy wrote in his diary, "I had a very interesting driver-colored, of course, who described in his own darky way the development of Jacksonville."[48] It was then on to Saint Augustine and Ormond. Ormond was famous during the years prior to World War I for its automobile races on the beach. Murphy seemed interested in everything and insisted on learning as much about whatever he came across. "We had a twenty mile ride on the beach over which the cars were to run and I learned on inquiry why Ormond was chosen for

Franklin Murphy circa 1910

Franklin Murphy statue at Weehaquic Park, Newark

these races. The beach is not a beach of sand as it is on the Jersey Coast, but made up of infinite small coquina shells. As soon as the tide reaches these shells, they become packed so hard that the tire of the heaviest car makes but a slight impression on them, and yet there is just enough elasticity to help the car along."[49]

After examining the beach, he rode up the Halifax River for about six miles to Bacon's Orange Grove, over a road covered with pine needles through groves of beautiful palms and orange trees. Murphy met Mr. Bacon who showed him over his grove pointing out the many different fruits and flowers. Bacon was happy when Murphy bought "all the marmalade and jelly that I thought we should be able to pay for."[50] They were soon back on the train speeding its way to Palm Beach where they arrived on Tuesday morning, March 3rd. They were greeted at the station by porters who took them to the hotel Royal Poinciana. It was a magnificent resort. Murphy recalled the impression it made on his party. "The Royal Poinciana astonished the members of our party who had never been there, as it does every first visitor."[51] It was over a quarter of a mile long. It was six or seven stories high with numerous wings and had some twelve hundred rooms. Its freshly painted white exterior and scrupulous cleanliness reminded Murphy of the White Mountain hotels of New Hampshire. He recalled meeting friends

everywhere; I should say more than fifty that I knew shook hands with me before night . . . the scene was one of indescribable beauty of what a western man would call "the outfit" . . . Everything that experience and taste and money, combined with the help of a favoring sun and a glorious climate, could provide for the delectation (I believe I have never used that word before, but this is the place to use it) of the visitors was there in perfection, and one seemed to desire a larger than normal capacity for enjoyment, in order that it all might be appreciated.[52]

Murphy often spent the afternoons enjoying ball games played by African-American athletes representing the various hotels. He recalled one such game where the "Breakers" beat the "Poinciana"

Franklin Murphy papers

Franklin Murphy and granddaughter, Janet, at the shore

team by a score of 4 to 3. Evenings were frequently spent in the Club House watching the "wheels go round." Murphy was not much of a gambler but was known, on occasion, to "contribute $20.00 to the support of the house."[53] His grandchildren, whom he affectionately referred to as the babies, were a continuous joy to his life. He wrote what "a comfort they were to me."[54]

Murphy was always on the lookout for something new and exciting. He discovered a favorite Palm Beach pastime; a "wheeled chair." This was a type of bicycle. He described it in his diary, "The thing to do at Palm Beach is to take a wheeled chair, which is of bicycle construction, the bicycle being on the rear and propelled by a darky, who takes you through the various roads and paths."[55] He visited Langhorne's Orange Grove this way and learned from the proprietor the origin of his coconuts. It seems that a ship had been stranded on the Florida beach loaded with coconuts for the northern market. Langhorne and some of his neighbors managed to gather up some sixteen thousand of them and plant them all over the neighborhood where they took hold and flourished. Murphy's analytical mind and business mentality soon determined that a coconut tree yielded 200 to 300 coconuts that could be sold to northern visitors for between 25 and 50 cents. He wrote, "with a few hundred orange trees on the side, it looks as though life in that neighborhood ought to be satisfactory."[56] Other days were spent enjoying the flora and fauna at the Garden of Eden or a sail on the lake until it was time to return home. How thoroughly he enjoyed his visit can been seen in his comment, "How much time one might spend with comfort at Palm Beach, I don't know, but our . . . days were delightful."[57] He returned home after two weeks of a most enjoyable vacation. His future trips to Florida became less frequent and his activities decidedly less rigorous. The years had taken their toll and he found himself slowing up and often not feeling well. He was plagued with a bad knee, injured years before when his horse stumbled and rolled over him and bouts of indigestion, which increasingly kept him up at night. As his overall health continued to decline, he turned over most of his business activities to his son, Frank Jr. He was determined to make another trip to Florida in hopes that the climate would restore his health. It, of course, could not.

To the Ages

While on a visit to the Royal Poinciana, his favorite resort in Palm Beach, he was stricken with severe abdominal distress. He was diagnosed with a serious intestinal obstruction which required immediate surgery. The operation was performed by Dr. Samuel Gant of New York, assisted by Dr. H.C. Russell of New York and Dr. Sherman Downs of Saratoga. The initial prognosis seemed favorable but complications soon developed and Murphy slumped into a coma, from which he never recovered. He died on February 24th, 1920, at the age of seventy-four. He now belonged, as Secretary of War Edwin Stanton had said of Lincoln, "to the ages." He was brought back to Newark and laid to rest in Mount Pleasant Cemetery. Thus ended the life of a man who, like Theodore Roosevelt, was "exactly right for his times," always living life to its fullest. He left a legacy filled with patriotism, of honesty, of decency, and integrity. He believed in public service, free entrepreneurial capitalism and what a later president would call, "rugged individualism." He always tempered these values with a gentle eye for those less fortunate. Above all, he believed in traditional family values; of fidelity and loyalty and morality. These all combined to set an example for future generations of Americans, to those who may study his life and perhaps, wish to follow in his footsteps "in the fairest land the sun ever shone upon."

In November 1925 a statue was dedicated to the memory of Franklin Murphy at Weequahic Park, New Jersey. The following inscription appears thereon:

"A friend of humanity endowed with rare civil zeal and executive foresight; an organizer and leader among men. Governor of this State 1902-1905."[58]

APPENDICES

Endnotes

Chapter 1

1. Viola, Herman J., *The National Archives of the United States*. New York, Harry N. Abrams, Inc., 1984, 14.

2. Bailey, Thomas. ed., *The American Spirit*. Lexington, MA: D.C. Heath Company, 1969, 273.

3. Donald, David, *Charles Sumner and the Coming of the Civil War*. Norwalk, CT: Easton Press, 1960, 118.

4. Joseph, Alvin M. Jr., *The Indian Heritage of America*. New York: Alfred A. Knopf Pub., 1969, 327.

5. Rostow, W.W. 3rd ed., *The Stages of Economic Growth: A Non-Communist Manifesto*. Cambridge, MA: Cambridge University Press, 1970, 36-37.

6. Barabba, Vincent P., *Historical Statistics of the U.S. Colonial Times to 1970*. U.S. Department of Commerce Bureau of the Census, 1975, 106.

7. Nevins, Allan, *Ordeal of the Union: A House Dividing 1852-1857. Vol. II*. New York: Scribner's Sons: 1947, 254.

8. McPherson, James M., *Battle Cry of Freedom, The Civil War Era*. New York, Oxford: Oxford University Press, 1988, 19.

9. *Ibid*, 251.

10. *The Smithsonian Experience Science-History-The Arts Treasures of the Nation*. New York: W.W. Norton & Company, 1977, 23.

11. Nevins, Allan, *Ordeal of the Union: A House Dividing 1852-1857. Vol. II*. 269.

12. Hunt, Livingston Rear Admiral Retired, *The Attempted Mutiny on the U.S. Brig "Somers."* U.S. Naval Institute Proceedings, 2100. Text provided by Alice S. Creighton-Head, Special Collections & Archives Nimitz Library U.S. Naval Academy.

13. Kobler, John, *The Rise and Fall of Prohibition*. New York: DaCapo Press, 1973, 81.

14. Cunningham, John T., *Newark*. Newark, New Jersey: The New Jersey Historical Society; 1988, 133.

15. Garraty, John A., *A Short History of the American Nation*. New York, Reading, MA, Menlo Park, CA: Addison Wesley Longman Inc., 1997, 186.

16. Gurko, Miriam, *The Ladies of Seneca Falls, The Birth of the Women's Rights Movement*. Norwalk, CT: Easton Press, 1974, 75.

17. *Ibid*, 75-76.

18. Cunningham, John T., *New Jersey's Main Road*. Garden City, New York: Doubleday & Company, 1965, 162-163.

19. Sculley, Bradley, Richard Croom Beatty, and E. Hudson Long, ed., *The American Tradition of Literature. Vol. I 3rd ed*. New York: W.W. Norton & Company, 1967, 1544.

20. *Ibid*, 1492.

21. Miller, Edwin Haviland, *Melville*. New York: George Braziller, Inc., 1975, 120.

22. Sculley, Bradley, Richard Croom Beatty and E. Hudson Long ed., *The American Tradition of Literature. Vol. I.*, 505.

23. Sculley, Bradley, Richard Croom Beatty and E. Hudson Long ed., *The American Tradition of Literature. Vol. II.*, 15.

24. Brinkley, Alan, *The Unfinished Nation*. New York, St. Louis, San Francisco: McGraw Hill, 1993, 308.

25. Garraty, John A. and Robert A. McCaughy, *The American Nation, A History of the United States*. New York: Harper & Row, 1987, 336; Eliot, Alexander, *Three Hundred Years of American Painting*. New York: Time Inc., 1957, 70-74.

26. *U.S. Military Academy Cadet Application Papers, 1805-1866*, Microfilm Pub. 688; Einstein, Alfred, *Music in the Roman-tic Era*. New York: W.W. Norton & Company Inc., 1947, 331; Chase, Gilbert, *American Music From the Pilgrims to the Present*. New York: McGraw Hill, 1955, 282-300.

27. Vexler, Robert I., and William F. Swindler, *Chronology & Documentary Handbook of the State of New Jersey*. Dobbs Ferry, New York: Oceana Pub. Inc.,1978, 21.

28. Valente, George, *The Wreck of the Ship John Minturn. Coast Fifty Anniversary Collector's Edition* June 1989: 62. Text provided by Michael Fowler, Professor Brookdale Community College.

29. Vexler, Robert I. and William F. Swindler, *Chronology & Documentary Handbook of the State of New Jersey*, 21.

30. Doane, George Washington, The Right Reverend Bishop of New Jersey, *"The Goodly Heritage of Jerseymen."* The First Annual Address before the New Jersey Historical Society January 1846. New Jersey Historical Society Reprint-Franklin Murphy Papers, in private possession.

31. Elizabeth LaFetra, Diary, entry of January 3, 1846, Rutgers University Libraries Special Collections and University Archives, text provided by Edward Skipworth.

32. Eaton, Harriet P., et al., *Jersey City & Its Historical Sites*, quoted in Wacker, Peter O., *Land And People-A Cultural Geography of Pre-Industrial New Jersey: Origins and Settlement Patterns*. New Brunswick: Rutgers University Press, 1975, 239.

33. Barber & Howe, *Historical Collections of New Jersey*. New York: S. Tuttle, 1844, 230.

34. Leiby, Adrian C., *The Early Dutch and Swedish Settlers of New Jersey*. Princeton: D. Van Nostrand Co., 1964 quoted in Wacker, Peter O., *Land And People A Cultural Geography of Pre-Industrial New Jersey: Origins And Settlement Patterns*. New Brunswick: Rutgers University Press, 1975, 123.

35. Barber & Howe. *Historical Collections of New Jersey*, 231.

36. *Ibid*, 231.

37. Gillette, William, *Jersey Blue Civil War Politics in New Jersey*. New Brunswick: Rutgers University Press, 1995, 14.

38. *Ibid*, 33.

39. Lewis, A.S., ed., *My Dear Parents The Civil War Seen By An English Soldier* by James Horrocks. San Diego, New York, London: Harcourt, Brace Jovanovich, 1982, 37. Text provided by Dr. Gregory Halligan.

40. Bailyn, Bernard, et al., *The Great Republic A History of the American People*. Boston, Toronto; Little Brown & Company, 1977, 759.

41. Franklin Murphy Papers-*extracts from* "Colonial Wars" *speech*, 18 and "Battle of Monmouth Anniversary" *speech*, 15, in private possession.

42. Quoted from the Franklin Murphy Papers, Genealogy in private possession.

43. For a more detailed discussion of these events in English history see Lunt, W.E., *History of England* 4th ed. New York, London: Harper & Row Pub., 1956, 220, 231-233.

44. Quoted from the Franklin Murphy Papers-Genealogy in private possession.

45. Quoted from Franklin Murphy Papers-Genealogy in private possession.

46. *Ibid.*

47. Barber & Howe, *Historical Collections of New Jersey*, 175.

48. Franklin Murphy Colonial Wars Speech at Lakewood, NJ, May 6, 1910, 11. Franklin Murphy Papers, in private possession.

49. Barber & Howe, *Historical Collections of New Jersey*, 182-183.

50 Franklin Murphy Newark Exposition Speech, May 17, 1916, 15. Franklin Murphy Papers, in private possession.

51. Kull, Irving S., Editor-In-Chief, *New Jersey, A History*. New York: The American Historical Society, 1930, 592.

52. *Ibid,* 592.

53. Nevins, Allan, *Ordeal of the Union A House Dividing 1852-1857.* Vol. II., 251.

54. Kull, Irving S., ed. *New Jersey, A History*, 592.

55. Doane, George Washington, *Goodly Heritage of Jerseymen.* ed., Edmund Morris 1846. Reprint New Jersey Historical Society, 9.

56. *Ibid,* 19.

57. Shaffer, Leon, *Business Relations of Newark With The South to 1861*, quoted in Kull, Irving S., Editor-In-Chief, *New Jersey, A History. Vol. II*. New York: The American Historical Society, 1930, 742.

58. *Ibid,* 242-243, For a detailed discussion of the views of Newark's clergy and examples.

59. Franklin Murphy, The Cost of the War Speech delivered at St. Paul's M.E. Church May 27, 1894, 4. Franklin Murphy Papers, in private possession.

60. *New York Tribune* May 2, 1861, quoted in Gillette, William, *Jersey Blue Civil War Politics In New Jersey*, 4.

61. Geissler, Suzanne, *A Widening Sphere of Usefulness Newark Academy 1774-1993*. West Kennebunk, Maine: Phoenix Publishing, 1993, 9.

62. *Ibid,* 9.

63. Cunningham, John T., *Newark*. Newark: New Jersey Historical Society, 1988, 94.

64. Geissler, Suzanne, *A Widening Sphere of Usefulness, Newark Academy, 1774-1993*, 9.

65. Pessen, Edward, *Jacksonian American Society, Personality, and Politics*. Homewood, IL: the Dorsey Press, 1969, 90-91.

66. *Ibid,* 91.

67. Geissler, Suzanne, *A Widening Sphere of Usefulness, Newark Academy, 1774-1993*, 53.

68. *Ibid,* 53.

69. Quoted from *The Fourth Annual Circular of the Newark Academy with Catalogue and Program of the Course of Instruction, July 1862*. Newark, New Jersey *Daily Adviser Office*, 16. New Jersey Historical Society, Newark, NJ.

70. Best, John Hardin and Robert T. Sidwell, ed., *The American Legacy of Learning-Readings in the History of Education*. Philadelphia-New York: J.B. Lippincott Company, 1967, 202.

71. *Ibid,* 203.

72. *Ibid,* 205.

73. Cunningham, John T., *Newark*, 94.

74. Franklin Murphy The Cost of the War Speech delivered at St. Paul's M.E. Church May 27, 1894, 3. Franklin Murphy Papers, in private possession.

75. McPherson, James M., *For Cause and Comrades Why Men Fought in the Civil War*. Oxford-New York: Oxford University Press, 1997, 104.

76. Franklin Murphy Speech delivered at Antietam, Maryland, September 17, 1903, 17. Franklin Murphy Papers, in private possession.

77. Franklin Murphy Colonial War's Speech at Lakewood, New Jersey, May 6, 1910, 17. Franklin Murphy Papers, in private possession.

Chapter 2

1. Brunt, P.A., *Thucydides The Peloponnesian Wars*. New York: Washington Square Press, Inc. 1963, ix Introduction. First published in manuscript in Greek circa 400 B.C.

2. *Ibid.*

3. Franklin Murphy, "Cost Of The War" speech delivered at Saint Paul's M.E. Church, Newark, New Jersey, May 27, 1894, 3. Franklin Murphy Papers in private possession.

4. *Pollard's Southern History of the War.* Quoted in Foster, John Y., *New Jersey and the Rebellion, A History of the Services of the Troops & People of New Jersey in Aid of the Union Cause.* Newark, New Jersey: Martin R. Dennis & Company, 1868, 2.

5. "The Course of American History," an address delivered by Professor Woodrow Wilson. Semi-Centennial Celebration of the founding of the New Jersey Historical Society at Newark, New Jersey, May 16, 1895, 188.

6. Commanger, Henry Steel, ed., *Documents of American History,* 7th edition. New York: Appleton-Century-Crofts, 1962, 442.

7. Foster, John Y., *New Jersey and the Rebellion: A History of the Services of the Troops and People of New Jersey in Aid of the Union Cause,* 27.

8. *Ibid,* 17.

9. *Ibid,* 27.

10. *Ibid,* 27.

11. *Ibid,* 30.

12. Franklin Murphy speech at Antietam, Maryland, September 17, 1903, 6. Franklin Murphy Papers in private possession.

13. Spader, P. Vanderbilt, *Weather Record For New Brunswick, New Jersey 1847-1890*. Somerville, New Jersey: Press of the *Union Gazette*, 1890, 73. Rutgers University Special Collections and University Archives text provided by Edward Skipworth.

14. Franklin Murphy Enlistment Document. New Jersey Archives, Department of State.

15. Marbaker, Thomas D. Sergeant, Company E., *History of the 11th NJ Volunteers from its Organization to Appomattox to which is added Experiences of Prison Life and Sketches of Individual Members*. MacCrellish & Quingley, Book & Job Printers, 1898. Reprint, Hightstown: Longstreet House, 1990, New Introduction by John W. Kuhl.

16. Pierson, David Lawrence, *Narratives of Newark In New Jersey from the Days of its Foundings*. Newark, New Jersey: Pierson Publishing Company, 1917, 292-295.

17. *Ibid.*; See also Urquhart, Frank, *A History of the City of Newark New Jersey Embracing Practically Two and a half Centuries, 1666-1913*. Volume II The Lewis Historical Publishing Company. New York, Chicago, 1913, 722-723.

18. Sergeant Albert C. Harrison, Alberton, Howard County, Maryland, to his mother in Red Bank, New Jersey September 14, 1862. Albert C. Harrison Papers in private possession.

19. Private Jacob Wolcott, Camp Vredenburgh near Freehold, New Jersey, to Friend Powers August 24, 1862. Private Jacob Wolcott Papers NJ Historical Society. Newark, New Jersey.

20. *Newark Daily Advertiser,* September 22, 1862, quoted in Siegel, Alan A., *For The Glory of the Union Myth, Reality, and the Media in Civil War New Jersey.* Cranbury, New Jersey: Associated University Presses, 1984, 207.

21. Shaw, William H., *History of Essex and Hudson Counties, New Jersey,* Volume I. Philadelphia: Everts & Peck, 1884, 136. Text provided by Edward Skipworth, Rutgers Special Collections University Archives.

22. Franklin Murphy, "Cost Of The War," speech delivered at Saint Paul's M.E. Church May 27, 1894, 9-10. Franklin Murphy Papers in private possession.

23. *New York Daily Tribune,* September 20, 1862, quoted in Hart, Albert Bushnell, ed. *American History Told by Contemporaries,* Volume IV, *Welding of the Nation 1845-1900.* New York, London: Macmillan Company, 1964, 347.

24. McPherson, James M., *For Cause and Comrades, Why Men Fought in the Civil War.* New York: Oxford University Press, 1997, 30-31, 33; McCagne, James, *Moguls and Iron Man, the Story of the First Transcontinental Railroad.* Norwalk, CT: Easton Press, 1964, 34.

25. *Newark Sunday News,* April 21, 1951, 74; see also Franklin Murphy Memorial Recorded at length in the *Journal of the Senate* by Clarence E. Case, President of the Senate, attest William H. Allbright Secretary of the Senate. Trenton, New Jersey: March 1, 1920, 14.

26. Foster, John Y., *New Jersey and the Rebellion,* 318.

27. McPherson, James M., *Battle Cry of Freedom, The Civil War Era.* New York: Oxford University Press, 1988, 544.

28. Franklin Murphy speech at Antietam, Maryland, September 17, 1903, 10. Franklin Murphy Papers in private possession.

29. *Ibid,* 12.

30. *Ibid,* 11.

31. Toombs, Samuel, *Reminiscences of the Thirteenth Regiment New Jersey Volunteers,* New Introduction by David G. Martin. Orange, New Jersey, 1878. Reprint Number 207, Heightstown, New Jersey: Longstreet House, 1994, 25-26. Original edition printed at the Journal Office 1878.

32. Colonel Carman to Captain Smith September 24, 1862, New Jersey Historical Society, Newark, New Jersey.

33. Franklin Murphy "Cost of the War Speech," 12-13. Franklin Murphy Papers in private possession.

34. Bradford, Ned, ed., *Battles & Leaders of the Civil War.* New York: Appleton-Century-Crofts, Inc., 1956, 260.

35. Toombs, Samuel, *Reminiscences of the Thirteenth Regiment New Jersey Volunteers,* 31.

36. Major Peter Vredenburgh, Jr., 14th New Jersey Volunteers from Camp Hooker, Monocacy, Maryland, to his mother in Freehold, New Jersey, September 19, 1862. Monmouth County Historical Association Library & Archives, Collection 1, Peter Vredenburgh Papers.

37. Toombs, 31.

38. Stryker, William S., *Record of Officers and Men of New Jersey in the Civil War 1861-1865, Vol. I.* Compiled in the Office of the Adjutant General. Published by the Authority of the Legislature: Trenton, New Jersey: Steam Book and Job Printers, 1876, 684.

39. Toombs, 41; See also Brandford, Ned, ed., *Battles & Leaders of the Civil War,* 591.

40. Franklin, John Hope, *From Slavery to Freedom: A History of Negro Americans.* New York: Alfred A. Knopf, 1967, 287.

41. Toombs, 47.

42. *Ibid.*

43. McPherson, James M., *Battle Cry of Freedom,* 644.

44. Toombs, 53.

45. *The War of the Rebellion:Official Records of the Union and Confederate Armies,* First Series (Washington), 1889, XXV, pt. i, 795-803, passim quoted in: *American History Told by Contemporaries,* Volume IV, *Welding of the Nation, 1845-1900.*ed. Hart, Albert Bushnell. New York, London: The MacMillian Company, 1896, 190l, 1924,1929,1964,363.

46. Toombs, 54.

47. McPherson, James M., *Battle Cry of Freedom,* 645.

48. Toombs, 62.

49. Franklin Murphy "Cost of the War" speech, 18-20, in private possession.

50. Catton, Bruce, *Never Call Retreat: The Centennial History of the Civil War,* Volume III. Garden City, New York: Doubleday & Company, 1965, 94.

51. Toombs, 68-69.

52. *Ibid,* 80.

53. Catton, Bruce, *Gettysburg: The Final Fury.* Norwalk, Connecticut: The Easton Press, 1974, 1986, 75.

54. *Ibid.*

55. Foster, John Y., *New Jersey and the Rebellion,* 326.

56. Hart, Albert Bushnel, *American History Told by Contemporaries,* Volume IV, *Welding of the Nation,1845-1900,* 375.

57. White, Edward G., *Justice Oliver Wendell Holmes Law and the Inner Self.* New York: Oxford University Press, 1993, 61.

58. Commanger Henry Steele, ed., *Documents of American History,* 429.

59. Sergeant Albert C. Harrison from Camp of the 14th New Jersey Volunteers, Bailey's Cross Roads, near Washington, D.C. to his cousin Clemmy in New York City, June 7, 1865. Sergeant Albert C. Harrison Papers in private possession.

60. Franklin Murphy address to the Carriage Builders' National Association, September 22, 1903, in response to the Address of Welcome made by Lieutenant Governor Curtis Guild, Jr., 4. Franklin Murphy Papers in private possession.

61. Bradford, Ned, ed., *Battles and Leaders of the Civil War,* 592.

62. Franklin, John Hope, *From Slavery to Freedom, A History of Negro Americans.* New York: Alfred A. Knopf, 1967, 279; see also Randall, J.G., David Donald, *The Civil War & Reconstruction.* Lexington, Massachusetts: D.C. Heath & Company, 1969, 316-317.

63. Hart, Albert Bushnel, *American History Told by Contemporaries,* Volume IV, *Welding of the Nation 1845-1900,* 376-377.

64. M.A. Day to James Augustus Grimstead, August 26, 1863. James Augustus Grimstead Papers in private possession.

65. Toombs, 86.

Chapter 3

1. Marszalek, John F., Sherman, *A Soldier's Passion For Order.* New York: The Free Press, a Division of Macmillan, Inc. 1993, 260-261.

2. Foster, John Y., *New Jersey and the Rebellion,* 331.

3. James Bullman, Company C, 14th New Jersey Volunteers, letter home to his family in New Jersey, May 17, 1863. James Bullman Papers, copies provided by Steven Freeman in private possession.

4. Confederate Veteran, Volume 10, 412. Information provided by Rebecca A. Ebert, Archive Librarian at the Handley Library, Winchester, Virginia.

5. Foster, John Y., *New Jersey and the Rebellion*, 329.

6. Hart, B.H. Liddell, *Sherman, Soldier, Realist, American*. Westport, Connecticut: Greenwood Press, 1978, 231.

7. Franklin Murphy speech, "The Republican Party in National Politics" 1900, 11. Franklin Murphy Papers in private possession.

8. Hart, B.H. Liddell, *Sherman, Soldier, Realist, American*, 239.

9. Toombs, 131.

10. Foster, John Y., *New Jersey and the Rebellion*, 322.

11. Sherman quoted in Hart, B.H. Liddell, Sherman, Soldier, Realist, American, 255.

12. Lieutenant William Burroughs Ross, 14th New Jersey Volunteers, letter to his father in Freehold, New Jersey, from the Wilderness near Chancellorsville, Virginia, May 9, 1864. Monmouth County Historical Association Library & Archives, Collection 9, William Burroughs Ross Papers.

13. M.A. Day from Brooklyn, New York, May 22, 1864, to Private James Augustus Grimstead, 14th New Jersey Volunteers. James Augustus Grimstead Papers in private possession.

14. Poem "Do They Miss Me At Home" written by James Bullman 14th New Jersey Volunteers-killed in action at Cold Harbor, VA, June 1, 1864. James Bullman Papers in private possession copies provided by Steven Freeman.

15. Marszalek, John F., Sherman, *A Soldier's Passion for Order*, 267.

16. Hart, B.H. Liddell, *Sherman, Soldier, Realist, American*, 264.

17. Letter written by a Union soldier identified only as George-no date. James Augustus Grimstead Papers in private possession.

18. McPherson, James M., *For Cause and Comrades, Why Men Fought in the Civil War*, 36.

19. Franklin Murphy, "Cost of the War Speech" delivered at Saint Paul's M.E. Church, May 27, 1894, 20. Franklin Murphy Papers in private possession.

20. Sherman quoted in Hart, B.H. Liddell, *Sherman, Soldier, Realist, American*, 266.

21. Cox, Jacob D. late Major-General commanding the 23rd Army Corps, *Sherman's Battle For Atlanta*-new introduction by Brooks D. Simpson. New York: DaCapo Press, 1864, 1994, 129; Markham, Felex, *Napoleon*. New York: Mentor Publishing, 1966, 37.

22. Toombs, 145.

23. Long, A.L., *Memoirs of Robert E. Lee, His Military and Personal History*. Secaucus, New Jersey: The Blue and Grey Press, 1983, 681; see also Donald, David Herbert, *Lincoln*. New York: Simon and Schuster, 1995, 531.

24. Castel, Albert, *Decision in the West, The Atlanta Campaign of 1864*. Lawrence, Kansas: University Press of Kansas: 1992, 365.

25. *Ibid*, 376-377.

26. *Ibid*, 380.

27. Toombs, 159.

28. Cox, Jacob D., *Sherman's Battle For Atlanta*, 159.

29. *Ibid*; see also Castel, Albert, *Decision in the West, the Atlanta Campaign of 1864*, 398-399.

30. Fellman, Michael, *Citizen Sherman, A Life of William Tecumseh Sherman*. New York: Random House, 1995, 323; see also Official Records Series I, Volume XLVII, Part III, 517.

31. Cox, Jacob D., *Sherman's Battle For Atlanta*, 183.

32. William Brown quoted in Tarbell, Ida M., *He Knew Lincoln*. New York: Mcclure, Phillips & Company, 1907, 24.

33. Sergeant Albert C. Harrison Company G. 14th NJ Volunteers to his mother and father in Red Bank, New Jersey, October 23, 1864. Papers in private possession.

34. Franklin Murphy speech at Antietam, Maryland, September 17, 1903, 15. Franklin Murphy Papers in private possession.

35. Abraham Lincoln to Albert G. Hodges April 14, 1864, quoted in Donald, David, Herbert, *Lincoln*. New York: Simon and Schuster, 1995, introduction.

36. Jefferson Davis to General John Bell Hood quoted in Castel, Albert, *Decision in the West, the Atlanta Campaign of 1864*, 448.

37. Cousin Amanda from Stockholm, New Jersey, to Cousin Frank Grimstead, November 1, 1861. James Augustus Grimstead Papers in private possession.

38. Private James Augustus Grimstead, Company C 14th New Jersey Volunteers, Five Miles from Fairfax Station, Virginia, to My Dear Brother Frank, Sabbath October 18, 1863. James Augustus Grimstead Papers in private possession.

39. Castel, Albert, *Decision in the West, the Atlanta Campaign of 1864*, 464.

40. *Ibid*, 461.

41. Toombs, 164.

42. Woodward, C. Van, ed., *Mary Chesnut's Civil War*. New Haven: Yale University Press, 1981, 642.

43. Toombs, 170.

44. Freidel, Frank, ed., *Union Pamphlets of the Civil War 1861-1865*. Cambridge, Massachusetts: Belknap Press of Harvard University, 1961, 1099-1100.

45. General Hood to General Sherman and response quoted in Marszalek, John F., *Sherman, A Soldier's Passion For Order*, 285; see also Hart, B.H. Liddell, *Sherman, Soldier, Realist, American*, 429.

46. *Official Records*, Series I, Volume 44, 977.

47. Hart, Albert Bushnell, ed., *American History Told by Contemporaries*, Volume IV, Welding of the Nation, 1845-1900, 429.

48. Toombs, 175.

49. Foster, John Y., *New Jersey and the Rebellion*, 340.

50. *Ibid*, 341.

51. Cousin Amanda from Stockholm, New Jersey, to Cousin Frank Grimstead, November 1, 1861. James Augustus Grimstead Papers in private possession.

52. Toombs, 184.

53. Letter from Federal soldier signed only George from Camp Seminary, Virginia, to James Augustus Grimstead in Metuchen, New Jersey, August 28, 1861. James Augustus Grimstead Papers in private possession.

54. Davis, Burke, *Sherman's March*. New York: Random House, 1980, 103-105.

55. Sherman quoted in Davis, Burke, *Sherman's March*, 105.

56. Raphael Semmes quoted in Spencer, Warren F., *Raphael Semmes, The Philosophical Mariner*. Tuscaloosa, London: University of Alabama Press, 1997, 181.

57. Woodward, C. Van, ed., *Mary Chesnut's War*, 623.

58. Sergeant Albert C. Harrison Company G 14th NJ Volunteers to his parents in Red Bank, New Jersey, March 31, 1865. Sergeant Albert C. Harrison Papers in private possession.

59. Fehrenbacher, Don E., *Abraham Lincoln Speeches and Writings 1859-1865, Speeches, Letters, and Miscellaneous Writings, Presidential Messages and Proclamations*. New York: The Library of America, 1989, 665. Text in this volume is from the *Collected works of Abraham Lincoln*, ed. Basler, Roy P., 1953; see also *Memoirs of General Sherman*. Saint Louis, Missouri, January 21, 1875, 231.

60. Franklin Murphy, "The Cost of the War Speech" delivered at Saint Paul's M.E. Church, May 27, 1894, 13-14. Franklin Murphy Papers in private possession.

61. Glatthaar, Joseph T., *The March to the Sea and Beyond, Sherman's Troops in the Savannah and Carolina's Campaigns*. New York, London: New York University Press, 1985, 105.

62. Fellman, Michael, *Citizen Sherman, A Life of William Tecumseh, Sherman*, 223; see also Marszalek, John F. Sherman, *A Soldier's Passion for Order*, 320.

63. Simms, William Gilmore, *Sack and Destruction of the City of Columbia, South Carolina*. Edited with notes by Salley, A.S., Freeport, New York: Books for Libraries Press, 1937, 1971, 28.

64. Toombs, 198.

65. Glatthaar, Joseph T., *The March to the Sea and Beyond, Sherman's Troops in the Savannah and Carolina's Campaigns*, 142.

66. McPherson, James M., *Battle Cry of Freedom*, 827.

67. Sherman quoted in Davis, Burke, *Sherman's March*, 139; see also Foster, John Y., *New Jersey and the Rebellion*, 347.

68. Davis, Burke, *Sherman's March*, 142.

69. Foster, John Y., *New Jersey and the Rebellion*, 345-346.

70. Long, A.L., *Memoirs of Robert E. Lee, His Military and Personal History*, 681.

71. Sherman, Hardee, Johnston quoted in Davis, Burke, *Sherman's March*, 147.

72. Hart, H.B. Liddell, *Sherman, Soldier, Realist, American*, 332.

73. Toombs, 203.

74. Harwell, Richard B., ed., *The Confederate Reader*. Secaucus, New Jersey: The Blue & Grey Press, 1957, 352-359.

75. Simms, William Gilmore, *The Sack and Destruction of the City of Columbia, South Carolina*, 29-39.

76. *Ibid*.

77. Toombs, 204.

78. Sherman quoted in Davis, Burke, *Sherman's March*, 189.

79. Davis, Burke, *Sherman's March*, 190.

80. Woodward, C. Van, ed., *Mary Chesnut's Civil War*, 767.

81. Cox, Jacob D., *Sherman's March to the Sea, Hood's Tennessee Campaign and the Carolina's Campaign of 1865*, 181-182.

82. Niccolls, Francis A., *Works of Eugene Sue; Illustrated with Etchings by Mercier, Poiteau, and Adrian Marcel*. Boston: (no date) Volume 4-6 "The Wandering Jew."

83. Glatthaar, Joseph T., *The March to the Sea and Beyond, Sherman's Troops in the Savannah and Carolina's Campaigns*, 137-138.

84. *Ibid*, 146.

85. Sherman quoted in Marszalek, John F. ,Sherman, *A Soldier's Passion for Order*, 327.

86. Foster, John Y., *New Jersey and the Rebellion*, 349.

87. Toombs, 211.

88. Official Records, Series I, Volume 47, 871.

89. Official Report on equipment lost at the Battle of Averasboro, March 16, 1865. Franklin Murphy Papers at the New Jersey Historical Society, Newark, New Jersey.

90. Wickham, John A., General, quoted in McPherson, James M., *For Cause & Comrades Why Men Fought in the Civil War*, Introduction.

91. Foster, John Y., *New Jersey and the Rebellion*, 353.

92. Bradford, Ned, ed., *Battles and Leaders of the Civil War*, 599.

93. *Official Records*, Series I, Volume 47, 909.

94. Glatthaar, Joseph T., *The March to the Sea and Beyond, Sherman's Troops in the Savannah and Carolina's Campaigns of 1865*, 176-177.

95. Randall, John G., Donald, David, *The Civil War and Reconstruction*. Lexington, Massachusetts: D.C. Heath and Company, 1969, 527-528.

96. Lincoln's last message to Sherman, quoted in Hertz, Emanuel, *Lincoln Talks, An Oral Biography*, collected and edited. New York: Branhall House, 1986, 555.

97. Sergeant Albert C. Harrison Company G 14th New Jersey Volunteers from Burkes Station, Virginia, to his mother and father in Red Bank, New Jersey, April 17, 1865. Papers in private possession.

98. Marszalek, John F., Sherman, *A Soldier's Passion for Order*, 342.

99. *Ibid*, 345; Hirshson, Stanley P., *The White Tecumseh, A Biography of General William T. Sherman*. New York: John Wiley & Sons, Inc., 1997, 307-310.

100. Donald, David Herbert, *Lincoln*. New York: Simon & Shuster, 1995, 254-255.

101. *Official Records*, Series I, Volume 47, 526.

102. Cox, Jacob D., *Sherman's March to the Sea, Hood's Tennessee Campaign and the Carolina's Campaign of 1865*, 117-118.

103. *Official Records*, Series I, Volume 47, 336.

104. Toombs, 224-226.

105. *Official Records Operations in NC, SC, South GA, and East FL.*, Chapter LIX, 526.

106. Toombs, 227-228.

107. Franklin Murphy, "The Cost of the War" Speech delivered at Saint Paul's M.E. Church, May 27, 1894, 15. Franklin Murphy Papers in private possession.

108. Sergeant Albert C., Harrison Company G 14th NJ Volunteers from Bailey's Crossroads near Washington, D.C., to his mother and father in Red Bank, New Jersey, June 10, 1865. Sergeant Albert C. Harrison Papers in private possession.

109. Franklin Murphy, "Cost of the War" Speech, 18.

110. Nellie at Winchester, Virginia, to James Augustus Grimstead, June 23, 1865. James Augustus Grimstead Papers in private possession.

111. E. Osbourn at Charleston, South Carolina, to James Augustus Grimstead, January 9, 1866. James Augustus Grimstead Papers in private possession.

112. Franklin Murphy "Speech to the New Jersey Society for the Daughters of the American Revolution," January 3, 1900, 17. Franklin Murphy Papers in private possession.

Chapter 4

1. "Some Boyhood Experiences," Essay, 2. Franklin Murphy Papers at the New Jersey Historical Society, Newark, New Jersey.
   2. *Ibid*, 3.
   3. *Ibid*, 3.
   4. *Ibid*, 4.
   5. *Ibid*.
   6. *Ibid*.
   7. *Ibid*.

8. *New Jersey, A Historical Biographical and Genealogical Record*, Volume V., The American Historical Society, Inc.: 1930, 181.

9. *Ibid.*

10. *Ibid.*

11. *Ibid.*

12. Willets, Gilson, *Workers of the Nation An Encyclopedia of the Occupations of the American People and a Record of Business, Professional and Industrial Achievement at the Beginning of the Twentieth Century*, Volume I. P.F. Collier and Son, 1903, 340.

13. Memorial to Franklin Murphy, Journal of the Senate. Clarence E. Case, President of the Senate, William H. Allright, Secretary of the Senate, Trenton, New Jersey, March 1, 1920, 23. Franklin Murphy Papers in private possession.

14. *The Industrial Directory of New Jersey*, compiled and published by the Bureau of Industrial Statistics of New Jersey. S. Chew & Sons Company, 1915, 355.

15. *The Book of Decoration*. Newark, New Jersey: The Murphy Varnish Company, 1923, 46.

16. *Newark, The City of Industry Facts and Figures Concerning the Metropolis of New Jersey*. Published under the Auspices of the Newark Board of Trade, 1912, 145.

17. "Personal Influence," Essay, 6-7. Franklin Murphy Papers at the New Jersey Historical Society, Newark, New Jersey.

18. "Kindness Is Policy" Essay, 8. Franklin Murphy Papers at the New Jersey Historical Society, Newark, New Jersey.

19. "A Corporation With A Soul" Essay, 10. Franklin Murphy Papers at the New Jersey Historical Society, Newark, New Jersey.

20. Franklin Murphy diary entry Friday, June 26, 1903. Franklin Murphy Papers in private possession.

21. Franklin Murphy diary entry December 24, 1904. Franklin Murphy Papers in private possession.

22. Josephson, Matthew, *The Robber Barons, The Great American Capitalists 1861-1900*. Norwalk, Connecticut: The Easton Press, 1934, 1962, 1987, 272.

23. *Ibid*, 365.

24. *Ibid*, 369.

25. Jackman, Michael, ed. *Macmillan Book of Business and Economic Quotations*. New York: Macmillan Publishing Company, 1984, 36.

26. Bailey, Thomas A., Kennedy, David M., *The American Pageant A History of the Republic*, 10th ed. Lexington, Massachusetts, Toronto: D.C. Heath & Company, 1994, 542.

27. Josephson, Matthew, *The Robber Barons, The Great American Capitalists 1861-1900*, 32.

28. Franklin Murphy, "Watch Night" Speech, December 31, 1884, 10. Franklin Murphy Papers in private possession.

29. *Ibid*, 13.

30. Franklin Murphy, "Business Men" Speech, January 30, 1886, 4-5. Franklin Murphy Papers in private possession.

31. Kull, Irving S., *New Jersey, A History*. New York: The American Historical Society, Inc., 1930, 1014.

32. "A Visit to the Newark Factory," Essay (no date), 2. Franklin Murphy Papers at the New Jersey Historical Society, Newark, New Jersey.

Chapter 5

1. "Mr. Murphy As A Citizen" Essay, 14. Franklin Murphy Papers in private possession.

2. Pierce, Frank H. Jr., "Governors of New Jersey," *Newark Sunday News*, April 29, 1951.

3. Murphy, Franklin. "Newark Exposition Speech," May 17, 1916, 7-8.

4. *Portraits of American Presidents-The Presidents of a National Struggle 1829-1901*. Questar Video, Inc. Produced by NBC News Productions: Chicago, Illinois MCMXCII.

5. Noble, Ransom E. Jr., *New Jersey Progressivism Before Wilson*. Princeton, New Jersey: Princeton University Press, 1946, 23.

6. *New Jersey, A History: Biographical & Genealogical Records*, Vol. V. New York: The American Historical Society Inc., 1930, 181-182.

7. Noble, 130.

8. Cunningham, John T., *New Jersey America's Main Road*. Garden City, New York: Doubleday & Company, 1966, 259; Pierce, Frank H., "Governors of New Jersey." Newark, New Jersey: *Newark Sunday News* April 29, 1951.

9. "Mr. Murphy As A Citizen," Essay, 15. Franklin Murphy Papers at the New Jersey Historical Society, Newark, NJ.

10. Memorial To Franklin Murphy in the Journal of the Senate: Clarence E. Case President of the Senate, William H. Allright, Secretary of the Senate. Trenton, NJ March 1, 1920, 16.

11. Noble, 23.

12. "My Experience in the Political Campaign of 92," Document, 2. Franklin Murphy Papers in private possession.

13. Stellhorn Paul A., Birkner, Michael J. ed., *The Governors of New Jersey: Biographical Essays*. Trenton, New Jersey: New Jersey Historical Commission, 1982, 170.

14. "My Experience in the Political Campaign of 92," Document, 26. Franklin Murphy Papers in private possession.

15. Franklin Murphy to William Nelson May 13, 1895. Franklin Murphy Papers in private possession.

16. "My Experience in the Political Campaign of 92," Document, 26. Franklin Murphy Papers in private possession.

17. *Ibid*, 36.

18. *State of New Jersey Manual of the Legislature of NJ*: One Hundred & Twenty Sixth Session 1902 by authority of the Legislature. Copyright 1900 by T.F. Fitzgerald: Trenton, NJ, 248-250.

19. Tobin, Eugene M., *George L. Record and the Progressive Spirit: New Jersey Portraits*. Trenton, New Jersey: New Jersey Historical Commission, 1979, 10.

20. *Ibid*, 12.

21. *Ibid*, 13.

22. Fitzgerald, 248-250.

23. Sackett William E., *Modern Battles of Trenton*, Volume II: *From Werts to Wilson*. New York: The Neale Publishing Company, 1914, 16.

24. *Ibid*, 17.

25. *Ibid*.

26. Sackett, 18.

27. *Ibid*, 49-50.

28. *Ibid*.

29. Vice President Garret A. Hobart to Franklin Murphy June 14, 1897. Franklin Murphy Papers in private possession.

30. Sackett, 117.

31. *Ibid*, 127.

32. Franklin Murphy Diary Entry March 24, 1902. Franklin Murphy Papers in private possession.

33. Memorial To Franklin Murphy: Journal of the Senate. Clarence E. Case President of the Senate, William H. Allright, Secretary of the Senate. Trenton, NJ, March 1, 1920, 18.

34. Morris, Edmund., *The Rise of Theodore Roosevelt*. New York: Coward, McCann & Geoghegan Inc., 1979, 738.

35. Sackett, 129.

36. *Ibid*.

37. Fitzgerald, 248-250; see also Kull, Irving S., A.M. *New Jersey, A History,* Volume III. New York: The American Historical Society, Inc., 1930, 1015.

38. Noble, 23.

39. Murphy, Franklin "Campaign Speech," (no place or date) , 1-2. Franklin Murphy Papers in private possession.

40. Noble, 1.

41. Pierce, Frank H. Jr., "Governors of New Jersey" *Newark Sunday News,* April 29, 1951.

42. Cunningham, John T., *New Jersey: America's Main Road,* 159.

43. Edge, Walter Evans., *A Jerseyman's Journal: Fifty Years of American Business.* Princeton, New Jersey: Princeton University Press, 1948, 60.

44. Franklin Murphy diary entry January 21, 1902. Franklin Murphy Papers in private possession.

45. *Ibid.*

46. *Ibid.*

47. Governor Franklin Murphy's Inaugural Address January 21, 1902, 12. Franklin Murphy Papers in private possession.

48. Sackett, 143.

49. *Ibid.*

50. *Ibid.* 144.

51. Franklin Murphy diary entry October 19, 1902. Franklin Murphy Papers in private possession.

52. *Ibid.*

53. *Ibid.*

54. Sackett, 144.

55. *A History of Trenton 1679-1929 Two Hundred and Fifty Years of a Notable Town With Links in Four Centuries.* Prepared Under the Auspices of the Trenton Historical Society With Illustrations by George A. Bradshaw, ed. Edwin, Robert Walker et. al: Trenton, New Jersey: Princeton University Press, 1929, 208-209, 332, 760.

56. First Annual Message of Franklin Murphy: Governor of New Jersey to the Legislature Session of 1903, 15. Franklin Murphy Papers in private possession.

57. Sackett, 144.

58. *Newark Advertiser,* February 11, 1904.

59. Franklin Murphy diary entry September 23, 1902. Franklin Murphy Papers in private possession.

60. "It Was Called Morvan," ed., Voss, Dorothy, *Tel-News,* September 1986, 2.

61. "Drumthwacket" ed., VanNote, Gloria, *Tel-News,* November 1981, 1.

62. Kull, Irving S., *New Jersey, A History.* Volume III, New York: The American Historical Society Inc., 1930, 1015.

63. Inaugural Address of Governor Franklin Murphy, January 21, 1902, 3. Franklin Murphy Papers in private possession.

64. *Ibid,* 5.

65. *Ibid,* 6.

66. *Ibid,* 10.

67. *Ibid,* 11.

68. Riss, J.A., *How The Other Half Lives, Studies Among the Tenements of New York.* Introduction By: Donald N. Bigelow. New York: Hill & Wang A Division of Farrar, Straus & Giroux, 1957, 34.

69. Pierce, Frank H. "Governors of New Jersey." *Newark Sunday News,* April 29, 1951.

70. Noble, 132.

71. Sackett, 156.

72. Interview with H.B. Walker, April 22, 1937 quoted in Noble, 132.

73. Noble, 133.

74. *Ibid.*

75. Senate Bill 87 Laws of New Jersey 1903, Chapter 248 quoted in Noble, 133.

76. Sackett, 131.

77. Edge, 62.

78. Franklin Murphy diary entry April 4, 1903. Franklin Murphy Papers in private possession.

79. "Mr. Murphy As Governor," Essay, 16. Franklin Murphy Papers at the New Jersey Historical Society, Newark, NJ.

80. Sackett, 131; see also Cunningham, 259.

81. Third Annual Message of Governor Franklin Murphy to the Legislature-Session of 1905, 5. Franklin Murphy Papers in private possession.

82. "Mr. Murphy As Governor," Essay, 17. Franklin Murphy Papers at the New Jersey Historical Society, Newark, NJ.

83. *Ibid.*

84. *Ibid,* 19.

85. Franklin Murphy diary entry October 20, 1903. Franklin Murphy Papers in private possession.

86. Pierce, Frank H., "Governors of New Jersey" *Newark Sunday News,* April 29, 1951.

87. Josephson, Matthew., *The Politicos, 1865-1896.* New York: Harcourt, Brace & World, Inc., 1938,1966, 473.

88. Faulkner, Harold U., *Politics, Reform and Expansion 1890-1900.* New York, Evanston, London: Harper & Row Publishers, 1959, 14; For a thorough explanation of the "single tax" see George, Henry, *Progress and Poverty: An Inquiry into the Cause of Industrial Depressions and of Increase Want With Increase of Wealth the Remedy.* New York: Walter J. Black Inc. For the Classics Club, 1942, 363-368.

89. Tobin, 13.

90. *Ibid.*

91. *Ibid,* 14.

92. *Ibid.*; see also Sackett, 184.

93. Tobin, 15.

94. *Ibid.*

95. Franklin Murphy diary entry October 13, 1902. Franklin Murphy Papers in private possession.

96. Franklin Murphy diary entry September 4, 1903. Franklin Murphy Papers in private possession

97. First Annual Message of Governor Franklin Murphy to the Legislature-Session of 1903, 11. Franklin Murphy Papers in private possession.

98. Sackett, 184.

99. New Jersey Journal March 24, 1904 quoted in Noble, 24.

100. *Newark News,* March 24, 1905 quoted in Noble, 26.

101. Sackett, 185.

102. *Ibid,* 207.

103. *Ibid,* 207.

104. Cunningham, 258.

105. Third Annual Message of Governor Franklin Murphy to the Legislature-Session of 1905, 6. Franklin Murphy Papers in private possession.

106. Ogburn, W.F., *Progress and Uniformity in Child Labor Legislation: Columbia University Studies in History, Economics, and Public Law,* Volume 48, number 2. New York, 1912, 53-54 quoted in Noble, 122.

107. *Ibid.*

108. Sackett, 145.

109. Franklin Murphy diary entry March 6, 1903. Franklin Murphy Papers in private possession.

110. Sackett, 144.

111. *Ibid.*

112. *Ibid,* 146.

113. *Ibid.*

114. *Ibid.*

115. Franklin Murphy diary entry January 8, 1904. Franklin Murphy Papers in private possession.

116. Ogburn, William F., *Progress and Uniformity in Child Labor Legislation: A Study in Statistical Measurement.* New York: AMS Press Inc., 1912, 184-185. Reprint Columbia University Press.

117. Franklin Murphy diary entry January 8, 1904. Franklin Murphy Papers in private possession.

118. Third Annual Message of Governor Franklin Murphy to the Legislature-Session of 1905, 15. Franklin Murphy Papers in private possession.

119. Faulkner, Harold U., *Politics, Reform, and Expansion 1890-1900.* New York, Evanston, London: Harper & Row Publishers, 1959, 32.

120. Sackett, 147.

121. *Ibid.*

122. Franklin Murphy diary entry May 28, 1903. Franklin Murphy Papers in private possession.

123. Franklin Murphy diary entry November 21, 1903. Franklin Murphy Papers in private possession.

124. Franklin Murphy diary entry August 26, 1903. Franklin Murphy Papers in private possession.

125. Second Annual Message of Governor Franklin Murphy to the Legislature-Session of 1904, 10. Franklin Murphy Papers in private possession.

126. First Annual Message of Governor Franklin Murphy to the Legislature-Session of 1903, 12-13. Franklin Murphy Papers in private possession.

127. A Bridgeton newspaper quoted in Wilson, Harold F., *The Story of the Jersey Shore.* Princeton, NJ: D. Van Nostrand Co. Inc., 1964, 87.

128. *Ibid,* 88.

129. Cunningham, 249-250.

130. *Ibid.*

131. *Ibid.*

132. "Mr. Murphy As Governor," Essay, 20. Franklin Murphy papers at the New Jersey Historical Society, Trenton, New Jersey.

133. First Annual Message of Governor Franklin Murphy to the Legislature-Session of 1903, 13-14. Franklin Murphy Papers in private possession.

134. Wilson, 88.

135. *Ibid,* 89.

136. *Ibid,* 90.

137. Mazour, Anatole G. & Peoples, John M., *Men And Nations A World History.* New York, Chicago, San Francisco: Harcourt Brace Jovanovich, 1975, 444.

138. Third Annual Message of Governor Franklin Murphy to the Legislature-Session of 1905, 23. Franklin Murphy Papers in private possession.

139. Wilson, 93.

140. *Ibid.*

141. Franklin Murphy diary entry September 14, 1903. Franklin Murphy Papers in private possession.

142. Wilson, 93.

143. Franklin Murphy diary entries: September 7, 1902; January 18, 1904; July 7, 1904; September 6, 1904; September 22, 1904. Franklin Murphy Papers in private possession.

144. Franklin Murphy diary entry February 22, 1904. Franklin Murphy Papers in private possession.

145. Grover Cleveland to Franklin Murphy. Princeton, February 15, 1904. Franklin Murphy Papers in private possession.

146. Woodrow Wilson to Franklin Murphy. President's Room, February 20, 1904. Franklin Murphy Papers in private possession.

147. Theodore Roosevelt to Franklin Murphy. White House, February 12, 1904. Franklin Murphy Papers in private possession.

148. F.M. diary entry March 4, 1904. Franklin Murphy Papers in private possession.

149. F.M. diary entry December 31, 1904. Franklin Murphy Papers in private possession.

150. F.M. diary entry July 12, 1902. Franklin Murphy Papers in private possession.

151. F.M. diary entry July 26, 1902. Franklin Murphy Papers in private possession.

152. *Ibid.*

153. *Ibid.*

154. *Ibid.*

155. *Ibid.*

156. F.M. diary entry September 15, 1902. Franklin Murphy Papers in private possession.

157. F.M. diary entry October 26, 1903. Franklin Murphy Papers in private possession.

158. F.M. diary entry September, 19, 1903. Franklin Murphy Papers in private possession.

159. Franklin Murphy "Antietam Speech," September 17, 1903, 18-19. Franklin Murphy Papers in private possession.

160. "The Battleship New Jersey Ceremonies: Attending the Launching and Presentation of a Silver Service by the State 1904-1907," 5. Franklin Murphy Papers in private possession.

161. *Ibid,* 4.

162. F.M. diary entry Friday, April 22, 1904. Franklin Murphy Papers in private possession.

163. F.M. diary entry Monday, October 10, 1904. Franklin Murphy Papers in private possession.

164. *Ibid.*

165. *Ibid.*

166. *Ibid.*

167. Franklin Murphy "New Jersey Day" Speech at Saint Louis, October 6, 1904. Franklin Murphy Papers in private possession.

168. F.M. diary entry October 10, 1904. Franklin Murphy Papers in private possession.

169. F.M. diary entry October 25, 1902. Franklin Murphy Papers in private possession.

170. *Ibid.*

171. Faragher, John Mark ed., *Encyclopedia of Colonial & Revolutionary America.* New York, Sydney: Facton File, 1990, 71; Alden, John R., *A History of the American Revolution.* New York: Alfred A. Knopf Inc., 1969, 359.

172. *Ibid.*

173. F.M. diary entry Saturday, June 27, 1903. Franklin Murphy Papers in private possession.

174. *Ibid.*

175. F.M. diary entry Sunday, June 28, 1903. Franklin Murphy Papers in private possession.

176. F.M. diary entry Thursday, January 17, 1905. Franklin Murphy Papers in private possession.

177. *Ibid.*

178. *Ibid.*

179. *Ibid.*

180. *Ibid.*

181. *Ibid.*

182. F.M. diary entry January 11, 1905. Franklin Murphy Papers in private possession.

Chapter 6

1. Franklin Murphy diary entry September 30, 1907, and subsequent Franklin Murphy diaries are part of his family Papers in private possession.

2. *Ibid.*

3. Franklin Murphy diary entry October 1, 1907.

4. Franklin Murphy diary entry December 25, 1907.

5. Franklin Murphy diary entry January 18, 1908.

6. Winthrop, Jordan D., Miriam, Greenblatt, Bowes, John S., *The Americans, A History.* Evanston, Illinois: McDougal Littell & Company, 1991, 404.

7. Franklin Murphy diary entry May 10, 1908.

8. Sackett, William E., *Modern Battles of Trenton Volume II: From Werts To Wilson.* New York: The Neale Publishing company, 1914, 16.

9. *Ibid.*

10. Franklin Murphy diary entry Saturday, March 29th, 1909.

11. Franklin Murphy Speech Delivered at the Dollar Dinner of the Orange Republican Club, May 26, 1910,

12. *bid.* 11.

13. William Howard Taft quoted in Franklin Murphy's Speech at the Dollar dinner of the Orange Republican Club, May 26, 1910, 5.

14. *Ibid.* 6.

15. Franklin Murphy diary entry Tuesday, June 9, 1908.

16. Franklin Murphy diary entry April 26th, 1909.

17. Franklin Murphy diary entry April 27th, 1909.

18. Franklin Murphy diary entry January 14th, 1908.

19. Franklin Murphy diary entry June 16, 1908.

20. Franklin Murphy Newark Exposition Speech, May 17, 1916, 1,2.

21. *Ibid.* 16,17.

22. *Ibid.* 18.

23. Franklin Murphy diary entry, Wednesday, January 22, 1908.

24. Franklin Murphy diary entry, Sunday, June 7, 1908.

25. Franklin Murphy diary entry, Sunday, October 11, 1908.

26. Franklin Murphy diary entry, March 17, 1909.

27. Franklin Murphy diary entry May 7, 1909.

28. Franklin Murphy diary entry May 19, 1909.

29. Franklin Murphy diary entry April 3, 1908.

30. Franklin Murphy diary entry Tuesday, November 17, 1908.

31. Franklin Murphy diary entry April 4, 1908.

32. Franklin Murphy diary entry January 29th, 1908.

33. Franklin Murphy diary entry October 31st, 1907.

34. "An Automobile Trip Through New England July 3-13, 1909," Franklin Murphy diary entry.

35. *Ibid.*

36. *Ibid.*

37. *Ibid.*

38. *Ibid.*

39. *Ibid.*

40. *Ibid.*

41. *Ibid.*

42. *Ibid.*

43. *Ibid.*

44. *Ibid.*

45. *Ibid.*

46. "Trip to Florida," Franklin Murphy diary entry February 29, 1908.

47. *Ibid.*

48. *Ibid.*

49. *Ibid.*

50. *Ibid.*

51. *Ibid.*

52. *Ibid.*

53. *Ibid.*

54. *Ibid.*

55. *Ibid.*

56. *Ibid.*

57. *Ibid.*

58. *New Jersey, A History, Biographical and Genealogical Records, Volume V,* The American Historical Society, Inc. New York: 1930, 183.

Sources

Books

A History of Trenton 1679-1929 Two Hundred and Fifty Years of a Notable Town With Links in Four Centuries. Prepared Under the Auspices of the Trenton Historical Society With Illustrations by George A. Bradshaw. ed., Edwin, Robert Walker et. al: Trenton: Princeton University Press, 1929.

Alden, John R., *A History of the American Revolution.* New York: Alfred A. Knopf Inc., 1969.

Bailey, Thomas A., Kennedy, David M., *The American Pageant A History of the Republic,* 10th ed. Lexington, Massachusetts, Toronto: D.C. Heath & Company, 1994.

Bailey, Thomas, ed., *The American Spirit.* Lexington, MA: D.C. Heath Company, 1969.

Bailyn, Bernard, et al., *The Great Republic A History of the American People.* Boston, Toronto; Little Brown & Company, 1977.

Barabba, Vincent P., *Historical Statistics of the U.S. Colonial Times to 1970.* U.S. Department of Commerce, Bureau of the Census, 1975.

Barber & Howe, *Historical Collections of New Jersey.* New York: S. Tuttle, 1844.

Best, John Hardin and Robert T. Sidwell, ed., *The American Legacy of Learning-Readings in the History of Education.* Philadelphia-New York: J.B. Lippincott Company, 1967.

Bradford, Ned, ed., *Battles & Leaders of the Civil War.* New York: Appleton-Century-Crofts, Inc., 1956.

Brinkley, Alan, *The Unfinished Nation.* New York, St. Louis, San Francisco: McGraw Hill, 1993.

Brunt, P.A., *Thucydides The Peloponnesian Wars.* New York: Washington Square Press, Inc., 1963.

Castel, Albert, *Decision in the West, The Atlanta Campaign of 1864.* Lawrence, KS: University Press of Kansas: 1992.

Catton, Bruce, *Gettysburg: The Final Fury.* Norwalk, Connecticut: The Easton Press, 1974, 1986.

Catton, Bruce, *Never Call Retreat: The Centennial History of the Civil War,* Volume III. Garden City, NY: Doubleday & Company, 1965.

Chase, Gilbert, *American Music From the Pilgrims to the Present.* New York: McGraw Hill, 1955.

Commanger, Henry Steel, ed., *Documents of American History,* 7th edition. New York: Appleton-Century-Crofts, 1962.

Cox, Jacob D. late Major-General commanding the 23rd Army Corps, *Sherman's Battle For Atlanta.* New York: DaCapo Press, 1864, 1994.

Cox, Jacob D., *Sherman's March to the Sea, Hood's Tennessee Campaign and the Carolina's Campaign of 1865.* New York: DaCapo Press, 1994.

Cunningham, John T., *Newark.* Newark: The New Jersey Historical Society, 1988.

Cunningham, John T., *New Jersey America's Main Road.* Garden City, NY: Doubleday & Company, 1966.

Davis, Burke, *Sherman's March.* New York: Random House, 1980.

Doane, George Washington, *Goodly Heritage of Jerseymen.* ed., Edmund Morris 1846. Reprint New Jersey Historical Society.

Donald, David Herbert, *Lincoln.* New York: Simon & Shuster 1995.

Donald, David Herbert, *Charles Sumner and the Coming of the Civil War.* Norwalk, CT: Easton Press, 1960.

Edge, Walter Evans., *A Jerseyman's Journal: Fifty Years of American Business.* Princeton: Princeton University Press, 1948.

Einstein, Alfred, *Music in the Romantic Era.* New York: W.W. Norton & Company Inc., 1947.

Eliot, Alexander, *Three Hundred Years of American Painting.* New York: Time Inc., 1957.

Faragher, John Mark ed., *Encyclopedia of Colonial & Revolutionary America.* New York, Sydney: Facts on File, 1990.

Faulkner, Harold U., *Politics, Reform and Expansion 1890-1900.* New York, Evanston, London: Harper & Row Publishers, 1959.

Fehrenbacher, Don E., *Abraham Lincoln Speeches and Writings 1859-1865, Speeches,*

Letters, and Miscellaneous Writings, Presidential Messages and Proclamations. New York: The Library of America, 1989.

Fellman, Michael, *Citizen Sherman, A Life of William Tecumseh Sherman.* New York: Random House, 1995.

Foster, John Y., *New Jersey and the Rebellion, A History of the Services of the Troops & People of New Jersey in Aid of the Union Cause.* Newark: Martin R. Dennis & Company, 1868.

Franklin, John Hope, *From Slavery to Freedom, A History of Negro Americans.* New York: Alfred A. Knopf, 1967.

Freidel, Frank, ed., *Union Pamphlets of the Civil War 1861-1865.* Cambridge, MA: Belknap Press of Harvard University, 1961.

Garraty, John A. *A Short History of the American Nation.* New York, Reading, MA, Menlo Park, CA: Addison Wesley Longman Inc., 1997.

Garraty, John A. and Robert A. McCaughy, *The American Nation, A History of the United States.* New York: Harper & Row, 1987.

Geissler, Suzanne, *A Widening Sphere of Usefulness, Newark Academy 1774-1993.* West Kennebunk, ME: Phoenix Publishing, 1993.

George, Henry, *Progress and Poverty: An Inquiry into the Cause of Industrial Depressions and of Increase Want With Increase of Wealth the Remedy.* New York: Walter J. Black Inc. For the Classics Club, 1942.

Gillette, William, *Jersey Blue Civil War Politics in New Jersey.* New Brunswick: Rutgers University Press, 1995.

Glatthaar, Joseph T., *The March to the Sea and Beyond, Sherman's Troops in the Savannah and Carolina's Campaigns.* New York, London: New York University Press, 1985.

Gurko, Miriam, *The Ladies of Seneca Falls, The Birth of the Women's Rights Movement.* Norwalk, CT: Easton Press, 1974.

Hart, Albert Bushnel, *American History Told by Contemporaries,* Volume IV, *Welding of the Nation ,1845-1900.* New York, London: Macmillan Company, 1964.

Hart, B.H. Liddell, *Sherman, Soldier, Realist, American.* Westport, CT: Greenwood Press, 1978.

Harwell, Richard B., ed., *The Confederate Reader.* Secaucus, NJ: The Blue & Grey Press, 1957.

Hertz, Emanuel, *Lincoln Talks, An Oral Biography,* collected and edited. New York: Branhall House, 1986.

Hirshson, Stanley P., *The White Tecumseh, A Biography of General William T. Sherman.* New York: John Wiley & Sons, Inc., 1997.

Hunt, Livingston, Rear Admiral Retired, *The Attempted Mutiny on the U.S. Brig "Somers."* U.S. Naval Institute Proceedings.

Jackman, Michael, ed., *Macmillan Book of Business and Economic Quotations.* New York: Macmillan Publishing Company, 1984.

Joseph, Alvin M. Jr., *The Indian Heritage of America*. New York: Alfred A. Knopf Pub., 1969.

Josephson, Matthew, *The Robber Barons, The Great American Capitalists 1861-1900*. Norwalk, CT: The Easton Press, 1934, 1962, 1987.

Josephson, Matthew, *The Politicos, 1865-1896*. New York: Harcourt, Brace & World, Inc., 1938, 1966.

Kobler, John, *The Rise and Fall of Prohibition*. New York: DaCapo Press, 1973.

Kull, Irving S., *New Jersey, A History*, Volume III. New York: The American Historical Society Inc., 1930.

Leiby, Adrian C., *The Early Dutch and Swedish Settlers of New Jersey*. Princeton: D. Van Nostrand Co., 1964.

Lewis, A.S., ed., *My Dear Parents The Civil War Seen By An English Soldier by James Horrocks*. San Diego, New York, London: Harcourt, Brace Jovanovich, 1982.

Long, A.L., *Memoirs of Robert E. Lee, His Military and Personal History*. Secaucus, NJ: The Blue and Grey Press, 1983.

Lunt, W.E., *History of England* 4th ed. New York, London: Harper & Row Pub., 1956.

Marbaker, Thomas D., Sergeant, Company E., *History of the 11th NJ Volunteers from its Organization to Appomattox to which is added Experiences of Prison Life and Sketches of Individual Members*. MacCrellish & Quingley, Book & Job Printers, 1898. Reprint, Hightstown: Longstreet House, 1990.

Markham, Felex, *Napoleon*. New York: Mentor Publishing, 1966.

Marszalek, John F., *Sherman, A Soldier's Passion For Order*. New York: The Free Press, a Division of Macmillan, Inc., 1993.

Mazour, Anatole G. & Peoples, John M., *Men And Nations A World History*. New York, Chicago, San Francisco: Harcourt Brace Jovanovich, 1975.

McCagne, James, *Mogels and Iron Man, the Story of the First Transcontinental Railroad*. Norwalk, CT: Easton Press, 1964.

McPherson, James M., *Battle Cry of Freedom, The Civil War Era*. New York, Oxford: Oxford University Press, 1988.

McPherson, James M., *For Cause and Comrades. Why Men Fought in the Civil War*. Oxford-New York: Oxford University Press, 1997.

Miller, Edwin Haviland, *Melville*. New York: George Braziller, Inc., 1975.

Morris, Edmund, *The Rise of Theodore Roosevelt*. New York: Coward, McCann & Geoghegan Inc., 1979.

Nevins, Allan, *Ordeal of the Union: A House Dividing 1852-1857. Vol. II*. New York: Scribner's Sons, 1947.

New Jersey, A History: Biographical & Genealogical Records, Vol. V. New York: The American Historical Society Inc., 1930.

Niccolls, Francis A., *Works of Eugene Sue; Illustrated with Etchings by Mercier, Poiteau, and Adrian Marcel*. Boston: (no date) Volume 4-6 "The Wandering Jew."

Noble, Ransom E. Jr., *New Jersey Progressivism Before Wilson*. Princeton: Princeton University Press, 1946.

Ogburn, W.F., *Progress and Uniformity in Child Labor Legislation: Columbia University Studies in History, Economics, and Public Law*, Volume 48, number 2. New York, 1912.

Ogburn, William F., *Progress and Uniformity in Child Labor Legislation: A Study in Statistical Measurement*. New York: AMS Press Inc., 1912. Reprint Columbia University Press.

Pessen, Edward, *Jacksonian American Society, Personality, and Politics*. Homewood, IL: The Dorsey Press, 1969.

Pierson, David Lawrence, *Narratives of Newark In New Jersey from the Days of its Foundings*. Newark: Pierson Publishing Company, 1917.

Randall, John G., Donald, David, *The Civil War and Reconstruction*. Lexington, MA: D.C. Heath and Company, 1969.

Riis, J.A., *How The Other Half Lives, Studies Among the Tenements of New York*. Introduction by: Donald N. Bigelow. New York: Hill & Wang, A Division of Farrar, Straus & Giroux, 1957.

Rostow, W.W. 3rd ed., *The Stages of Economic Growth: A Non-Communist Manifesto*. Cambridge, MA: Cambridge University Press, 1970, 36-37.

Sackett, William E., *Modern Battles of Trenton*, Volume II: *From Werts to Wilson*. New York: The Neale Publishing Company, 1914.

Sculley, Bradley, Richard Croom Beatty, and E. Hudson Long, ed., *The American Tradition of Literature, Vol. I 3rd ed*. New York: W.W. Norton & Company, 1967.

Sculley, Bradley, Richard Croom Beatty and E. Hudson Long, ed., *The American Tradition of Literature. Vol. II*. New York: W.W. Norton & Company, 1967.

Shaffer, Leon, *Business Relations of Newark With The South to 1861*, quoted in Kull, Irving S., Editor-In-Chief, *New Jersey, A History. Vol. II*. New York: The American Historical Society, 1930.

Shaw, William H., *History of Essex and Hudson Counties, New Jersey*, Volume I. Philadelphia: Everts & Peck, 1884.

Siegel, Alan A., *For The Glory of the Union Myth, Reality, and the Media in Civil War New Jersey*. Cranbury, NJ: Associated University Presses, 1984.

Simms, William Gilmore, *Sack and Destruction of the City of Columbia, South Carolina*. Edited with notes by Salley, A.S. Freeport, NY: Books for Libraries Press, 1937, 1971.

Spader, P. Vanderbilt, *Weather Record For New Brunswick, New Jersey 1847-1890*. Somerville, NJ: Press of the *Union Gazette*, 1890.

Spencer, Warren F., *Raphael Semmes, The Philosophical Mariner*. Tuscaloosa, London: University of Alabama Press, 1997.

Stellhorn, Paul A., Birkner, Michael J., ed., *The Governors of New Jersey: Biographical Essays*. Trenton: New Jersey Historical Commission, 1982.

Stryker, William S., *Record of Officers and Men of New Jersey in the Civil War 1861-1865*. Compiled in the Office of the Adjutant General. Trenton: Steam, 1866. Book and Job Printers, 1876.

Tarbell, Ida M., *He Knew Lincoln*. New York: McClure, Phillips & Company, 1907.

The Book of Decoration. Newark: The Murphy Varnish Company, 1923.

The Industrial Directory of New Jersey, compiled and published by the Bureau of Industrial Statistics of New Jersey. S. Chew & Sons Company, 1915.

The Smithsonian Experience, Science-History-The Arts Treasures of the Nation. New York: W.W. Norton & Company, 1977.

The War of the Rebellion: Official Records of the Union and Confederate Armies, First Series (Washington), 1889, XXV, pt. I.

Tobin, Eugene M., *George L. Record and the Progressive Spirit: New Jersey Portraits*. Trenton: New Jersey Historical Commission, 1979.

Toombs, Samuel, *Reminiscences of the Thirteenth Regiment New Jersey Volunteers*, New Introduction by David G. Martin. Orange, New Jersey, 1878. Reprint Number 207, Heightstown, New Jersey: Longstreet House, 1994. Original edition printed at the Journal Office 1878.

U.S. Military Academy Cadet Application Papers, 1805-1866, Microfilm Pub. 688.

Urquhart, Frank, *A History of the City of Newark New Jersey Embracing Practically Two and a half Centuries, 1666-1913*. Volume II. New York, Chicago: The Lewis Historical Publishing Company. 1913.

Valente, George, *The Wreck of the Ship John Minturn. Coast Fifty Anniversary Collector's Edition,* June 1989.

Vexler, Robert I., and William F. Swindler, *Chronology & Documentary Handbook of the State of New Jersey*. Dobbs Ferry, NY: Oceana Pub. Inc., 1978.

Viola, Herman J., *The National Archives of the United States*. New York: Harry N. Abrams, Inc., 1984.

Wacker, Peter O., *Land And People A Cultural Geography of Pre-Industrial New Jersey: Origins And Settlement Patterns*. New Brunswick: Rutgers University Press, 1975.

White, Edward G., *Justice Oliver Wendell Holmes Law and the Inner Self*. New York: Oxford University Press, 1993.

Willets, Gilson, *Workers of the Nation An Encyclopedia of the Occupations of the American People and a Record of Business, Professional and Industrial Achievement at the Beginning of the Twentieth Century*, Volume I. P.F. Collier and Son, 1903.

Wilson, Harold F., *The Story of the Jersey Shore*. Princeton: D. Van Nostrand Co. Inc., 1964.

Woodward, C. Van, ed., *Mary Chesnut's Civil War*. New Haven: Yale University Press, 1981.

Government Documents

Journal of the New Jersey Senate
Manual of the Legislature of New Jersey

Newspapers

New Jersey Advertiser
New Jersey Daily Advertiser
New York Daily Tribune

Newark News
Newark Daily News
Newark Sunday News

Personal Papers

James Bullman papers in private possession
James Augustus Grimstead papers in private possession
Albert C. Harrison papers in private possession
Franklin Murphy papers in private possession
Franklin Murphy papers at the New Jersey Historical Society
Jacob Wolcott papers at the New Jersey Historical Society
Monmouth County Historical Association Library & Archives, Collection 1, Peter Vredenburgh Papers; Collection 9, William Burroughs Ross Papers

Educational Institutions and Historical Societies

Monmouth County Historical Association Library & Archives
New Jersey Historical Society
Princeton University Rare Books and Special Collections
Rutgers University Library
Special Collections and University Archives
Monmouth University
Frederick, MD Historical Society
Library of Congress
National Archives
National Park Service
Newark Academy
State Library of New Jersey
United States Military History Institute
United States Military Academy Library
Nimitz Library, United States Naval Academy

Videotapes

Questor Video Inc.

Index

Abbet, Leon, 132, 139
Abbettism, 132
Abolitionists, 15
Ackworth, GA, 58
African-Americans, 5, 181
Alabama, C.S.S., 4, 80
Albemarle Hotel, 143
Aldrich, Nelson, 179
Alexandria, VA, 111
"All Quiet Along The Potomac Tonight,"
    illus., 118
Allatoona Pass, 55, 57
Allen, Ethan, 172
Allen, Secretary, 146
Amanda, Cousin, 67, 78
American Institute of Instruction, 16
American Pottery Company, 7-8
Anderson, GA, 52
Anderson, General, 143
André, John, 48
Anthony, Susan B., 4
Antietam Creek, 33
Antietam, Battle of, 28, 159; illus., 31, 160,
    161, 162
Anti-Injunction plank, 184
Apprentice System, 5
Aqueduct Bridge, 28, 111; illus., 120
Aquia Creek, 35
Arese-houck, 7
Areseck-heck, 7
Arey, John H. 13th NJ Vols., 41, illus., 42
Argyle Island, 78
Arlington Heights, VA, 27
Armistead, Lewis A., 41
Army of Georgia, 82, 111
Army of Tennessee, 52, 82
Army of the Cumberland, 52
Arnold, Benedict, 48, 172
Art Organ Company, 189
Asbury Park Press, 148
Aspinwall Hotel, 195
Athenaeum, 13
Athens, Greece, 19
Atlanta & Augusta Railroad, 75
Atlanta campaign, 66; illus., 68-69
Atlanta, GA., 57; illus.,73,74
Atlantic City, NJ, 150
Auditorium, 190
Augusta & Carolina Railroad, 86
Augusta, GA, 74, 86
Averasboro, NC, 99, 100-101

Babies' Hospital, 123
Backus, William, 13th NJ Vols., 62
Bacon's Orange Grove, 199
Baird, Mr., 16
Baitzel, Lieutenant, 13th NJ Vols., 55
Baldwin, Robert C., 13th NJ Vols., 53
Ballantine, Robert, 150
Ballinger-Pinchot Controversy, 181, 184
Baltimore Road, 27

Barnett, James G., 122
Barnwell, 83
Barony of Ballaghkeen, 10
Barrymore, Ethel, 190
Baseball, 6
Bates, Governor, 163, 168
Battle Creek Valley, 52
Battle Fatigue, 39
Baxter, Archibald, 159
Bayonne, NJ, 7
Beardsley, George A., 13th NJ Vols., 36, 37;
    illus., 37
Beauford Bridge, 86
Beauregard, Pierre G.T., 15, 80, 87, 92
Beck, Reverend, 48
Bellows Falls, VT, 195
Bennett, James, 108
Bentonville, Battle of, 101, 106; illus., 103
Bessemer Process, 13
Best's Battery, 36
Billboards, 147
Bissell, 143
Black River, 103
Black, Captain, 158
Black, Charles C., 144
Blackburn, 86
Blackville, 83, 86
Blandesburg Road, 113
Blanket Toss, 26
Bliss, Cornelius N., 177
Bliven, C.H., 13th NJ Vols., 93 110; illus., 93
Blue Bridge, 97
Blue Ridge, 43
Bluff Church, 99
Board of Managers of the National Home for
    Disabled Volunteer Soldiers, 178, 190
Board of Visitors of the Military Academy at
    West Point, 177
Bohwell, 13th NJ Vols., 97
Bolles, Francis T., 163, 168
Bonhamtown, NJ, 114
Booth, John Wilkes, 107
Booth, John, 13th NJ Vols., 55
Boston, MA, 4, 163, 190
Boutwell, George S., 16
Brady, "Diamond Jim," 147
Branchbrook Park, 123
Brandy Station, VA, 40
Brattleboro, VT, 195
Breckenridge, J.C., 87
Briand, Aristide, 4
Bridgeport, AL, 52
Bridgeport, GA, 66
Brientnall, R. Heber, 138, 163
Briggs, Frank, 182-183; illus., 182
Broad River, 91
Broad Street, Newark, 27
Bronson, Captain, 168
Brook Farm, MA, 4
Brooker, Mr. 167
Brooklyn, NY, 55

Brooklyn Eagle, 4
Brown Bess, 59
Brown, Joseph E., 75
Brown, Richard, 13th NJ Vols., 63
Brown, William 65
Bryant, Lewis T. 145, 146, 163, 171
Brice's Crossroads, 100
Buckhead, 59
Bucklish, William, 13th NJ Vols. illus., 77
Buffalo Creek, 75
Buffalo Exposition, 169
Buffalo's Temple of Music, 135
Buford, John, 100
Bull Run Battlefield, 111
Bullman, James, 14th NJ Vols., 47; illus., poem
    56
Bummers, illus., 80, 89, 90
Burkes Station, 107
Burnside, Ambrose E., 33

Cabinet Meetings, 139
Calhoun, John C., 22
Cambell, General, 138
Camden Battery, 173
Camden Citadel, 134
Cammeyer, Alfred J. to Franklin Murphy,
    illus., 14
Camp Frelinghuysen, 25, 27
Camp Lawton, 76, 77; illus., 78
Cannon, Joseph, 181, 183, 184
Cape Fear River, 98, 99, 107
Cape May County, NJ, 148
Cape May, NJ, 23
Capitalism, 143
Carman, Ezra A. 13th NJ Vols., 25, 26, 30, 31,
    35, 41, 61, 75, 78, 161; illus., 25
Carmen, James L., 13th NJ Vols., illus., 77
Carnegie, Andrew, 128, 186
Carolinas Campaign, 82
Carpenter, Frederick, 163
Carver, Dr., 171
Cassville, 53
Castle Thunder, 111
Castell, Albert, 64
Catawba River, 92
Catford, James, 13th NJ Vols., 61, 62
Catletts Station, illus., 96
Catoctin Mountains, 28
Cedar Creek, 55
Cemetery Ridge, 41
Chadwick, Major, 13th NJ Vols., 35
Chadwick, Samuel, 13th NJ Vols., 25
Chambersburg, PA, 64

Chancellor House, 35
Chancellorsville, Battle of, 35, 36, 111
Charles VI, 9
Charleston, SC, 74, 86 114
Charleston & Savannah Railroad, 78
Charleston Brigade, 101
Charleston Pike, 78
Charlestown Bridge, 193
Charlotte, NC, 197
Chattahoochee River, 58, 59; illus., 60
Chattanooga, 47, 52
Cheraw, SC, 95, 96; illus., 95
Chesapeake & Ohio Canal, 33
Chesterfield, SC, 94, 95
Chestnut Street, Newark, NJ, 27
Chestnut, Mary, 71, 80, 92
Chevaux-de-frise, illus., 58
Chicago, IL, 121, 125
Chicago Exposition, 169, 170
Chicago Platform, 65
Chicago Republican Convention, 180; illus.,
  185
Chickahominy River, 111
Christmas, 48, 127, 151, 178
Cincinnati, Lucius Quintius, 172
Cincinnati, Society of, illus., 172
City Beautiful Movement, 131
Civil War, 7, 151
Clark, 13th NJ Vols., 98
Clark, Dr., 150
Clark, John G., 80
Clark's Mills, 75
Clay, Henry, 13, 109
Clayton Anti-Trust Act, 125
Clemmy, 43
Cleveland, OH, 125
Cleveland, Grover, 132, 150
Clinton, Sir Henry, 48, 173, 174
Clysdale Creek, 80
Cobb, Howard, 73, 74
Colby, Everett, 144, 146
Coldstream Guards, 112
Cole, Thomas, 5
Coleman, Robert, 64
Collegiate Preparatory School, Carlisle, PA, 11
Color Battalion, 156
Columbia & Augusta Railroad, 88
Columbia, SC, 86, 88, 91,197
Colyers Mill Pond, 115
Combat Stress Disorder, 39
Committee of One Hundred, 184
Committee of the Legislature, 138
Compact Theory of States' Rights, 22
Confederate States of America, 15
Congaree River, 91
Conklin, Judson, 138

Connecticut River, 195
Connecticut Valley, 192
Connelly, James F., 131
Connesauga River, 52
Constitution, The United States, 22
Coosawatchie River, 86
Corduroying the Road, 94; illus., 94
Cornwallis, Charles Earl, 67, 108, 174
Cortelyou, George, 186
Cosmopolitan, The, 129
Cost Of The War Speech, 115-120
Cotton Gin, 21
Court of Errors, 142
Cox, Jacob D., 32, 59
Crane, Josiah, 10, 173
Crater, 64
Crawford, Isaac, 13th NJ Vols., 29
Crawford, Lieutenant, 84
Crawford Notch, NH, 194
Crittenden, John J., 22
Cromwell, Oliver, 10
Crowell, J.E., 161
Culp's Hill, Gettysburg, 41, 42, 158, 159
Cumberland Mountains, 52
Cunningham, John, 148
Czar, 22
Czar's Court at Saint Petersburg, 134
Czolgosz, Leon, 135

Dale, Jimmy, 150
Dallas, 53
Dallas, Battle of, 57
Dalton, GA, 52
Danville Railroad, 91
Davis, Burke, 80
Davis, Jefferson C., General, 83
Davis, Jefferson, 66, 81, 93, 111 178; illus.,
  21
Dawes Commission, 134
Dawes, Charles G., 186
Day, Israel, 122
Day, M.A., 45, 55
Deal Lake, 156
Decatur, GA, 52
DeKalb County, 75
Delargny, Mr., 16
Delaware Bay, 23
Delmonicos, 149
Democrat, 130
Democratic Copperheads, 132
Demon Rum, 3
Dermot, King of the Danes & Leinster, 10
Desertion, 39
Devil's Den, Gettysburg, illus., 44
Dickinson, Anna Elizabeth, 45
Dickinson, Colonel, 135
Dingley Tariff, 181
Distant Shore, ix
Divine Right of Kings, 174
Doane, George Washington, 6, 13, 15
Doane, Hannah, 10
Dodd, Pierson G., 131
Dollar Dinner of the Orange Republican
  Club, 180, 182

Dollar Diplomacy, 178
Donald, David Herbert, 66
Donnelly, Arthur, 13th NJ Vols., 100
Donner Party, 2
Downing, Henry, 13th NJ Vols., 41
Downs, Sherman, 200
Drainsville, VA, 40
Dred Scott, 2
Drew, John, 190
Drumthwacket, 140
Dryden, John F., 152, 159, 160, 170
Dumfries, VA, 33, 40
Duncan's Bridge, 86
Dunker Church, 29
Durand, Asher, B, 5
Durham Station, NC, 108
Dutch East India Company, 7

Eagle Rock, NJ, 131
East Point, GA, 66
Easy Boss Platt, 135
Edgar Thompson Works, 128
Edge, Walter Evans, 137, 140, 141, 163; illus.,
  153
Edison, Thomas, 121
Edison, Thomas Jr., 148
Edwards Ferry, 40
Edwards, Misses, 7
Eighty-Second Ohio Vols., 55, 61
Elberon, NJ, 123, 149, 151, 173
Electrics, 147
Eleventh Corps, 36, 47
Elkwood Park, 148
Elysian Field, 6
Emerald Isle, 8
Essex Caucus, 134
Essex County, 25, 131
Essex Park System, 177
Essex Troop, 138, 176; illus., 174
Etowah River, 53, 55, 57
Ettinger, Mr., 127
Ewell's Corps, 40
Executive Committee, 135

Fabyan House, NH, 194; illus., 193
Fagan, Mark, 142, 143, 144
Fairbanks, Charles, 173, 175, 186
Fairfax Station, VA, 33, 67
Fayetteville, NC, 97, 98, 99
Fayetteville Arsenal, 98
Fidelity Trust, 142
Field Orders No. One hundred and Twenty,
  74
Field Orders No. Sixty-Seven, 72
Fifteenth Corps, 74, 83, 91, 107
Fifth Corps, 43
Fifth Georgia Regiment, 94
Fifth Light Artillery Battery NJ Vols., 9
Fifth Tennessee Confederate Regiment,
  64
Fifty-Four Forty or Fight, 2
Fingal, 140
First Centennial of the Republic of Mexico,
  178

First Michigan Engineers, 87
First South Carolina Regiment, 114
First Virginia Cavalry, 48
Flappers, 16
Florences, The, 188
Flume House, NH, 194
Foote, Captain, 161
Ford, Henry, 121, 148
Fore River Ship Building Company, 163, 167
Forrest, Nathan Bedford, 47, 100
Fort Delaware, 23
Fort Hancock, 158
Fort McAllister, 80
Fort Richardson, 27; illus., 28
Fort Stark, 193
Fort Sumter, 15, 22, 82
Fort Ticonderoga, 172
Fort Worth, 111
Forty-Niners, 5
Fortress Monroe, 178
Forty-Sixth Pennsylvania Regiment, 39, 78
Foster, Stephen Collins, 5
Fourteenth Corps, 74, 76, 88, 91, 104
Fourth Corps, 61
Francis, Governor, 169
Franklin, Benjamin, 13
Franklin, John Hope, 35
Frederick, MD, 28
Fredericksburg, VA, 33
Free Silver Issue, 132
Freeborne, Thomas, 6
Freiday, Jacob A., 13th NJ Vols., 55
Frelinghuysen, Joseph, 180
Fremont Campaign, 109
French Bayonet Drill, 25
Fryeburg, 194
Fuller, Colonel, 186
Fuller, Margaret, 4
Furman, Moore, 139

Gaddis, Elisa B., 131
Gale, Cathrine Cox, 122
Gallagher, Mr., 188
Garden of Eden, 200
Garden State, 5
Garden, Mary, 190
Garrabrant, Moses, 13th NJ Vols., 55
Garrison, Charles G., 144
Geary, John W., 40, 55, 62, 63, 82, 86, 88
George, 19, 58, 79
George, Henry, 142
Georgia Railroad, 71, 76
Germania Ford, 35
Gettysburg, Battle of, 40-42, 158, 161; illus., 40, 43, 44
Gibbons Family, 79
Gilded Age, 121, 142, 178
Gillisonville, SC, 83
Gillmore, General, 151
Glenn, Colonel, 74
Golden Age of Greece, 19
Goldsboro, NC, 85, 100, 105
Goodley Heritage of Jerseymen, 6

Gordon, John B., 28, 29, 31
Gough, John B, 4
Gould, Jay, 128
Governor's Day, 139
Grahamville, 83
Grand Army of the Republic, ix, 109, 178
Grand Old Party, 131, 178, 184
Grand Review, 110; illus., 111, 112
Granliden, NH, 195
Grant, Samuel, 200
Grant, Ulysses S., 42, 49, 64, 65, 74, 108, 109, 110; illus., 49
Gray, Mr., 146
Great Barrington, MA, 195
Great Pee Dee River, 95, 96
Great Seal of the State of New Jersey, 138
Great Skedaddle, 26
Great White Fleet, 162
Greeley, Horace, 65; illus., 65
Green Mountains, 190
Greene, George S., 29, 31
Greene, Nathanael, 10, 108, 171
Greenfield, 195
Greensborough, NC, 107, 110
Grenadiers, 112
Griffith, Thomas, 13th NJ Vols., 61
Griggs, Governor, 185
Grimes, John, 13th NJ Vols., 35, 36, 37, 48, 55, 71; illus., 35
Grimstead, Frank, 67, 78
Grimstead, James Augustus, 14th NJ Vols., 45, 55, 67, 79, 113, 114; illus., 45
Gripps, Governor, 138
Groito de Delores, 178
Gummere, W.S., 138, 144, 152, 171, 177, 186
Guyer, Captain, 13th NJ Vols., 62, 83

Habersham Street, Savannah, 82
Hager, Abigail, Elizabeth, 10
Hagerstown Road, 29
Hagerstown, 43, 161
"Hail To The Chief," 135, 156
Half-Holiday, 127
Halifax River, 199
Halleck, Henry W., 40
Haltiwanger, R.J., 83
Hamilton, Alexander, 171
Hampton, VA, 178
Handkerchief Campaign, 135
Hanna, Mark, 134
Hannegan, Edward A., 2
Hapsburgs, ix
Hardee, William J., 52, 70, 87; illus., 70
Hardeeville, SC, 83
Harding, Warren G., 114
Hardman, Wickliffe, 13th NJ Vols., 100
Hargreaves, James, 121
Harpers Ferry, VA, 28, 32, 33, 40; illus., 32
Harris, Captain, 13th NJ Vols., 36, 59, 66, 71, 94
Harris, Major, 190, 195
Harrison, Albert C. 14th NJ Vols., 25, 43, 65, 107

Harrison, Benjamin, 132
Harte, Bret, 112
Hartford, CT, 192
Hatch, William B., 22
Haussling, Mayor, 184
Havre de Grace, MD, 27
Hawley, Colonel, 86, 104, 105
Hawthorne, Nathaniel, 4
Hay, Samuel C., 13th NJ Vols., 48
Haymarket Square Riot, 143
Hazen, William, 80
Hemmenway, Congressman, 175
Henry, 84
Henry of Lancaster, 9
Hewitt, Edward R., 148, 150
Hidalgo, Miguel, 178
Highlands, NJ, 157
Hill, Ambrose P., 36
Hill, Jim, 128
Hillsborough, 33, 107
Hinchliffe, Mayor, 143
Hindman's Division, 58
Hobart, Garret A., 134
Hohenzollerns, ix
Hood, John B., 52, 58, 61, 62, 63, 64, 66; illus., 62
Hooker, Joseph, 29, 31, 33, 35, 40, 52, 63; illus., 48
Horrocks, James, 8
Hot Springs, AK, 150
Hotel Sommerset, 163, 168
Hotel Touraine, 168, 192
Hotel Wentworth, 193
How The Other Half Lives, 140
Howard, Oliver O., 63, 64, 74, 75, 80, 89, 111, 158
Howe, Elias, 3
Hudson County, 7
Hudson River School, 5
Hughes, Charles Evans, 184
Hunt, Livingston, 4
Hunt, Mr., 167
Hunt, William T., 190, 192
Hy-Kinsellagh County, Ireland, 9

Indian Spring Farm, 149
Industrial Revolution, 3, 22
Inside Inn, 168
Intervale, NH, 194
Irish Immigrants, 45
Irish, H.C., 13th NJ Vols., 29
Iron-Willed Bismark of the Republican Party, 133
Irving, Washington, 18

Jackson, Andrew, 1

Jackson, Thomas J. (Stonewall) 36; illus., 37
Jacksonian Era, 3, 4, 14, 16
Jacksonville, FL, 197
Jacobson, Dr., 167
James River, 111
Jeff Davis, 66
Jefferson, Thomas, 22
Jersey City Glass Company, 8
Jersey City, 7, 10, 11, 132, 163
John Minturn, Packet, 5
John's Crossroads, 43
Johnson, Alexander H., 131
Johnson, Andrew, 109
Johnson, Lieutenant, 13th NJ Vols., 66
Johnson's Division, 40
Johnston, Joseph E., 52, 53, 55, 59, 61, 81, 87,
    92, 95, 103, 104, 106, 107, 108, 110; illus.,
    61
Jonesboro, GA, 66

Kean Family of Elizabeth, NJ, 147
Kean, John, 132, 138, 152, 159, 160, 163,
    179
Kearney, Dennis, 9
Kearny, Philip, 35
Kearsarge U.S.S., 80
Kellogg, Frank, B., 4
Kelly's Ford, 35, 43
Kelsey, H.C., 138
Kenesaw Mountain, 57, 58, 59, 60, 61
Kennebec Valley, 193
Kennebunkport, ME, 193
Kensett, John, 5
Kentucky Resolutions, 22
Kerens, Dick, 184
Kilpatrick, Judson, 22, 66, 67, 75, 83, 86, 99;
    illus., 67, 99
Kilroy, James, 13th NJ Vols., 31
Kimbel, W.W., 163
Kingston, 58
Kinney, Helen, ix, 42, 163, 167, 168, 197;
    illus., 165, 166
Kinney, William, 163
Kip, 86, 88, 95, 105, 186
Kissam, Mr., 150
Knapp, Nicholas, 10
Knights Templar, 177
Knipe's Brigade, 53
Know-Nothings, 8
Knox, Henry, 171, 172
Krubart, Christopher, 13th NJ Vols., 39
Kuhl, John, 25
Kull, Irving, 129
Kulp's Farm, Battle of, 58

Ladd, William, 4

Lafayette College, 171
Lamb Hill Railroad, 97
Landell, Miss, 26
Langhorne's Orange Grove, 199, 200
Larger Political Experience, 132
Lawtonville, SC, 83, 85
"Lead Kindly Light," 135, 152
Lee, B.F. 138
Lee, Charles, 173
Lee, Harry, Light Horse, 171
Lee, Robert E., 61, 93, 106, 108, 114; illus.,
    114
Leesburg, VA, 33, 40
Leighton, 92
Leinster, 9
Lentz, Carl, 144
Leopold, Andrew, 47, 48
Levy, Reverend, 26
Lexington Court House, SC, 88, 90
Lexington, SC, 83
Libby Prison, 111
Liberia, 5
Lichtman, Allan, 131
Lincoln, Abraham, 2, 20, 22, 23, 33, 64, 65,
    66, 81, 107, 108, 132, 135; illus., 3, 20
Little, H.S., 138
Little Lynch's Creek, 94
Little River, 75
Lockwood's Hotel, 113
Locomobiles, 148
Lodge, Henry Cabot, 186
Loeb, Ass. Secretary, 153
Logan, John A. 64, 107; illus., 107
Long Branch, NJ, 149
Long, Governor, 192
Long Island, Battle of, 10
Long, John D., 135, 168
Longfellow, Henry Wadsworth, 4
Longstreet, Jas. C., 40, 41
Lookout Valley, 52
Lord, Assemblyman, 145
Lost Mountain, 58, 61
Lotos Club, 186
Lounge-lizards, 16
Lowden, Colonel, 186
Lower Green, Newark, NJ, illus., 11
Luger, 92
Lumber River, 97
Lunatic Fringe, 131
Lusitania, 188
Lynchburg, VA, 197
Lynn, MA, 193
Lyon, Benjamin & Phebe (Crane), 10
Lyon, Cecil, 186
Lyon, Henry, 10
Lyon, Sarah, 10

MacFall, Bishop, 175
MacKenzie, Alexander Slidell, 4
Mackie, Arthur H., 163
MacMurrough (MacMurphy or Murphy), 9
MacMurrough, Art, 9
Macon, GA, 74
Madison, James, 22

Magnus, Cathirus, 9
Magonigle, Mr., 177
Mahon, Alfred Thayer, 162
Malefactors of Great Wealth, 145
Malvern Hill, 41
Manchester, VA, 111
Manifest Destiny, 2
Mansfield, Joseph K., 28
Manual of Arms, 25
March to the Sea, 82
Marietta, GA, 58, 59, 61
Marion, Frances, 108
Marion's Grave, 96
Markland, A.H., 107
Martha's Vineyard, 106
Martyrdom of Saint Crispin, 9
Marx, Karl, 128
Mary Benton, The, 83
Marye's Heights, 36; illus., 36
Maryland Heights, 30, 32
Mason & Dixon Cut, 97
Mason-Dixon Line, 20
Massasoit House, 192
Mat River, 111
Mathews. A.M., 13th NJ Vols., 53, 83, 84, 86,
    88, 97, 105, 110; illus., 54
Mayflower Compact, 11
Mayflower, 153
Mayors' Equal Taxation League, 142
McAdam, John, 148
McCarter, Robert, 150
McCarter, Senator, 135
McCarter, Thomas, 150, 183
McClellan, George B., 65, 132, 137
McCullough, David, 1
McIntosh, Miss, 97
McKinley Memorial Commission, 177
McKinley, William, 132, 134, 135, 168, 186
McPherson, James B., 52, 63, 64; illus., 64, 65
McPherson, James M., 18
McPhersonville, 83
McWhorter Street, Newark
Meade, George G., 40, 112
Medzgar, Abram, 14th NJ Vols., 33
Meherin River, 111
Melville, Herman, 4
Mendham, NJ, 188
Meriden, CT, 192
Merrimac River, 193
Methodist Episcopal Church, 11, 15
Mexican-American War, 5
Middletown Valley, 28
Midway, GA, 83
Milburn, John G., 177
Military Board in Philadelphia, 150
Mill Creek Gap, 52
Milledgeville, GA, 75
Millen, GA, 76, 77
Miller, W.H. 13th NJ Vols., illus., 63
Mindell, Colonel, 84, 86
Mingo Creek, 101
Minutemen, 31
Miss A., 167
Missouri Compromise Line, 22

Monmouth Court House, NJ, 173
Monmouth Park, 173
Monmouth, Battle of, Anniversary Address of Gov. Murphy, 173-175
Montgomery Street, Jersey City, illus., 8
Montieth Swamp, 78
Montieth Turnpike, 78
Montreal, Canada, 125
Morganthau, Hans J., 20
Morris Canal, 25
Morristown, NJ, 79, 174
Morrows, 10
Morton, William, 2
Morven, 140
Mosby, John S., 47; illus., 49
Motor Vehicle Department, 149
Mount Washington House, 194; illus., 192
Mt. Kisco, NY, 195
Mt. Pleasant Cemetery, Newark, NJ, 200
Mt. Vernon, NY, 195
Mulbury Street, Newark, NJ, 15
Munn, Joseph L., 141
Murphy, Abby Hager, 6
Murphy Coat of Arms, illus., 10
Murphy, Frank Jr., 151, 163, 168, 171, 183, 186, 200
Murphy, Franklin, illus., circa 1880, 131; circa 1885, 134; illus., invitation to the inauguration of Murphy as Governor, 136; illus., F.M. awaiting arrival of Pres. Roosevelt, 154; illus., escorting Pres. Roosevelt, 155; illus., Gov. Murphy and Pres. Roosevelt, 156; illus., Gov. Murphy, his daughter Helen and dignitaries at the launching of the U.S.S. *New Jersey*, 166; illus., home in Newark, 175; illus., Gov. Murphy and William Howard Taft, 181; illus., home in Mendham, 186; illus., music room in Newark, 187; illus., library in Newark 188; illus., study in Newark 189; illus., Franklin Murphy portrait circa 1908, 191; illus., Franklin Murphy circa 1910, 197; illus., Franklin Murphy statue at Weehaquic Park, Newark, NJ, 198; illus., Franklin Murphy with granddaughter Janet at the shore, 199
Murphy, Franklin, Lieutenant, illus., 20, promotion document, 34
Murphy, Franklin, Murphy Frank Jr., Murphy, William H., illus., 133
Murphy, Janet, 123, 138, 149, 151; illus., 123
Murphy, Robert, 10
Murphy Varnish Company ix, 122, 125; illus., 125, 127
Murphy, William Hayes, 10
Murphy-Colwell Wedding Ceremony Announcement, illus., 124
Murruff, 9

Nancy's Creek, 61
Naples, 194
Nassau Hotel, 171
Nast, Thomas, 9
National Guard, 151

National Hymn, 152
National Intelligence, 13
National Republican Committee, 135
Nativism, 8
Naval Academy, 168
"Nearer My God To Thee," 152
Nellie, 114
Nelson, William, 132
Neuse River, 111
New Britain, CT, 192
New Haven, CT, 190
"New Idea," 142, 144
New Idea In Business, 122
New Jersey Day At Saint Louis World's Fair, 168; illus., 169, Gov. Murphy's Speech, 169-171
New Jersey Historical Society, 6
New Jersey House Assembly, 132
New Jersey Society, 11
New Jersey, 5, 22
New Rochelle, NY, 190
New York Draft Riots, 45
New York Tribune, 13
Newark Academy, 15, 16, 25
Newark Advertiser, 53
Newark Common Council, 130, 131
Newark Exchange For Women's Work, 123
Newark, NJ, 15, 25, 26, 113, 132, 184, 190
Newark, NJ, Mid-19th Century Description, 11-12
Newburyport, MA, 193
Newcastle, NH, 193
Newcomen, Thomas, 121
Newport, NH, 195
Normandy, 47
North River, 101
Nullification Proclamation, 22

O'Connor, Thomas, 131
O'Neal, Edward, 62
O'Sullivan, John, 2
Oakey, Daniel, 43, 106
Obear Home, 92
Occoquan Creek, 33
Ogeechee River, 76
Old Bourbon, 137
Old Ford Tavern, 171
Old Guard, 142, 144
Old Susanna, 5
Old Wilderness Tavern, 35
Olden, Charles, 23, 140
Oliphant, Dr., 150
Oliphant, General & Mrs., 175; Mrs. 176
Olmstead, Frederick Law, 188
Oostanaula River, 53
Open Letter to Governor Murphy, 144
Orange & Alexandria Railroad, 33
Orange Mountains, 131
Orange Street, Newark, NJ, 25, 26
Orangeburg, 83
Oranges, NJ, 25
Order of the Star Spangled Banner, 8
Oregon Trail, 2
Ormond, FL, 197

Osbourn, E., 114
Ossabaw Sound, 80
Ostend Manifesto, 2
Outing Day, 127
Oyster Bay, NY, 153, 159

Paice's Ferry, 59
Palm Beach, FL, 197, 200
Palmer, MA, 192
Pamunkey River, 111
Paris Commissionership, 134
Parker, Charles W., 163
Parker, Joel, illus., 23
Parliament, James H., 13th NJ Vols., 100, 101
Parrot Guns, 67
Passaic River, 140
Paterson, 132
Pauw, Michael, 7
Pavonia, 7
Payne-Aldrich Tariff, 181, 182
Pea Patch Island, 23
Peabody, Elizabeth, 4
Peach Orchard, Gettysburg, 41
Peachtree Creek, Battle of, 61
Peculiar Institution, 3, 21
Pee Dee River, 95
Peirson, Captain, 13th NJ Vols., 97, 100, 101
Pelleas And Mesalinde, 190
Peloponnesian Wars, 19
Peninsular War, 59
Pennsylvania Railroad, 168
Pennyworth Island, 80
Penrose, Senator, 186
Personal Influence Interview, 126
Peters, W.C., 5
Pettigrew, J. Johnston, 41
Phalanx, 4; illus., 5
Philadelphia, PA, 22, 27
Philippine Exhibit, 168
Pickett, George E. (Division), 41, 42
Pierson, David Lawrence, 26
Pierson, Lieutenant, 13th NJ Vols., 48
Pinchot, Gifford, 184
Pine Knob, 58
Pine Mountain, 58
Pipemaker's Creek, 78
Piscataqua River, 193
Plato, 4
Plume, Joseph W. 177
Po River, 111
Poland Springs, ME, 193
Polk, James K. 2; illus., 2
Polk, Leonidas, 58
Poncho Villa, 178
Pope, John, 30
Porter, Fitz John, illus., 33

219

Portland, ME, 190
Potomac River, 33
Price, Thompson, 122
Princeton, Battle of, 171, 174
Princeton University, 171
Profile House, illus., 195
Progress and Poverty, 142
Progressive "Bull Moose" Faction, 180
Progressive era, 137
Protestant Foster Home, 123
Prudential Insurance Corporation, 142, 170
Public School Law, 142
Public Service Corporation, 142
Pullman Car "Rover," 197
Pullman Cars, 168
Pumpkin Vine Creek, 57
Putnam, Israel, 171
Pyne, Moses Taylor, 140

Quincy, MA, 168

Raleigh Road, 100
Raleigh, NC, 106, 107, 110, 111
Rappahonnock River, 35, 43, 111,
Rappelyea, Mr., 167
Record, George L., 135, 141, 142, 143, 144
Red Bank, NJ, 107
Red Bank, Battle of, 174
Red Bank Troop, 173
Republican, 130
Republican National Convention at Saint
    Louis 1896, 132, 134; at Philadelphia
    1900, 132
Republican State Committee, 132
Revere Beach, MA, 193
Rhett, Alfred, 98
Rhett, Robert B., illus., 98
Rhode Island Day, 168
Richard II, 9
Richmond, VA, 111
Riis, Jacob, 140
Riker, Chandler W., 144
Riker, Joseph M. 131
Riley, James Whitcomb, 177
Ringgold, GA, 52
Ripley, Sarah, 4
Road Law, 148
Roanoke River, 111
Robertsville, SC, 83, 84, 85
Robinson, Henry R., 138
Rock Creek, 41
Rockville, 28
Rocky Face Ridge, illus., 52, 53
Rogers, General, 159
Rogers, Mr., 188
Roosevelt, Emlin, Mr. & Mrs., 153
Roosevelt, Miss., 153

oosevelt, Mrs., 153
Roosevelt, Theodore, x, 1, 66, 129, 131, 135,
    145, 150, 152, 153, 154, 156, 157, 159,
    160, 177, 179, 180, 181, 186, 200; illus.,
    154, 155, 156, 157, 158, 161, 162
Root, Elihu, 185; illus., 159
Roseville Avenue, Newark, NJ, 25-26
Ross, Andrew, 9
Ross, Edmund, 109
Ross, William Burroughs, 14th NJ Vols., 55
Rossville, 52
Rostow, W.W., 3
Rough Riders, 152
Round Top, 40
Royal House of Leinster, 9
Royal Poinciana Hotel, 199; illus., 196
Ruger, Thomas H., 43, 52, 53, 106
"Rugged Individualism," 200
Rumson Neck, NJ, 149
Runyon, Mayor, 113
Russell, H.C., 200
Russell, Lillian, 148
Russian Ministership, 134
Rye Beach, NH, 193
Ryerson, Captain, 13th NJ Vols., 36, 41, 58

Sagamore Hill, 159
Saint Augustine, FL, 197
Saint Louis Limited, 168, 169
Saint Paul's Methodist Episcopal Church,
    122, 150
Saint Petersburg, 22
Salem, MA, 193
Salisbury Beach, MA, 193
Salisbury, NH, 193
San Jaun Hill, 152
Sandersville, GA, 75, 76
Sandy Hook, MD, 43
Sandy Hook, NJ, 157
Santa Claus, 151, 178
Santa Fe Trail, 2
Saratoga, NY, 173
Savannah, GA, 21, 61, 74, 75, 78, 80, 81, 82,
    86, 197
Scarborough, Bishop, 173
Scarlet Letter, 4
Schofield, John M., 52, 106, 110; illus., 105
Schuyler, Philip J., 171
Scientific Management, 128
Scorched Earth Policy, 73
Scott, Senator & Mrs., 186
Scott's Alabamans & Louisianans, 62
Scudder Home, 139
Scudder, Mr., 167
Sea Gull, illus., 163; Invitation to a reception
    for Gov. Murphy aboard
Second Massachusetts Volunteers, 29, 43,
    45, 106,
Second-Class Properties, 144
Seddon, James A. 73, 74
Sedgwick, John, 36, 55; illus., 54
"Seeing the Elephant," 28
Semmes, Raphael, 4, 80; illus., 80

Senate Committee, 145
Seneca Falls, NY, 4
Seventeenth Corps, 74, 93, 95
Seward, William H., 13
Sewell, William J., 133, 134, 135
Seymour, James M., 135
Sharpsburg Peninsula, 28
Sharpsburg, MD, 33, 161
Shell-shock, 39
Shepherdstown, VA, 33, 48
Sheppard, Mr., 173
Sheridan, Philip, 132
Sherman Anti-Trust Act, 125
Sherman, James, 179
Sherman, William Tecumseh, 43, 47, 49, 52,
    57, 58, 59, 64, 65, 66, 67, 72, 74, 75, 78,
    80, 81, 92, 96, 98, 101, 106, 107, 108,
    110, 111, 112; illus., 55, 59, 76, 85, 87
Shinn, Colonel, 151
Shrewsbury, MA, 192
Sickles, Daniel E., 40, 158, 159
Simonson, Captain, 52
Simonson's Battery, 58
Single Tax, 142
Slater, Samuel, 3
Slocum, Henry W., 37, 72, 74, 75, 82, 83, 88,
    101, 103, 104, 106, 111 158, 159; illus., 72
Smedley, Mr., 190
Smith, A.A. General, 30
Smith, J.O., 161
Smith, T.B., 13th NJ Vols., 37
Smithsonian Institution, 3
Snake Creek Gap, 52
Snickerville, 43
Society of the Army of the Potomac, 158
Soldier's Friend, 33
Sons of the American Revolution, 11, 173
South Egremont, MA, 195
South Jersey Bosses, 132
South Mountain, Battle of, 28
South River, 75
Southern Road, 197
Spanish-American War, 152, 162, 168
Spaulding, Bishop, 177
Spence, John A., 13th NJ Vols., 53
Spencer, Philip, 4
Spier's Station #13, 76
Spot Resolutions, 2
Springfield Rifle-Musket, 25, 55
Springfield, MA, 174, 190, 192
Square Deal, 66, 179
Stafford Court House, 33, 37
Stamford, 192
Stanton, Edwin, 108, 200; illus., 108
Stanton, Elizabeth Cady, 4
Stark, Captain, 6
State House Commission, 139
State Street House, 139
Sterling Hotel, 139
Steuben, Baron von, 171, 173
Stevens, Alexander, 21; illus., 21
Stevens's Georgians, 62
Stevenson, 47

Stevenson's Division, 58
Stewart, Lt. Col., 158
Stockbridge, MA, 195
Stockton Family, 140
Stockton, Adjutant-General, 22
Stokes, E.C., 135, 141
Stokes, Governor, 175, 176, 185; illus. of
    inaugural review, 174
Stone, Governor, 159
Stone, Lucy, 4
Stone Mountain, 75
Stone, Paymaster, 33
Story of the Jersey Shore, The, 147
Stryker Mansion, 139
Stuart, Jas. E.B. ("Jeb"), 35
Sumner, Charles, 2, 4
Sumner, Edwin, 29
Sunapee Lake, 195
Susquehanna River, 27
Swain, Samuel, 11
Swayze, John, 139, 150
Swords, Lt. Col., 13th NJ Vols., 35

Ta River, 111
Taft, William Howard, x, 178, 179, 180; illus.,
    181, 182
Takahira, Baron, 185
Take-Off, 3
Tally-Ho Coaches, 168
Tally-Ho Parties, 148
Tavaraz, Master, 16
Taylor, Frederick W., 128
Taylor Opera House, 138, 176
Tenement House Commission, 146
Tenements, 146
Tennessee, 46, 47
Tennille Station #13, 76
"Tenting On The Old Camp Ground," illus.,
    38
Terry, Alfred, 106
Texas, 46
Thanksgiving, 48, 127
Thayer, Slyvanus, 177
The Belfry of Bruges, 4
*The Influence of Sea Power Upon History
    1660-1783*, 162
The Lofty And The Lowly, 97
The Man From Home, 190
The Outfit, 199
The Voyage of Life, 5
Theberath, Charles M., 131
Third Wisconsin Regiment, 43
Thirteenth New Jersey Vols., 19, 23, 27, 138;
    illus., Flags of, 27
Thirty-Third New Jersey Regiment, 62, 84
Thomas, George H., 74
Thompson, Lieutenant, 13th NJ Vols., 93
Thompson's Creek, 94
Thoreau, Henry David, 5
Thucydides, 19
Tin Lizzies, 16
Tocqueville, Alexis de, 16
Toffey, John J., 161

Toombs, Samuel, 13th NJ Vols., 35, 42, 52, 61,
    79, 90
Townsend, E.D., 111
Treat, Robert, 11
Treaty of Guadalupe Hidalgo, 2
Treaty of Paris 1898, 168
Trenton House, 176
Trenton, 150; Battle of, 171, 174
Trout House, 72
Truex, William S., 22
Twain, Mark, 121, 186, 188
Twelfth Corps, 36, 40, 47
Twentieth Army Corps Insignia, illus., 33
Twentieth Corps, 52, 53, 61, 74, 101, 106
Twenty-Fifth Corps, 106
Twenty-Fourth Corps, 106
Twenty-Seventh Indiana Regiment, 37, 40,
    42, 43
Twin Mountain House, illus., 194
Typee
Tyrolean Alps, 169

U-20, 188
Underwood, Lieutenant, 93
Union, 22
United Gas Improvement Company, 142
United States Ford, 35, 111
United States Lifesaving Service, 6
United States Lifesaving Station # 10, illus.,
    6
U.S.S. *Connecticut*, 168
U.S.S. *Georgia*, 163
U.S.S. *Missouri*, 167
U.S.S. *Nebraska*, 163
U.S.S. *New Jersey*, 162, 163; illus., 164; chris-
    tening, 165; Gov. Murphy and staff at
    launching, 165; silver setting, 167; snap-
    shot, 167
U.S.S. *Oregon*, 162
U.S.S. *Somers*, 4
U.S.S. *Virginia*, 163

Valley Forge, PA, 173, 174
Van Leer, Miss, 145
Van Resselear, D. 13th NJ Vols., illus., 88
Van Vorst, Cornelius, 25
Van Woert, Mr., 190
Vanderbilt, William H., 128
Victoria, Queen, 111
Victorian Era, 1, 138
Virginia Resolutions, 22
Vixen, 157
Voices Of Freedom, 4
Voorhees, Foster M., 137, 138, 185

Wadsworth, Major, 190, 192
Walker Tariff, 3
Wallingford, CT, 192
Ward, J.C., 145
Ward, Leslie D., 177
Ward, Marcus, 33
Ward, U.S. Army General Hospital, 33
Warner, J.F. 67

Warren, MA, 192
Warren, Orem, 13th NJ Vols., 100
Warren Square, Savannah, 82
Warrenton Junction, 43
Washington, DC, 26, 111, 112, 137
Washington, George, 174
Washingtonians, 4
Wayne, Mad Anthony, 171
Webb, General, 159
Wellington, Duke of, 59
Werts, Governor George T., 185
West End, Long Branch, NJ, illus., 6
West Point, NY, 5, 22, 177
Westervelt, Cornelius, 13th NJ Vols., 101
Westminster Abby, England, 111
Wheeler, Joseph, 52, 66, 75, 92; illus., 75
Whigs, 109
White House Landing, 35
White Mountains, 190
White Plains, 195
White Scourge, 146
Whitfield, George G., 13th NJ Vols., 37
Whitman, Walt, 4
Whitmans, 2
Whittier, John Greenleaf, 4
Wickham, John A., 104
Wide-A-Wakes, 109
Wiley, William H., 163
Williams, Alpheus S., 30, 37, 49, 53, 62, 86,
    88, 101, 106; illus., 63
Williams, John R., 13th NJ Vols., 111, 178
Williamsburg, VA, 58
Wilmington, NC, 85
Wilmington, Lamb Hill & Charlotte Railroad,
    97
Wilmont Proviso, 2
Wilson, Harold F., 147
Wilson, R.G., 13th NJ Vols., 53
Wilson, Woodrow, x, 4, 20, 137, 138, 143,
    145, 150, 171, 184
Winnsborough, SC, 91, 92
Winthrop, John, 10
Wiss, Jacob, 13
Wolcott, Jacob, 14th NJ Vols., 25
Wolfe Run Shoals, 33
Wonder, 148
Woodstock, 194
Worcester, MA, 192
World War I, 179
World's Fair Commissioners, 168

Yale College, 192
York Beach, 193
Yorktown, VA, 173, 175

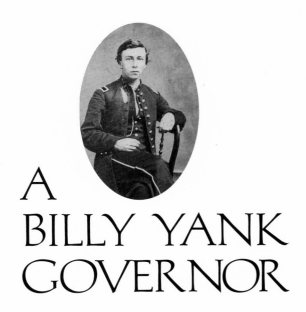

A
BILLY YANK
GOVERNOR

has been published in a first edition
of three thousand copies.
Designed by A. L. Morris,
the text was composed in Garamond Light and Michaelangelo
and printed by J.S. McCarthy / Letter Systems
in Augusta, Maine, on Potlatch Vintage Velvet.
The endleaves were printed on Strathmore Americana Text,
and the binding in ICG Arrestox and Rainbow Antique
was executed by New Hampshire Bindery
in Concord, New Hampshire.